FACULTY PRIORITIES RECONSIDERED

FACULTY PRIORITIES RECONSIDERED

Rewarding Multiple
Forms of Scholarship

KerryAnn O'Meara

R. Eugene Rice

Foreword by Russell Edgerton

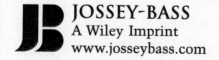

JOSSEY-BASS
A Wiley Imprint
www.josseybass.com

Published by Jossey-Bass
A Wiley Imprint
989 Market Street, San Francisco, CA 94103-1741   www.josseybass.com

Jossey-Bass books and products are available through most bookstores. To contact Jossey-Bass directly
call our Customer Care Department within the U.S. at 800-956-7739, outside the U.S. at 317-572-3986,
or fax 317-572-4002.

Jossey-Bass also publishes its books in a variety of electronic formats. Some content that appears in
print may not be available in electronic books.

Library of Congress Cataloging-in-Publication Data
O'Meara, KerryAnn
  Faculty priorities reconsidered : rewarding multiple forms of scholarship / by KerryAnn O'Meara
and R. Eugene Rice ; Foreword by Russell Edgerton.
      p. cm.
  Includes bibliographical references.
  ISBN 0-7879-7920-1 (alk. paper)
  1. Education, Higher—United States. 2. College teachers—United States. 3. Learning and
scholarship—United States. 4. Research—United States. I. Rice, R. Eugene. II. Title.
  LA227.3.O43 2005
  378.1'2—dc22
                                2005006483

Printed in the United States of America
FIRST EDITION
HB Printing 10 9 8 7 6 5 4 3 2 1

CONTENTS

PART THREE: NATIONAL PERSPECTIVES

APPENDIX: SURVEY TABLES

The Jossey-Bass Higher and Adult Education Series

FOREWORD

Russell Edgerton, President Emeritus
American Association for Higher Education

This book covers the rise and evolution of concern about whether the priorities of America's faculty are in sync with the nation's most important needs. Inside this story is a second story—about how *Scholarship Reconsidered: Priorities of the Professoriate* (Boyer, 1990), a publication of the Carnegie Foundation for the Advancement of Teaching, transformed the issue and introduced a different way to think about faculty priorities. Drawing together evidence and perspectives from three diverse sources—leading thinkers about the scholarly roles of faculty, campus leaders who have tried to put the ideas into practice, and a national survey of provosts—the authors give us an up-to-date picture of where things now stand.

What I would underscore for readers is that these stories are real political struggles that are still going on. Questions such as why *Scholarship Reconsidered* had the reach it did and what its impact was are not just of academic interest. The lessons we draw about why things happened as they did can shape the next chapters of the story. Accordingly, I would like to give you a participant's feel for how the story began, some of my own thoughts about the way things turned out, and what lessons can be learned.

During the years I served as president of the American Association for Higher Education (AAHE), I periodically scanned the horizon for the next big issue that would emerge and require a response from campuses—and possibly the services of a national association like AAHE. Around the mid-1980s, new issues—assessment, active learning, cost containment, accountability—started coming in like waves whipped up by a tropical storm.

I remember at the time wondering whether and when the faculty—and especially the incentives and rewards that shape what priorities faculty pursue—would ever come into focus. And then, rather suddenly in 1990, it happened.

First there was Syracuse University. At the initiative of Vice Chancellor Robert Diamond, the faculty, department chairs, and deans were surveyed about their views of the priorities the university attached to teaching and research. Each group thought that there was too much emphasis on research, and each also assumed that their colleagues thought otherwise. When the survey revealed a university full of "closet teachers," the university concluded that the balance between teaching and research had to be addressed. Diamond went on to turn the survey into a national project, eventually involving 46 other research universities. And every single institution reported findings similar to those of Syracuse.

In April 1990, Stanford President Donald Kennedy gave a high-profile address to his faculty, calling upon them to recognize teaching as "the first among our labors." In September, University of California President David Gardner established a university-wide task force on faculty rewards. By mid-fall, I counted 30 campuses that had initiated similar evaluations.

Finally, at the end of the year, the Carnegie Foundation for the Advancement of Teaching released *Scholarship Reconsidered*. Scores of campuses placed bulk orders for the report, which soon became the best-selling special report ever issued by the Carnegie Foundation.

Scholarship Reconsidered transformed the discussion. Instead of describing faculty roles in terms of the familiar trilogy of teaching, research, and service, it argued that faculty were responsible for four basic tasks: discovering, integrating, applying, and representing the knowledge of their scholarly fields. This formula, originally developed by R. Eugene Rice as a scholar in residence at the Carnegie Foundation, spoke to the faculty not in their role as "professors" (members of a university) but as "scholars" (members of an intellectual community). The issue of faculty priorities was no longer just a matter of reconciling competing claims for faculty time. It was also a matter of having a narrower or broader view of one's scholarly identity and responsibilities.

From my perch at AAHE, it was obvious that here was a *big* issue that our organization was well positioned to address. My colleagues and I established the AAHE Forum on Faculty Roles and Rewards—an annual conference and other services that provided an infrastructure for campuses to work through their responses in a collaborative setting.

How did things turn out? For over a decade, more than a thousand faculty and administrators each year attended AAHE's annual forum. So we know that the issue of faculty priorities had staying power. But what really happened? Did Gene Rice's generative formula truly transform the way campuses dealt with and thought about faculty roles? Have faculty priorities—and the way faculty are evaluated and rewarded—truly changed? If so, why, and if not, why not? Are there lessons to be drawn from this story about what are the necessary and sufficient conditions for improvement to occur?

These are the kind of questions we should be asking and that this book helps us answer. I leave you with some of my own thoughts and propositions in the hope that these will stimulate your own.

Had *Scholarship Reconsidered* never appeared, faculty priorities would still have surfaced as a major issue. The conditions under which colleges and universities do business were clearly changing. Rather than just grow, colleges found themselves dealing with expectations to become more effective, more productive, and more accountable. It was just a matter of time before the faculty would come into focus.

By reframing the issue of faculty priorities as a matter of identity and professional responsibility, *Scholarship Reconsidered* presented the issue in a way that tapped into the intrinsic interest of faculty. This elicited a surge of faculty interest and energy that wouldn't otherwise have emerged.

At the same time, it's clear from the campus reports in this book that there has been lots of confusion at the campus level about what the various dimensions of scholarship really entail, and how these should be documented and evaluated. The discussion seems to have resulted in a somewhat more inclusive view of what activities and products deserve to be regarded as scholarly. But this view, in most cases, simply lies on top of existing practices. It has not generated new practices. Nor has there been any letup in the pressure to do research.

In retrospect, the initial presentation of the idea in *Scholarship Reconsidered* was rather thin: the whole concept was developed in fewer than 150 pages. And the implications for how faculty performance was to be documented and evaluated came only much later, when the Carnegie Foundation issued a companion volume,

Scholarship Assessed (Glassick, Huber, & Maeroff, 1997). Hence, the national conversation that took place focused on vague and general goals and priorities, divorced from the concrete examples of what were the implications and stakes involved in embracing the vision.

Would an intellectually richer presentation of the idea, coupled with concrete illustrations of how performance could be documented, displayed, and reviewed, have deepened the impact of the idea? We don't need to speculate about the answer because we have a body of experience to draw on. With respect to the fourth dimension of scholarly activity—the representation of knowledge through teaching—AAHE and the Carnegie Foundation have been pursuing a distinctive line of work that now flies under the banner of Scholarship of Teaching and Learning. This effort has yielded concrete prototypes for documenting and displaying teaching as scholarly work, for reviewing these portfolios by peers, and for considering this evidence for promotion and tenure. Faculty who have been involved have been transformed by the experience.

In sum, a number of ingredients for successful reform were in place, but some are still missing. *Scholarship Reconsidered* provided an energizing idea. AAHE's Forum on Faculty Roles and Rewards provided continuity, staying power, and good company. But only in the case of teaching have practitioners been shown specific ways *how* to enact the idea into practice. And as usual, the actors that might reinforce the importance of this work—such as accrediting bodies—have been focused on other things. Further progress will require providing more detailed itineraries for the journey and clearer signals from various authorities that the journey must be taken.

References

Boyer, E. (1990). *Scholarship reconsidered.* Princeton, NJ: Carnegie Foundation for the Advancement of Teaching.

Glassick, C. E., Huber, M. T., & Maeroff, G. I. (1997). *Scholarship assessed: Evaluation of the professoriate.* San Francisco: Jossey-Bass.

ACKNOWLEDGMENTS

KerryAnn O'Meara and R. Eugene Rice

One of the joys of working on a project of this sort is that you become a part of a special community with a wide variety of talents collaborating over an extended period of time. We can't possibly thank all involved in this endeavor, but we want to begin with those who provided the original inspiration and, then, the resources that made it possible. Russell Edgerton, then President of the American Association for Higher Education (AAHE), provided the key leadership in launching both the Forum on Faculty Roles and Rewards and the New Pathways Projects, of which this effort was one component. The Atlantic Philanthropies supplied the financial support that made this collaborative effort possible. And, of course, none of this would have happened without the rich intellectual foundations on which *Scholarship Reconsidered: Priorities of the Professoriate* was constructed and the creative imagination and savvy of Ernest Boyer, who brought it together and initiated what became an enduring national debate. Both of us were honored to work with the late Ernest Lynton on the scholarship of engagement and the assessment of the professional service of faculty—he cared deeply about faculty and developing a rewards system that has integrity.

At AAHE, we were fortunate to have the talented administrative and editorial support of Melinda Majors, Jane Hamblin, and William Zeisel. At the University of Massachusetts, Amherst, KerryAnn O'Meara drew on a wide range of contributions from that vital academic community. She wants to express her special appreciation to Marni Presnall, Aaron Kuntz, William Skorupski, Anne Garner, and Jeff Hauger.

Central to this project was the work of the authors of the campus studies. We are grateful for their patience and resilience through the exchange of drafts and their capacity to be the best

kind of reflective practitioners. They have enriched our understanding of the changing faculty role—what we mean by scholarship and what should be rewarded. We wish also to thank the
provosts—the chief academic officers of four-year institutions—
who responded to our survey. The data they helped generate enriched the reliability of our reconsideration of faculty priorities.

As we were designing the survey and interpreting the results,
we took counsel with colleagues who were also exploring similar
issues, either as researchers or academic leaders. We want to thank
John Braxton, Cathy Burack, Deborah Hirsch, Mary Deane Sorcinelli, Larry Braskamp, Cathy Trower, Bob Diamond, and Mary
Huber for their thoughtful feedback and reflections on our survey, results, and the many chapters we sent them. They enabled us
to reflect more deeply, think more broadly, and write a study that
was of finer quality.

Finally, we both want to thank our families. KerryAnn was living
the experience of the early-career faculty member as we were studying it. KerryAnn wishes to thank her husband, Dan, who was a constant support and sometime editor, and her three children, Molly,
Emma, and Caroline (who was born just as this book was completed) for the joy, patience, and perspective they add to her life.

Gene is grateful to Sandra Cheldelin, his wife, best friend, and
perennial discussant of the ups and downs of academic life. Her
loving critique of this senior professor greatly enriches his understanding of the agonies and rewards of faculty work, and provides
the faithful reminder that there is more to life.

The Authors

Talya Bauer, School of Business, Portland State University.

Dennis Bozyk, Department of History, Madonna University.

David G. Brailow, Franklin College.

Victoria L. Clegg, Kansas State University.

Robert M. Diamond, Syracuse University and National Academy for Academic Leadership.

Amy Driscoll, Carnegie Foundation for the Advancement of Teaching.

Gretchen R. Esping, Kansas State University.

Don Evans, Center for Research on Education in Science, Mathematics, Engineering and Technology, Arizona State University.

Jerry G. Gaff, Association of American Colleges and Universities and American Association for Higher Education.

Catherine Garner, In-Hospital Schools Division of HealthStream, University of Phoenix.

Judy Grace, Center for Learning and Teaching Excellence, Arizona State University.

Robin A. Harvan, Office of Education, University of Colorado School of Medicine.

Barbara DeVeaux Holmes, Department of Educational Leadership, Albany State University.

Mary Taylor Huber, Carnegie Foundation for the Advancement of Teaching.

Pat Hutchings, Carnegie Foundation for the Advancement of Teaching.

Diane Kayongo-Male, Department of Sociology, South Dakota State University.

Steven R. Lowenstein, Office of the Dean and the Departments of Surgery, Medicine and Preventive Medicine/Biometrics, University of Colorado School of Medicine.

KerryAnn O'Meara, School of Education, University of Massachusetts, Amherst.

William Pepicello, the University of Phoenix.

Carol J. Peterson, Office of the Vice President for Academic Affairs, South Dakota State University.

John Rueter, Environmental Science Program, Portland State University.

R. Eugene Rice, American Association for Higher Education.

Duane Roen, Center for Learning and Teaching Excellence, Arizona State University.

David K. Scott, University of Massachusetts, Amherst.

Lee S. Shulman, Carnegie Foundation for the Advancement of Teaching.

Craig Swenson, Vice President's Office, University of Phoenix.

George E. Walker, Indiana University Graduate School and Carnegie Foundation for the Advancement of Teaching.

Kenneth J. Zahorski, St. Norbert College.

FACULTY PRIORITIES RECONSIDERED

INTRODUCTION

KerryAnn O'Meara and R. Eugene Rice

> *Scholarship is a choice of how to live as well as a choice of a career.*
> —C. WRIGHT MILLS, 1959

RETHINKING SCHOLARSHIP AND NEW PRACTICE: THE CHALLENGE

During the 1980s there was a growing concern about the misalignment of the priorities of faculty and the central missions of the institutions in which they worked. Parents, trustees, and legislators became increasingly vocal about the quality of undergraduate teaching and what they regarded as "absentee professors." Journalistic diatribes such as Charles Sykes's *ProfScam* (1988) grew in popularity. The scholarly work of faculty was seen by many as disconnected from the larger purposes of American society.

This was the environment that spawned a number of reform initiatives aimed at addressing concerns about the changing faculty role and the reward system. Much of this effort came to focus on the scholarly work of faculty and led to the Carnegie report *Scholarship Reconsidered: Priorities of the Professoriate*. In this report, Ernest Boyer (1990) and others fundamentally reframed the terms of the discussion and challenged higher education to expand the definition of scholarship used to evaluate and reward faculty work. Boyer's expanded definition included the discovery, teaching, integration, and application of knowledge. Since that time a movement of faculty members, department chairs, chief academic officers, presidents, associations, and foundations has worked to encourage, assess, and reward multiple forms of scholarship in all institutional types across the country and abroad.

There is evidence that this movement has had a significant impact. Over more than a decade, major changes have altered how faculty work is defined, structured, assessed, and rewarded. Just four years after its publication, 62 percent of chief academic officers in four-year institutions reported that *Scholarship Reconsidered* had informed discussions of faculty roles and rewards (Glassick, Huber, & Maeroff, 1997). Adrianna Kezar (2000) conducted focus groups with practitioners and researchers and asked them to identify the most memorable piece of writing that they had read in the last five, 10, or more years. Almost every focus group member mentioned *Scholarship Reconsidered* and said the work "fueled and provided a language for a change that had been discussed for years" (p. 450). A search of the Institute for Scientific Information's citation database reveals that *Scholarship Reconsidered* was one of the most frequently cited publications of the past decade (Braxton, Luckey, & Holland, 2002). While an argument could be made that *Scholarship Reconsidered* was something of a watershed for American higher education, as momentous a document for higher education as *A Nation at Risk* (National Commission on Excellence in Education, 1983) was for K–12, or the Yale report of 1828 was for the defense of liberal education, celebrating the importance of this one document is not the purpose of this book.

Many have attempted to understand the extent of reform in faculty roles and rewards prompted by *Scholarship Reconsidered,* but most cite individual case studies, examining the impact in one area such as teaching or engagement, or describing how these reforms influenced one institutional type (for example, liberal arts colleges). There is one notable exception. Braxton et al. (2002) recently completed a national study of faculty professional performance, to understand the degree to which faculty in four disciplines had institutionalized the four domains of scholarship in their everyday work. The researchers found that all four domains of scholarship had attained the most basic, or structural-level institutionalization; the scholarships of discovery and teaching had attained procedural-level institutionalization (wherein the activity is a regular part of workload); but only the scholarship of discovery had achieved incorporation-level institutionalization (wherein faculty values and assumptions support the activity).

This important study helped us understand how discipline influences faculty involvement in multiple forms of scholarship. It also provides insight into the most pervasive barriers to the institutionalization of multiple forms of scholarship and how they operate in the work life of faculty members. Despite this study, however, little research had examined the extent or impact of policy changes to encourage multiple forms of scholarship on all types of four-year colleges and universities (Braxton et al., 2002). Also, while several important books explored redefining faculty roles and rewards conceptually (Moxley & Lenker, 1995; Zahorski, 2002), academic administrators had few roadmaps for initiating reform and evaluating whether it was working. There was, in addition, a lack of information on how redefining scholarship was interacting with other internal and external forces affecting the professoriate. Session after session at AAHE's annual Forum on Faculty Roles and Rewards conference included testimonials by administrators about campus transformations, but little solid evidence demonstrated the national impact of efforts to redefine scholarship.

With this kind of exploration in mind, AAHE's Forum on Faculty Roles and Rewards launched a two-year project in fall 2001, "Toward an Enlarged Understanding of Scholarship: A Project Exploring How Institutions Encourage Multiple Forms of Scholarly Excellence." The project was led by us and funded by the Atlantic Philanthropies and an anonymous donor. It had two main components. The first was a nationwide survey of chief academic officers (CAOs) of four-year colleges and universities, to determine the national impact of the effort to encourage multiple forms of scholarship on faculty work life, institutional effectiveness, and academic cultures.

The second component was the "Reflecting on Best Practice Project," January 2001 through spring 2003, which solicited proposals from entire institutions, specific departments, or colleges that had encouraged multiple forms of scholarship through faculty rewards, incentives, or other support structures over the past decade and were interested in completing campus studies of their own change process and outcomes. Nine institutions were chosen and received modest honoraria to facilitate participation. We selected the nine institutions with an eye to diversity. They included non-profit institutions and one for-profit; public and private institutions; small liberal arts colleges and large research universities; institutions that initiated reform a decade ago and just recently; institutions that describe one unit's efforts and those that describe institution-wide efforts.

Each campus study team wrote a chapter for this book: Franklin College, Madonna University, Albany State University, the University of Phoenix, South Dakota State University, Kansas State University, Portland State University, Arizona State University, and the University of Colorado School of Medicine. While a few of the institutions might be considered primary leaders in the movement to redefine scholarship, most were not, and they wrote about their efforts for the first time.

ORGANIZATION OF THIS BOOK

Although the campus studies are interesting in their own right as illustrations of significant reform, they have even more value when placed in the context of national developments, for they are local expressions of a much larger phenomenon. We have therefore organized this book so as to begin with historical and conceptual background, move through the nine campus studies, and finish with a detailed examination of AAHE's survey of CAOs and the impact of the movement nationwide.

The book has three parts. Part One, "Context," begins with a chapter by one of the editors, R. Eugene Rice, that sketches the history of the movement to redefine scholarship and the context around the development of *Scholarship Reconsidered*. Rice was a senior scholar at the Carnegie Foundation and was intimately involved in conceptualizing *Scholarship Reconsidered*. He also served as director of AAHE's Forum on Faculty Roles and Rewards, where redefining scholarship was a primary focus. Through visits to hundreds of campuses since 1990, he has assisted academic leaders in the United States and abroad in reforming faculty roles and rewards to acknowledge and support a greater diversity of talent and approaches to scholarship.

Next come two chapters in which pioneers of the movement reflect on their own work with campuses nationwide. We are grateful that such a distinguished group of leaders agreed to write short narrative essays. In Chapter Two, Mary Taylor Huber, Pat Hutchings, Lee S. Shulman, Amy Driscoll, George E. Walker, and David K. Scott discuss issues relating to the four categories of scholarship identified by Boyer. In Chapter Three, Robert M. Diamond, Kenneth J. Zahorski, and Jerry G. Gaff examine some of the more concrete issues relating to bringing a new perspective on scholarship to the campus.

Part Two of this book, "Lessons Learned from Campus Studies" (Chapters Four–Twelve), presents studies of the nine institutions involved in the "Reflecting on Best Practice" project. Whenever the radio host and author Garrison Keillor performs for an audience in a new city, he begins by helping them and the listeners to understand where they are. He locates himself by reflecting on both the obvious and the idiosyncratic character, values, and history of the place. Because redefining scholarship in faculty roles and rewards is so dependent on an institution's culture and history, we asked each campus study team to describe the *history* of faculty roles and rewards at their institution, and how distinct aspects of institutional culture, institutional type, and internal and external forces influenced reform efforts. We also asked authors to describe the *process* of making the change. This included all stakeholders and external agents, forces working for and against change, how the process was organized, the infrastructure or financial investment required, and how it was approved through campus governance structures. We then asked each author to outline their campus study's *research questions and methods for collecting data* (surveys, focus groups, individual interviews, and so forth). Guided by scholars of organizational culture, such as Schein (1992) and Masland (1985), authors were encouraged to record artifacts or surface-level changes, changes in values and beliefs, and deeper cultural changes, such as alterations in basic assumptions. Authors examined promotion and tenure rates of faculty involved in the scholarships of teaching or engagement, and changes in language and beliefs regarding scholarship among faculty, department chairs, and deans. They examined and reported both obvious *outcomes* of policy reform and more subliminal signs. In the final section of each study, the authors provide advice to others considering similar change. Authors *reflected* on what they would have done differently, what aspect of their change process worked well, and where they were struggling. Chapters end with *questions* for the future about encouraging, supporting, assessing, and rewarding multiple forms of scholarship.[1]

We asked authors to be frank and honest about where policy reform was not working, the unanticipated consequences of redefining scholarship, and the problems it did not solve or made worse. We are grateful to them for having the courage to air their struggles and questions for the benefit of other campuses with similar concerns.

THE NINE CAMPUS STUDIES

Franklin College (Chapter Four) and Madonna University (Chapter Five) are stories of redefining scholarship in a liberal arts context. They underscore the important role of institutional mission and faculty workload in defining faculty work. They also illustrate the limits of policy reform: many faculty members had only a vague recollection of why the definitions of scholarship were changed, or what these changes meant for them, until their campus studies began. Franklin College's campus study explores the dilemmas that small liberal arts colleges face in trying to raise the bar of expectations for faculty scholarship without losing their character and mission (for example, a commitment to student learning and development). At Franklin, faculty members raised concerns about being expected to engage in scholarship at the expense of students, or "selfish scholarship," while the provost was concerned about the insular nature of the faculty, who reviewed each other's teaching and research for promotion and tenure rather than using external reviews. The study at Madonna University generated excitement and encouraged the faculty to reflect on new opportunities to engage in multiple forms of scholarship, such as working collaboratively with student affairs and academic affairs administrators, and reciprocal mentoring between junior and senior faculty.

Albany State University's campus study (Chapter Six) partly answers the question posed by the previous two chapters, of how an institution that has traditionally emphasized teaching and service might increase scholarship without deviating from its mission or hurting students. Albany State is a historically black university with a mission of recruiting, retaining, and graduating at-risk students. In 2002, Georgia's Board of Regents and the legislature cut funding for developmental studies and programs that were critical to student enrollment, retention, and persistence. At the same time, the regents required the institution to press for more research from its faculty. The academic administration made the best of this situation by redefining scholarship and encouraging the faculty to engage in forms that would directly influence the retention and success of students. Faculty members began studying the relationship between their own pedagogy and student study habits and test-taking skills. Administrators developed programs to support discovery, engagement, integration, and teaching scholarship that addressed the university's crisis and the fundamental mission of preparing, recruiting, and retaining at-risk students.

Many would consider the University of Phoenix—a for-profit institution—an unlikely choice for a book about redefining scholarship. However, its story (Chapter Seven) offers lessons for non-profit and for-profit education alike. An underlying question framing the University of Phoenix campus study is, How are faculty accomplishments in any form of scholarship linked to student success? The University of Phoenix is well known for its model of "unbundling" the faculty role and its focus on adult learners and professional education. Less well known is the degree to which its faculty members engage in discovery, integration, or application of knowledge outside of their teaching role, and what influence those activities have on the university's bottom line—student success and profitable programs. While this campus study does not answer the question, its findings raise important issues about the place of scholarship in faculty roles and rewards: Is there a direct link between faculty involvement in any form of scholarship and student engagement or success? Are there ways to make the linkages more useful to students, faculty, or institutions? If we assume doctoral programs require faculty who are involved in the scholarship of discovery, what do undergraduate programs require?

Chapters Four–Seven describe campuses where redefining scholarship was used as a strategy to encourage faculty to engage in any of the four forms of scholarship in addition to effective teaching, advising, and service. In the following chapters (Eight–Twelve) about research, doctoral, and comprehensive universities, however, redefining scholarship was a strategy to give greater legitimacy to the scholarships of teaching, application, and integration, and to challenge the trend toward ever higher research expectations at the expense of other kinds of scholarly work.

The authors of the studies of South Dakota State University (SDSU; Chapter Eight) and Kansas State University (KSU; Chapter Nine) observe that the larger the university, the more any kind of reform in faculty roles and rewards is dependent on departmental culture. Rather than fighting the culture of departmental autonomy and disciplinary influence in defining faculty roles and rewards, academic leaders at SDSU embraced it by facilitating the development of a university standards document and departmental documents outlining standards for multiple forms of scholarship. These documents had a significant impact on promotion and tenure decisions and on merit pay, and served to clarify department missions and relate them to faculty workload and rewards. At KSU, the provost, realizing that faculty who emphasized the scholarships of teaching or engagement were in particular jeopardy, decided that "flexible allocation of faculty time and talent" was needed to align mission, workload, and reward system more effectively. The university devised individualized faculty assignments, not unlike Boyer's (1990) "creativity contracts," and created a vehicle through which faculty could emphasize any form of scholarship for one or more years, in agreement with their department chairs, and be evaluated based on that evidence. On both campuses, the lack of reform in disciplinary associations and among other prestigious research universities put limits on innovative reforms, though both found concrete benefits for institutional effectiveness and faculty satisfaction from initiating reform.

Portland State University (PSU; Chapter Ten) has been an exemplar for redefining scholarship since Judith Ramaley's tenure there as president. Rather than detailing the strategies employed, the authors critically examined the culture shift that occurred over the past decade at PSU, assessing its effects on how faculty and administrators define scholarship. Those who study organizational change in reward systems will appreciate the different perspectives the authors bring to bear on what did or did not happen at PSU during a decade that saw both reform and the discussion of "second-generation" issues, such as socializing and being influenced by new and junior faculty values and expectations, and the effects of the departure of key change agents.

Arizona State University (ASU; Chapter Eleven) is the kind of premier research institution other campuses try to emulate in their reward systems. Yet, many of ASU's faculty and administrators realized the need for paying greater attention to the scholarship of teaching. Arizona State's campus study looks closely at one small but far-reaching attempt at supporting faculty involvement in the scholarship of teaching, the Center for Research on Education in Science, Mathematics, Engineering and Technology (CRESMET), which served as both a protective environment for faculty members engaged in the scholarship of teaching and as a catalyst for changing the discourse on the scholarship of teaching. ASU learned the important role of enclaves in cultivating talent and initiating reforms to encourage an enlarged view of scholarship.

The University of Colorado School of Medicine campus study (Chapter Twelve) is remarkable for several reasons. It begins by explaining recent changes in medical education, as well as the practice of tracking medical faculty (researchers, clinicians, teachers, and others), which consigned faculty who emphasized teaching and clinical practice to second-class status. By restructuring faculty appointments on a single track and redefining scholarship to include teaching, integration, and application, as well as research, the university sought to create a more equitable and supportive environment. The study describes the university's attempt to reform policies and procedures for promotion and tenure in ways that recognize and reward teaching and clinician practice. Embedded in the discussion is a detailed look at the scholarships of teaching, discovery, application, and integration within a single discipline, medicine. The vignettes provide an inspiring window into the major contributions faculty are making to society through these different forms of scholarship, as well as the ways committees are actually evaluating this work.

ASSESSING THE IMPACT OF REFORM

Part Three of the book, "National Perspectives," draws upon diverse sources and evidence to understand the impact of the movement to redefine scholarship, but with a national more than a local emphasis. Chapter Thirteen reports on AAHE's national survey of CAOs. Written by one of the editors, KerryAnn O'Meara, it uses a nationally representative sample of four-year institutions to explore key questions, such as the extent to which campuses have made formal changes to their reward systems to encourage multiple forms of scholarship over the past decade; the catalysts for making these changes and the barriers to implementing them; and the impact of formal policy changes on faculty work life, reward systems, and academic culture. Another important question is whether there were noticeable differences between campuses that made formal changes and those that did not, in terms of faculty work life, reward systems, or academic cultures. The findings are presented in three categories: the extent and kinds of formal policy reform; catalysts and barriers to change; and the impact of policy reform on faculty work life and institutional effectiveness, reward systems, and academic culture. Tables of survey data are provided in the Appendix, which enable readers to compare campus studies and survey findings, to explore the effects of changes in mission and planning documents, revisions in promotion and tenure documents and criteria, development of flexible workload programs, and creation of incentive grants on faculty reward systems and work life.

As noted previously, the national movement to encourage multiple forms of scholarship has meant different things to different types of institutions. While some of the barriers to reform are similar across institutional types, others are very different. O'Meara draws on many sources of data to analyze the barriers that thwart and the strategies that support faculty involvement in multiple forms of scholarship. The discussion includes the role of institutional type in defining the kinds of barriers that exist and the most effective strategies for addressing them.

In Chapter Fourteen, O'Meara provides a guide to best practices, strategies, and campus examples, modeled after Mary Deane Sorcinelli's "Best Practices for Supporting Early Career Faculty." Chapter Fifteen, written by Rice, sets out the lessons learned from this inquiry into the scholarly work of faculty. He identifies key lines of work growing out of the effort and asks about the future of a broader understanding of scholarship in a rapidly changing environment.

ADDRESSING THE GAP BETWEEN POLICY AND PRACTICE

By presenting historical background, campus studies of the current situation for all types of four-year institutions, and qualitative and quantitative analysis, we have tried to convey an idea of the breadth and depth of real change during the years since *Scholarship Reconsidered* appeared. We believe that readers of this book will conclude that, unquestionably, many colleges and universities have experienced a shift in their understanding of scholarship and in their capacity to reward it. But beyond that, the essays collected here address an issue raised often during the past 20 years, as scholars and practitioners have critiqued higher education research for its lack of utility and relevance. Practitioners have argued that higher education literature would be more useful if it provided information about best practices, looked at issues within specific contexts, drew implications, and provided advice; while researchers felt that it would be more helpful if it "pushed theoretical boundaries or questioned commonly held assumptions" (Kezar, 2000, p. 453).

The chapters in this book accomplish each of these objectives. Their authors demonstrate a depth of understanding in exploring the gap between policy and practice. Rather than completing research that sits on a shelf, authors used the results of their investigations to improve faculty satisfaction, institutional effectiveness, and academic culture. New questions and frameworks from their findings challenge the national discourse on how we think about and reward faculty work. The book's diversity of institutional types and attention to issues specific to different kinds of institutional contexts provide deans and provosts an opportunity to see their own issues addressed and to compare their own institutions with national trends. Scholars who study organizational change in academic reward systems or who study faculty role performance will find this volume helpful for its insight into the benefits and limitations of reforming faculty reward systems.

Colleges and universities will not be able to genuinely recognize and reward multiple forms of scholarly work unless faculty have confidence in the integrity of the institution's mission, aspiration and goals, and values. The definition of scholarship, accordingly, must be aligned with the basic institutional mission, and the various forms of scholarship—whether discovery, teaching, integration, or engagement—must be rewarded in ways that encourage faculty members to contribute to the fulfillment of institutional goals as well as their own disciplinary aspirations. Our intention is that this book will enable administrators and faculty members, both individually and institutionally, to reflect on their own definition of scholarship, understand how the several forms of scholarship can be rewarded, and recognize how faculty members can contribute significantly to strengthening the mission while finding greater personal and professional fulfillment.

Note

1. We provided each campus liaison person with studies on faculty roles and rewards, and asked them to read Andrew T. Masland's article "Organizational Culture in the Study of Higher Education" (1985), which includes recommendations for collecting cultural data and evidence of change, and excerpts from the American Council on Education's series *On Change* (Eckel, Green, Hill, & Mallon, 1999), as resources for thinking about how to collect evidence of campus change. One of the challenges of writing the campus studies was deciding which aspects of reform to focus on, because most of the institutions had tried more than one kind of reform over the previous decade. We worked with each campus liaison to focus on one "unit of analysis," as the case-study methodologist Robert K. Yin (1994) would describe the focus of a case, so that each could contribute something unique to the entire project. Each campus liaison formed a committee or invited additional authors to the project, to gather evidence about the changes and their potential outcomes for faculty and institution. We labeled Chapters Four–Twelve "campus studies" to underscore that they are not case studies as defined by scholars of that methodology. However, we did ask each campus to use many of the principles employed by case-study methodologists. In our function as editors, we pushed each campus to make their stories interesting and distinctive, to articulate questions and issues that went beyond their own kind of policy reform or institutional type, and to analyze the data and make them meaningful for readers.

References

Boyer, E. (1990). *Scholarship reconsidered: Priorities of the professoriate.* Princeton, NJ: Carnegie Foundation for the Advancement of Teaching.

Braxton, J., Luckey, W., & Holland, P. (2002). *Institutionalizing a broader view of scholarship through Boyer's four domains.* ASHE-ERIC Higher Education Report, Vol. 29, No. 2. San Francisco: Jossey-Bass.

Eckel, P., Green, M., Hill, B., & Mallon, W. (1999). *On Change III: Taking charge of change. A primer for colleges and universities.* Washington, DC: American Association for Higher Education.

Glassick, C. E., Huber, M. T., & Maeroff, G. I. (1997). *Scholarship assessed: Evaluation of the professoriate.* San Francisco: Jossey-Bass.

Kezar, A. (2000). Higher education research at the millennium: Still trees without fruit? *Review of Higher Education, 23*(4): 443–468.

Masland, A. T. (1985). Organizational culture in the study of higher education. *Review of Higher Education, 8*(2): 157–168.

Mills, C. W. (1959). *The sociological imagination.* New York: Oxford University Press.

Moxley, J. M., & Lenker, L. (Eds.). (1995). *The politics and processes of scholarship.* Westport, CT: Greenwood.

National Commission on Excellence in Education. (1983). *A nation at risk: The imperative for educational reform.* Washington, DC: Author.

Schein, E. H. (1992). *Organizational culture and leadership* (2nd ed.) San Francisco: Jossey-Bass.

Sykes, C. (1988). *ProfScam: Professors and the demise of higher education.* New York: St. Martin's.

Yin, R. K. (1994). *Case study research* (2nd ed.). Applied Social Research Methods Series, Vol. 5. Thousand Oaks, CA: Sage.

Zahorski, K. J. (Ed.). (2002, Summer). *Scholarship in the postmodern era: New venues, new values, new visions.* New Directions for Teaching and Learning, no. 90. San Francisco: Jossey-Bass.

PART ONE

CONTEXT

CHAPTER ONE

"SCHOLARSHIP RECONSIDERED"
History and Context

R. Eugene Rice

Scholarship Reconsidered: Priorities of the Professoriate (Boyer, 1990b) is a concise document of fewer than 150 pages that tells us little that we did not know already. What makes it significant, however, is that it came along at the right time and addressed the major strains that had developed around what was central to the scholarly work of faculty and should be valued and rewarded. More important, it reframed the issues so that we could get beyond the old teaching-versus-research debate, rise above the theory/practice hierarchy plaguing the discussion of scholarship, and begin to think in new ways about the alignment of faculty priorities and institutional mission.

The primary intent of the Carnegie report was to be heuristic— to reframe the discussion about what faculty do as scholars on a broad range of fronts, and to open a lively conversation across higher education on this important topic. At no time was the purpose to impose a particular formulation of the meaning of scholarship and what should be encompassed. Rather, the intention was to enlarge the debate, generating fresh conceptions of faculty work in a way that would reintegrate personal and institutional priorities, and to bring a new kind of wholeness to what it means to be a scholar while at the same time responding more adequately to the changing educational needs of society.

THE CHANGING CONTEXT

Following World War II, American higher education experienced enormous growth and development—change that was genuinely transformative but also disjointed. Much has been made of the rich mosaic that evolved from a radically decentralized system that placed a high priority on autonomy—both individual and institutional. The divisions were across state, region, sector, public/private boundaries, and, for faculty particularly, disciplines and departments. While we must all acknowledge the strengths of this arrangement, which has been widely praised, it also became clear that not a lot was invested in integration and connection, a sense of the whole. *Scholarship Reconsidered* was an attempt to address this systemic need.

The understanding of scholarship in the American context was fundamentally shaped by events leading up to World War II and its aftermath. The conflict with the Third Reich precipitated an intellectual sea change as leading scholars in many fields migrated across the Atlantic. Two additional events, largely external, had a critical impact on how we thought about scholarship: passage of the GI Bill and the Soviet Union's launching of *Sputnik I,* in 1957. These significant events cut two ways. The GI Bill funded greater diversity and access, heightening pressures for broader engagement with elements of society that earlier had been largely neglected. Competition with the Soviet Union triggered by the launching of *Sputnik* led to the funding of a particular kind of scholarship—a narrowly circumscribed form of scientific and technical research. Scholarship, especially in the sciences and engineering, became increasingly defined by funding sources and the availability of grant money. In a very real sense, the Cold War redefined scholarly priorities on our college and university campuses; scholarship became research, funded and publishable.

During the 1960s and early '70s, American higher education expanded dramatically. To meet the demand for faculty generated by the influx of students and the rapid proliferation of colleges and universities across the country, the number of doctorates granted between 1960 and 1970 tripled, and the prestige of being a professor rose significantly. During these heady days of expansion and growth, what I have referred to elsewhere as the "assumptive world of the academic professional" took hold (Rice, 1996). The constituent parts of this influential professional consensus can be traced back in the history of American higher education, imported in part from Germany, of course, but being rooted in Britain and Scotland as well. This powerful conception of scholarly work had seven key parts:

1. Research is the central professional endeavor and focus of academic life.
2. Quality in the profession is maintained by peer review and professional autonomy.
3. Knowledge is pursued for its own sake.
4. The pursuit of knowledge is best organized by discipline (that is, by discipline-based departments).
5. Reputations are established in national and international professional associations.
6. Professional rewards and mobility accrue to those who persistently accentuate their specializations.
7. The distinctive task of the academic professional is the pursuit of cognitive truth.

This vision of scholarship and the interrelated complex of assumptions on which it was built contributed to major advancements of knowledge. How often we have heard the American research university referred to as "the envy of the world"?

The "scholarship of discovery," as this conception of scholarly work was identified in *Scholarship Reconsidered,* became normative for most of American higher education and was linked to an influential economy of prestige. As higher education expanded and differentiated further, this narrow conception of scholarship became the gold standard, and, most important, drove the expanding graduate programs that were preparing the faculty who would be responsible for setting the criteria of excellence for the remainder of the 20th century.

While research productivity escalated under this dominant but narrow view of scholarship, questions were soon being raised by higher education's major constituents—legislators, trustees, parents, and others—about the quality of undergraduate teaching. Internally, students and faculty as well as academic administrators grew increasingly concerned about the scholarly investment in teaching and its place in the reward system. During the mid-1970s, faculty development became an institutional priority and teaching and learning the primary emphasis. Foundations invested heavily in teaching improvement strategies; a new national association was formed, with regular assemblies and a journal, the *Professional and Organizational Development Network in Higher Education*. Disciplinary associations began to attend to teaching as a scholarly endeavor, several starting journals about scholarly teaching and what is now called "the scholarship of teaching."

A second major concern focused on the extent to which the scholarly work of professors engaged the nation's critical societal issues. Faculty scholarship was seen as too narrowly specialized and self-referential. Exaggerated but popular diatribes such as Charles J. Sykes's *ProfScam* (1988) were widely discussed. By 1990, Harvard's Derek Bok would render this stinging indictment in his book *Universities and the Future of America*:

> Armed with the security of tenure and the time to study the world with care, professors would appear to have a unique opportunity to act as society scouts to signal impending problems long before they are visible to others. Yet rarely have members of the academy succeeded in discovering the emerging issues and bringing them vividly to the attention of the public. What Rachel Carson did for risks to the environment, Ralph Nader for consumer protection, Michael Harrington for problems of poverty, Betty Friedan for women's rights, they did as independent critics, not as members of the faculty. Even the seminal work on the plight of blacks in America was written by a Swedish social scientist, not a member of an American university. After a major social problem has been recognized, universities will usually continue to respond weakly unless outside support is available and the subjects involved command prestige in academic circles. These limitations have hampered efforts to address many of the most critical challenges to the nation. (p. 105)

Toward the end of the 1980s, the demand for change gathered enough attention to require a response. Discontent with the way faculty were using their scholarly talents was gaining momentum: the neglect of undergraduate teaching, particularly at the large research universities, was being broadly attacked across the country;

the disconnect from the larger social problems facing the nation was being roundly criticized; and, perhaps most important, the lack of integration—the sense of fragmentation—in a highly specialized, differentiated system of higher education was being blamed (often unfairly) on the professoriate. The time was ripe for rethinking the scholarly work of faculty.

From the Margins to the Heart of the Academic Enterprise

Most efforts to change higher education begin on the margins of institutions and stay there. *Scholarship Reconsidered,* in contrast to almost all of the reports calling for reform published by foundations and associations interested in initiating change, struck at the heart of the academic enterprise. The report began with the faculty role and had the audacity to raise questions about the meaning of scholarship. More important, it called into question the academic reward system—the criteria used in making decisions about tenure and promotion.

Scholarship Reconsidered immediately struck a responsive chord, becoming the best-selling publication in the history of the Carnegie Foundation. Ernest Boyer's leadership was critical in drawing widespread attention to the report and the call to reexamine the faculty role and reward structure. In this effort Boyer's charismatic and positional authority came together in a way that was virtually unique in recent American higher education. Few others combined the public presence, persuasiveness, and national visibility required to effectively take on the task of redefining the meaning of scholarship and raising substantive questions about the relationship between the scholarly priorities of individuals and institutional missions. Years of political experience in Washington, D.C., and Albany, New York, had given Boyer an uncanny sense of timing, nowhere more evident than in the process of developing and releasing the report. Following the publication of *Scholarship Reconsidered,* Boyer committed his very active speaking schedule and much of his extensive writing to the dissemination of the new conception of scholarship set forth in the report. On more than one university campus where provosts and deans pressed to get the broader definition of scholarly work adopted, resistant faculty were heard to complain of being "Boyerized."

Scholarship Reconsidered had a broader impact than most foundation reports, not only because it was a timely response to a widely articulated demand for change but also because it drew together ideas that were already being developed and were just waiting to be appropriated and built into a larger perspective. In addition, the report had an ongoing life, because the American Association for Higher Education (AAHE) developed an organizational initiative to ensure that the ideas it sparked would not disappear. Russell Edgerton, president of AAHE at the time, and a group of major university provosts founded the Forum on Faculty Roles and Rewards, with significant financial support from the Fund for the Improvement of Post-Secondary Education. In the keynote address at one of the forum's early annual conferences, Boyer (1990a) described what was happening to the discourse on the scholarly work of faculty: "We are beginning to find a new language, a common language . . . that will help revitalize research, give dignity to teaching, and help the academy be more responsive."

Most faculty members have at least three stands in their careers. Donald Light (1974) has identified these as the institutional, external, and disciplinary dimensions of faculty work. Those familiar with academic culture know that disciplinary commitments must be addressed if progress is going to be made in reconsidering scholarship. The majority of the faculty have their identities imbedded in their disciplines, and align themselves institutionally with their departments.

Any effort to enlarge the conception of scholarly work requires beginning with the disciplines and the departmental structure. This means serious work with the discipline-based scholarly societies and the professional associations. Therefore, Robert Diamond and his colleagues at Syracuse University launched a series of major projects aimed at bringing the disciplinary and professional associations into the process of developing guidelines for evaluating and rewarding an enlarged conception of scholarly work. The results can be found in two volumes edited by Diamond and Bronwyn Adam (1995, 2000), in which 20 disciplinary and professional associations presented the conclusions of long and involved discussions among their members and within their representative boards. The Syracuse projects advanced the reconsideration of scholarship and gave it a special kind of legitimacy, by going to the associations where the scholarly identities of the more scholarly faculty are shaped and to which the individual departments look for guidance on what counts as scholarship.

Another practical approach that made the reconsideration of scholarship more than an interesting peripheral phenomenon was the way in which AAHE's Forum on Faculty Roles and Rewards was organized. Colleges and universities were encouraged to send "teams" of faculty leaders and academic administrators to the annual conference to work on issues central to the mission of the institution. The team members interacted with one another across administrative and faculty lines and with participants from other institutions struggling with similar issues. Over the 10-year period that the forum convened annually, hundreds of institutions sent teams. In addition, associations representing particular sectors of higher education picked up on the agenda. For instance, the Council of Independent Colleges launched a large, well-funded initiative focused on changing faculty roles and rewards. The land-grant universities, with strong support from the W. K. Kellogg Foundation, waded in with the aim of renewing their founding mission of outreach and civic engagement; Ohio State, Oregon State, and Clemson led the way. Small private universities joined to form the Association of New American Colleges, to establish a distinctive niche, a new kind of excellence, for liberal arts institutions with growing professional programs. An enlarged conception of scholarship and an innovative approach to faculty work were at the heart of this endeavor (McMillin & Berberet, 2002).

AAHE's 2000 Conference on Faculty Roles and Rewards marked the tenth anniversary of the publication of *Scholarship Reconsidered* by choosing as the central theme for that year "*Scholarship Reconsidered* Reconsidered: Update and New Directions." More than a celebration of what had been accomplished, the conference was a critical assessment. The meeting was organized around the four forms of scholarship and their interrelationship: the scholarships of teaching and learning, engagement, integration, and discovery.

Since publication of the Carnegie report, the largest advances have been made, as might be expected, in the scholarship of teaching and learning. The Carnegie Foundation and AAHE have collaborated in giving this form of scholarly work both viability and substance. Additionally, Campus Compact and AAHE worked together on what is now referred to as "the scholarship of engagement." In setting the context for understanding what follows in this volume, the extensive work on these two forms of scholarship needs to be introduced.

THE SCHOLARSHIP OF TEACHING AND LEARNING

When the conceptual framework for the Carnegie report was being constructed, many distinguished scholars were already devoting their professional lives to what later took on the designation "scholarship of teaching." William Perry, Joseph Katz, Patricia Cross, and Lee Schulman were among those who laid a firm intellectual foundation for recognizing teaching as a scholarly endeavor. Disciplinary associations as diverse as sociology and chemistry were grappling with the challenge. The AAHE Assessment Forum was gaining recognition, and a new "teaching initiative" had been created.

One of AAHE's great success stories is the peer-review-of-teaching project, led by Pat Hutchings, Russell Edgerton, and Lee Shulman. Much of the work on the scholarship of teaching and learning we are now engaged in builds on lessons learned through that initiative, which called for an approach to teaching that transcends the older content/process, theory/practice, teacher/student dichotomies that usually shape our thinking. The project involved having campuses work together to create new scholarly roles for faculty members in improving and ensuring the quality of teaching and learning. The work was organized largely around disciplines and specific scholarly societies.

Institutions are now beginning to make teaching and the focus on learning a public, documented endeavor, with the same kind of community of discourse and the open sharing and critiquing of scholarly work as in traditional approaches to research. Teaching as scholarly inquiry becomes subject to empirical evidence and the focus of collaborative, intellectual deliberation. As Randy Bass, professor at Georgetown University, puts it, the scholarship of teaching and learning has become a movement to "think of teaching practice, and the evidence of student learning, as problems to be investigated, analyzed, represented and debated" (Bass, 1998).

The phrase "scholarship of teaching" has been widely debated since first appearing in *Scholarship Reconsidered*. It was also a topic of major contention even as the book was being prepared. A number of terms considered—including the "presentation of knowledge" and the "transmission and dissemination of knowledge"—were found to be one-sided and did not encompass the interactive character of this aspect of scholarly work. They also reinforced the misperception that teaching is a one-way street, merely a packaging and distribution function, and suggested that teaching and learning stand in a hierarchical relationship, with knowledge being viewed as a finished product, to be refined and then passed down. The questions raised about this perspective led to the adoption of the more inclusive "scholarship of teaching and learning."

Lee Shulman's seminal essay "Knowledge and Teaching: Foundations of the New Reform" (1987) reminded us that teaching is a more dynamic, relational endeavor, transcending the old process/content dichotomy that had long plagued the discussion of teaching. Shulman and his colleagues at Stanford introduced the awkward but useful phrase "pedagogical content knowledge." Their work with faculty members in specific disciplines revealed that effective teaching requires a content-specific knowledge base. In Shulman's words, it is "the capacity of a teacher to transform the content knowledge he or she possesses into forms that are pedagogically powerful and yet adaptive to the variations in an ability and background presented by students" (p. 5).

A key element for ensuring that the scholarship of teaching and learning would continue to receive vigorous attention was the appointment of Lee Shulman as president of the Carnegie Foundation for the Advancement of Teaching, following the passing of Ernest Boyer. Shulman had provided the intellectual underpinnings for AAHE's project on the peer review of teaching and, in his new position, made a special place for the scholarship of teaching and learning. Under his leadership and the guidance of Barbara Cambridge and Pat Hutchings, the Carnegie Foundation collaborated with AAHE in establishing the Carnegie Academy for the Scholarship of Teaching and Learning (CASTL). This national program has three parts, structured around the three ways faculty members pursue their professional lives: as individual scholars, as members of a campus community, and as participants in a discipline.

1. *The Carnegie Scholars Program.* Outstanding individual faculty, selected from designated disciplines, convene to engage in serious conversation with colleagues about the scholarship of teaching and learning. They look at their own classroom experience and document their scholarly work in teaching and learning in ways that can be reviewed on their campuses and by disciplinary peers in the United States and abroad. Through course portfolios, conference presentations, published papers, and a genuinely open discourse focusing on teaching and learning, these creative scholars are developing a body of literature, practical examples, assessment strategies, and new research methods lending greater coherence and substance to this form of scholarly inquiry. A growing cadre of scholars is emerging in the field of teaching and learning that can now be looked to for leadership and new ideas. A community of scholarly discourse extends beyond the classroom and the local campus.

2. *The Campus Program.* CASTL also has a substantial institutional dimension, one that is campus based and being implemented through AAHE. A national network of cross-sectoral institutions is exploring how to build the scholarship of teaching and learning into the institutional life of colleges and universities. The program has developed at more than a hundred campuses, ranging from Brown University to Augustana College and from Middlesex Community College to Ohio State University. These institutions have tailored their approaches to address the specific characteristics and needs of their own campuses. Campus conversations on teaching and learning are cultivated, and the network of institutions facilitates the sharing of what is learned. The AAHE WebCenter offers resources, the opportunity to try out new ideas, and the chance to engage in open conversation about this challenging form of scholarly work.

3. *Disciplinary Associations.* Working through the disciplines is essential, because so much work on the scholarship of teaching and learning focuses on the relationship between process and con-

tent in specific disciplines, and because faculty identify so thoroughly with the discipline. Increasingly, professional associations are sponsoring sessions on the scholarship of teaching and learning at their national conferences. The Academy of Management, the American Chemical Society, and the American Sociological Association have been particularly attentive to this. Several disciplinary associations, notably the American Studies Association, are now beginning to attend to the instructional role of technology in teaching.

The scholarship of teaching and learning has come a long way since the publication of *Scholarship Reconsidered*. It is receiving impressive attention internationally, and its conceptual framework continues to be a source of challenge and debate. Particularly contentious is the argument about the differences among good teaching, scholarly teaching, and the scholarship of teaching and learning. Teaching and learning are emerging as topics of provocative, scholarly discourse that have the potential for becoming the basis for cosmopolitan and intrinsically rewarding public exchange—a form of scholarly work that can be evaluated and assessed with increasing confidence.

THE SCHOLARSHIP OF ENGAGEMENT

Scholarship Reconsidered was introduced into a climate receptive to receiving an enlarged conception of scholarly work. The commitment to research—the scholarship of discovery—was still firmly in place and provided a major source of suspicion and resistance, but a significant constituency acknowledged the importance of the faculty's scholarly dimensions in teaching undergraduates and the assessment of learning—the scholarship of teaching. However, another form of scholarship, now called the scholarship of engagement, long marginalized but deeply rooted in the land-grant tradition, was also ripe for recognition.

The scholarship of engagement goes beyond what was identified in *Scholarship Reconsidered* as "the scholarship of application." Although the report attempted to honor what can be learned from practice, the scholarship of application, which builds on the established academic epistemology, assumes that knowledge is generated in the university or college and then applied to external contexts, with knowledge flowing in one direction, out of the academy.

The scholarship of engagement, in contrast, requires going beyond the "expert" model that often gets in the way of constructive university-community collaboration. It builds on the important work done by the late Ernest Lynton in his book *Making a Case for Professional Service* (1995) and the handbook that followed (coedited by Driscoll and Lynton), *Making Outreach Visible: A Guide to Documenting Professional Service and Outreach* (1999). These contributions advanced our ability to document and reward the scholarly work of faculty engaged in the application of knowledge.

We are now prepared to alter the approach taken by Lynton and Driscoll in fundamental ways. The scholarship of engagement calls on faculty to move beyond "outreach," as it was conceptualized in the land-grant colleges with their agricultural roots. It also asks that the scholar go beyond "service," with its overtones of noblesse oblige. What it emphasizes is genuine *collaboration:* that the learning and the teaching be multidirectional and the expertise shared. This represents a basic reconceptualization of faculty involvement in community-based work and will require our working in new ways across disciplines and institutional sectors. It will not only involve sharing the results of such work with the wider community as well as academic colleagues, but will also involve bringing representatives of the community into the planning and discussion at the beginning of the task. The mutuality implied here raises interesting, if thorny, questions about peer review. In this kind of scholarly work, who are the peers?

Thinking about the scholarship of engagement has benefited greatly from the substantive work of the late Donald Schön (1983, 1995) and his conception of the "reflective practitioner." He contributed to the reconsideration of scholarship, and his contention that "the new scholarship requires a new epistemology" continues to be especially influential. More persuasively than anyone else, he argued that theory and research, on the one hand, and practice, on the other, must be realigned—that theory and practice are hierarchically related but should not be. He also contended that every university develops an "institutional epistemology," an implicit theory of knowledge, and holds "conceptions of what counts as legitimate knowledge and how you know what you claim to know" (1995, p. 34). This epistemology is built into institutional structures, policies, and practices and becomes most evident in the faculty reward system's assessment of what counts as scholarship.

In broadening the conception of scholarship, the designation "scholarship of engagement" can serve as an umbrella category encompassing what in the past has been pursued under the rubrics of outreach, the scholarship of application, and professional service. This more inclusive approach is gaining growing acceptance.

With the epistemological challenge discussed previously, the scholarship of engagement also opens the way for a very different approach to scholarly work in all three of the traditional areas of faculty responsibility—teaching, research, and service. On the pedagogical front, the scholarship of engagement understood in this way requires a radically different approach to teaching and learning. In both the emergence of service-learning and the development of learning communities, faculty members have to rethink their relationship to students, the larger community, and many of their assumptions about teaching.

In pursuing the growing interest in community-based research, the scholarship of engagement calls for a realignment of the relationship of local and cosmopolitan knowledge. Community-based research is of necessity local, rooted in a particular time and place, calling for shared expertise and challenging established academic criteria. The scholarship of engagement puts a priority on collaboration with the larger community and an emphasis on learning that is multidirectional, extending beyond the boundaries of the campus and university. It transforms community service into collaborative practice.

CONCLUSION

Scholarship Reconsidered has clearly achieved its heuristic goal of stimulating a debate about the function of scholarship and the relationship between faculty priorities and the intent and expectations of colleges and universities. The many and varied directions of this widespread discourse are evident in the essays that follow.

The Carnegie report encouraged a wide-ranging set of conversations that occasionally developed a life of their own and moved off in disparate directions. A primary intent of *Scholarship*

Reconsidered was to foster a diverse dialogue while maintaining a unified conception of scholarship that would be broader and more inclusive, yet provide an integrated conception of scholarly work. Much of the discussion generated by the report and by changing conditions in higher education gravitated toward disaggregating the different forms of scholarship that were moving toward specialization, not only by field but by function. The campus studies found in this volume show the tension generated by this pull in the face of the need for greater coherence and more purposeful direction. But before presenting the campus studies, we should consider the thoughts offered in the next two chapters by pioneers in the movement to advance alternative forms of scholarship.

References

Bass, R. (1998). The scholarship of teaching: What's the problem? *Inventio: Creative Thinking About Teaching and Learning, 1*(1). Retrieved November 1, 2002 from http://www.doit.gmu.edu/Archives.feb98/randybass.htm

Bok, D. (1990). *Universities and the future of America.* Durham: Duke University Press.

Boyer, E. L. (1990a). *The new American scholar.* Keynote address presented at the AAHE National Conference on Higher Education, San Francisco, April.

Boyer, E. L. (1990b). *Scholarship reconsidered: Priorities of the professoriate.* Princeton, NJ: Carnegie Foundation for the Advancement of Teaching.

Diamond, R., & Adam, B. (1995). *The disciplines speak: Rewarding the scholarly, professional, and creative work of faculty.* Washington, DC: American Association for Higher Education.

Diamond, R., & Adam, B. (2000). *The disciplines speak II: More statements on rewarding the scholarly, professional, and creative work of faculty.* Washington, DC: American Association for Higher Education.

Driscoll, A., & Lynton, E. (1999). *Making outreach visible: A guide to documenting professional service and outreach.* Washington, DC: American Association for Higher Education.

Light, D. (1974). Introduction: The structure of the academic profession. *Sociology of Education, 47:* 2–28.

Lynton, E. (1995). *Making a case for professional service.* Washington, DC: American Association for Higher Education.

McMillin, L., & Berberet, W. (2002). *New academic compact.* Bolton, MA: Anker.

Rice, R. Eugene. (1996). *Making a place for the new American scholar.* Washington, DC: American Association for Higher Education.

Shulman , L. (1987). Knowledge and teaching: Foundations of the new reform. *Harvard Educational Review, 36*(4): 1–22.

Schön, D. A. (1983). *The reflective practitioner: How professionals think in action.* New York: Basic Books.

Schön, D. A. (1995). Knowing in action: The new scholarship requires a new epistemology. *Change, 27*(6): 27–34.

Sykes, C. J. (1988). *ProfScam: Professors and the demise of higher education.* New York: St. Martin's.

CHAPTER TWO

THE FOUR FORMS
OF SCHOLARSHIP

The effort to enlarge our understanding of the scholarly work of faculty would not have gone much beyond *Scholarship Reconsidered* without the serious intellectual work and dogged persistence of key leaders in higher education who were already engaged in rethinking what it means to be a scholar. The authors of the first section of this chapter, Mary Taylor Huber, Pat Hutchings, and Lee S. Shulman, have focused on the scholarship of teaching and learning. Through the Carnegie Scholars program, particularly, they have cultivated a cadre of talented teacher-scholars and created a body of literature that has given visibility and prestige to this important form of scholarship and practice. In the second section of the chapter, Amy Driscoll chronicles developments in the scholarship of engagement, a burgeoning field, through a highly personal statement. Her professional memoir explores the risks and benefits involved when young faculty try to incorporate a concern for community needs into their scholarly lives. In the chapter's third section, George E. Walker places the scholarship of discovery in its broader context. He comes to this work from years of experience as vice president and dean of the Graduate School at Indiana University, and his recent appointment as senior scholar and director of the Carnegie Initiative on the Doctorate has enriched his perspective. In the fourth and final section of the chapter, David K. Scott takes on the form of scholarship that has received the least attention and yet holds the greatest promise—the scholarship of integration. While serving as the chancellor of the University of Massachusetts,

Amherst, Scott chaired the advisory board of AAHE's Forum on Faculty Roles and Rewards. In that role he championed the broader definition of scholarship and framed it, as he argues in his essay, as an anticipation of a "much larger movement toward transformation of the academy."

—R.E.R.

The Scholarship of Teaching and Learning Today

Mary Taylor Huber, Pat Hutchings, and Lee S. Shulman

Teaching and learning is a vigorous, emergent field of thought and practice, engendering new forums and outlets for scholarship in departments, programs, and centers in colleges and universities across the country. Building and using knowledge to improve curricula, classroom teaching, and the quality of learning is no longer just a priority for specialists in education. Mainstream faculty in all the disciplines are beginning to consult the pedagogical literature, look critically at education in their fields, examine teaching and learning in their own classrooms, and improve practice with the knowledge produced by this inquiry. They are beginning to document their scholarly work on teaching and learning in course portfolios, conference presentations, and published papers, making it available to campus and disciplinary peers. The scholarship of teaching and learning is drawing interest both in the United States and abroad that will promote its critique and continued development (Healey, 2000; Lyons, Hyland, & Ryan, 2002; Martin, Benjamin, Prosser, & Trigwell, 1999).

The idea of treating teaching and learning as subjects for scholarship, when introduced into the vocabulary of higher education as "the scholarship of teaching" by *Scholarship Reconsidered* (Boyer, 1990), gained a hearing less because of its novelty than because it showed the place of teaching within a broader vision of scholarship. Boyer expanded scholarship to include discovery through basic research and efforts to advance the integration and application of knowledge. "As a scholarly enterprise," Boyer wrote, "teaching is a dynamic endeavor that begins with what the teacher knows" and "builds bridges between the teacher's understanding and the student's learning. Pedagogical procedures must be carefully planned, continuously examined, and relate directly to the subject taught" (p. 121). By focusing on the intellectual demands of teaching in *Scholarship Reconsidered* and especially in its sequel, *Scholarship Assessed,* Boyer and his colleagues foregrounded what the scholarship of teaching shares with other kinds of scholarly work (Glassick, Huber, & Maeroff, 1997; Rice, 1991).

Scholarship Reconsidered entered and helped shape a lively debate about higher education. Attention to teaching and learning increased during the 1990s, spurred by public concern about faculty commitment to the education of undergraduate students, issues of equity and access, the explosion of new media, the appeal of new pedagogies, and growing pressures for accountability. Key educators recognized that the scholarship of teaching added institutional *gravitas* and momentum to the efforts of faculty who were rethinking their work with students in ways that might address these developments (Edgerton, 1993; Lazerson, Wagnener, & Shumanis, 2000). Also important, as these reformers began to focus more centrally on students and their learning, they gradually shifted the language from "the scholarship of *teaching*" to "the scholarship of teaching *and learning.*"

Meanwhile, a host of related developments gave further momentum and substance to the work. Scholars of teaching and learning were able to draw upon a long-standing literature on the nature of "teacher knowledge" (Grossman, Wilson, & Shulman, 1989; Shulman, 1987), and on more recent research into the character of learning itself (Bransford, Brown, & Cocking, 1999; Marchese, 1997). The assessment movement, and especially the phenomenon of classroom assessment, sharpened higher education's focus on student learning and provided tools for faculty members seeking to investigate the impact of their course designs and pedagogies on learning (Angelo & Cross, 1993; Cross & Steadman, 1996). An interest in course and teaching portfolios, and other strategies for the peer review of teaching, widened the concept of the teaching audience to include peers as well as students (Centra, 1993; Edgerton,

Hutchings, & Quinlan, 1991; Hutchings, 1996; Seldin, 1997; Shulman, 1993). This decade also saw the establishment and growth of teaching and learning centers, which, on many campuses, provide programming and support for faculty reflecting upon and sharing their teaching practice. Indeed, more recently, many of these centers have explicitly embraced the agenda and language of the scholarship of teaching and learning.

Many of the educational reform projects of the past two decades have also fueled the development of the scholarship of teaching and learning. Projects of national scope include initiatives in undergraduate curriculum, teaching, technology, assessment, and graduate education led by the National Science Foundation, the American Association for Higher Education, the American Association of Colleges and Universities, the U.S. Department of Education's Fund for the Improvement of Postsecondary Education, the Carnegie Foundation for the Advancement of Teaching, and a host of other higher education associations, scholarly societies, and funding agencies. Many of these efforts have reinforced and advanced key principles of the scholarship of teaching and learning: that it is serious intellectual work and raises questions calling for systematic investigation and public exchange (Cambridge, 2002). As 1998 Carnegie Scholar and Georgetown University professor Randy Bass remarked, the scholarship of teaching and learning is a movement to "think of teaching practice, and the evidence of student learning, as problems to be investigated, analyzed, represented, and debated" (Bass, 1999, p. 1).

As the scholarship of teaching and learning has evolved and been enriched by intersections with related initiatives, its boundaries have become less clear. It is taking shape somewhat differently in different disciplines (Huber & Morreale, 2002). To be sure, many issues cut across fields, but most faculty members think about teaching and learning within the framework of their own disciplines. Biologists, historians, and psychologists may all agree that they want to foster "deep understanding" in their classrooms, but what they mean by "deep understanding" is different (Becher & Trowler, 2001; Donald, 2002), and so too is the way they are likely to go about the scholarship of teaching and learning itself.

We have begun to distinguish distinctive elements of discovery, integration, and application within the scholarship of teaching, because this work typically involves classroom inquiry, synthesizing ideas from different fields, and the improvement of practice all at the same time. But while Boyer and his colleagues productively parsed the notion of "scholarship" at the beginning of the 1990s, it became clear by the end of the decade that some new distinctions were needed to better map the scholarship of teaching and learning. For example, two of us—Lee Shulman, who succeeded Boyer as president of the Carnegie Foundation, and Carnegie vice president Pat Hutchings—argued that all faculty members have an obligation to be excellent teachers, well versed in their own fields and able to promote the development of real learning. When they also use what is known about teaching and learning and "invite peer collaboration and review," they may well be called scholarly teachers. But the scholarship of teaching and learning goes even further. As we wrote, "It requires a kind of 'going meta' in which faculty frame and systematically investigate questions related to student learning—the conditions under which it occurs, what it looks like, how to deepen it, and so forth—and to do so with an eye not only to improving their own classroom but to advancing practice beyond it" (Hutchings & Shulman, 1999, p. 13).

Disagreement on definitions promotes dialogue and continued scholarship under the broad canopy of teaching and learning. For many, the boundaries separating discovery, integration, and application are situational, depending on one's discipline, institution, and purpose. Scholarship may include work of elaborate design and formal execution, but it may also involve the kinds of action research that faculty members do when they make inquiries into their classroom practice and document their work and make it available to peers. Inviting mainstream faculty to see inquiry, documentation, and sharing about teaching and learning as part of their scholarly repertoire promotes dialogue on definitions as well as innovation (Hutchings, 2000).

Pathfinders in any new or emergent field of theory and practice face a familiar set of problems in winning support and acceptance for their work (Gumport, 2002). Scholars of teaching and learning are no exception. In many fields, "pedagogy" is both new and suspect as a topic, and the methods available for classroom inquiry are neither well understood nor well regarded. Some work may be presented as a form of reflection on teaching and learning, some may qualify as scholarship of discovery (research). The work may involve unusual cross-disciplinary collaborations, making it difficult to get the findings accepted in discipline-specific journals and conference sessions. Scholars of teaching and learning face institutional hurdles as well, ranging from working with colleagues to write appropriate human-subjects guidelines (Hutchings, 2002), to gaining eligibility for additional resources of time, money, and assistance, or to finding recognition for their work in the system of faculty roles and rewards. Rules written in the standard language of teaching, research, and service scholarship will likely place cross-cut categories at a disadvantage. Scholars of teaching and learning and their advocates must be prepared to make a strong case for the legitimacy and value of this work (Huber, 2001, 2002).

The placement of the scholarship of teaching and learning in the academy is very much at issue now. Its genres, topics, and methods are being invented as we speak; its role in academic careers is being written case by case; new practitioners announce themselves every day, and they are just beginning to seek each other out. Institutional realities and disciplinary styles are influencing the way scholars approach teaching and student learning, but, fortunately, boundaries in this area are not that well established, facilitating the emergence of a new "trading zone" for intellectual exchange and collaboration across countries, institutions, and fields (Huber & Morreale, 2002). It is in this space that we may find the best chances for the future of the scholarship of teaching.

Tracing the Scholarship of Engagement Through My Professional Memoirs

Amy Driscoll

"A faculty life can be a long life of doing essentially the same thing—teaching, publishing, serving on committees" (Secor, 2002, p. 10). That describes my life in academe until 1994, when I turned my work world upside down and applied for the position of director of community/university partnerships at Portland State University (PSU), in Portland, Oregon. The campus wanted someone to begin an ambitious program of service-learning in the context of collaborative relationships with the surrounding city. I was one of those faculty who had situated both teaching and research and my publishing pursuits in community for most of my career. The new position offered an opportunity to support colleagues who had similar commitments. Unfortunately, I had only recently stumbled upon the term "service-learning," so I had to do a quick study to qualify for the new position.

During my cramming, I encountered the early scholarship of civic engagement. I read the passionate anecdotes and the compelling theoretical rationales of work in varied communities, and the inspiring descriptions of what happened to students who learned while providing service. Their writings prepared me for the interviews and informed the energy and commitment I would bring to the civic engagement agenda before me.

I also read with intensity the exquisitely crafted recommendations of Ernest Boyer (1990) to expand our notions of scholarship, and the possibilities encouraged by R. Eugene Rice (1996) when

he described a more integrated potential for faculty roles and responsibilities. They gave me a vision of how to motivate and support faculty members engaged in community. Fortunately, I was
based on a campus that had begun taking Boyer's suggestions seriously and had revisited the institutional thinking about rewards
for promotion and tenure.

Within a month, I left the position of professor behind and continued to study the rapidly growing scholarship of engagement. I
realized that I was not alone in my pursuits and that a great many
pioneers were already deep into civic engagement. Fortunately for
me, they were writing about their service-learning programs, about
their faculty development efforts, and about the integration of the
academic curriculum and the curriculum of engagement. Their insights and innovations provided scholarly descriptions of early "best
practices" in service-learning, scholarship sorely needed in the swell
of civic engagement and scholarship still brimming with passion.

By the end of my first year, colleagues (Gelmon, Holland,
Driscoll, Spring, & Kerrigan, 2001) and I began an ambitious and
comprehensive exploration of ways to study and assess the impact
of service-learning on the major constituencies. We were not alone.
Colleagues across the country pursued quantitative measures, while
we designed case studies. As the pressure to produce results grew,
the responding scholarship balanced between replications of traditional experimental research and newly emerging narratives and
collaborative studies. Passion emerged amid the data and interpretations, even between the lines of reported results.

I pause here to laud Ernest Lynton, who entered my life
through his writing about the scholarship of professional service,
and later through his presence as we codirected projects funded
by the W. K. Kellogg Foundation that explored documentation of
new forms of community outreach scholarship. Together with 16
faculty and four administrators, we engaged in a three-year endeavor to document the scholarship of civic engagement. The following questions directed our struggles:

1. How would this differ from traditional forms of scholarship?
2. How could we document the ongoing collaboration or learning partnerships with community, while demonstrating our
   own scholarly contributions?

3. How could we capture the diverse results of this work and demonstrate its value?

We turned the community work of the participating faculty inside out to come up with effective ways to describe and document their scholarship. We combined the resulting framework, guidelines, examples, and mini-portfolios with Lynton's wisdom and my observations to create *Making Outreach Visible: A Guidebook to Documenting Professional Service and Outreach* (Driscoll & Lynton, 1999).

Once we gained clarity about the how-to's of documentation and a profile of the kind of institutional support needed for the scholarship of civic engagement, we faced an even more significant question. For the participating faculty and for faculty we encountered around the country, the worry was, "Who will review and evaluate this work?" Much inspired by Lynton's vision and guidance, I teamed with Lorilee Sandman to create the National Review Board for the Scholarship of Engagement, supported by Kellogg-funded clearinghouses. Faculty members who engaged with community and created new forms of scholarship needed assurance that their work would be understood and valued by credible evaluators. The National Review Board responded to their needs and provided external review for the scholarship of engagement.

The first years of the National Review Board revealed challenges for our work as well as important lessons. The challenges revolved around the issues of visibility and credibility for the board, as the members worked to gain acceptance in higher education in general and in the disciplines. The lessons for those faculty who contemplate future engagement or have been engaged in community scholarship come from successful portfolios. Those portfolios consistently reflect, first, an *ongoing* and *substantive* agenda of community partnership work, be it teaching or research. They pay attention to the *collaborative aspects* of the work and clearly acknowledge each constituency's contribution. The portfolios display a seamless *integration of teaching, research, and service* that is powerful and undeniably scholarly. *Reflection* is critical to the documentation, enabling readers to understand rationales for decisions, interpretation of successes and failures, and implications of work for future agendas. Those reflections affirm the continuing passion that characterizes faculty engagement in community.

Here I sit today, so grateful that I have been able to make this journey but unsettled in my reverie by remaining issues. One is a concern for junior faculty and their lack of ease and security about pursuing the scholarship of engagement, even on campuses with revised guidelines for promotion and tenure. In the words of one observer, "The studied silence and subtle disapproval regarding public service, advocacy, and community work leave many younger scholars discouraged" (Sabin, 2002, p. 5). It is not uncommon for administrators to advise new faculty to wait until after they have been granted tenure before pursuing the scholarship of civic engagement. There is a spirit (even on engaged campuses) of being "safe," of staying within the box of traditional scholarship to protect academic positions. With that kind of message, one can hardly blame a new scholar for deciding that pioneering work is too risky.

My second concern is an unspoken lack of credibility for alternative forms of scholarship. Applause greets scholarly products such as new policy manuals, legislation, increased funding, and community reports, as well as scholarly results such as improved services for clients, changes in thinking about issues, improved retention rates for students from disadvantaged neighborhoods, and so on. However, there continues to be an unspoken message that these products and results must be accompanied by traditional, refereed publications to be rewarded as scholarship.

As I look to the future, I commit myself to continued work for the "wholeness" described by David Cooper (2002) in his role as a public scholar—the "convergence of separate pathways of scholarship, teaching, and professional service into the thoroughfare of an integrated professional and personal life" (p. 18). Like him, I hold tightly to the aspects of our work that build community for learning together and respect our responsibilities to society.

The Scholarship of Discovery

George E. Walker

The four areas of scholarship that Boyer discussed in *Scholarship Reconsidered* (1990) have considerable overlap. In addition, a given scholar may focus on different forms of scholarship over the span of a career. From my perspective as scientist, administrator, and director of the Carnegie Initiative on the Doctorate, I have had the chance to see how each of these forms of scholarship has evolved over the past decade. For the purposes of this brief essay, it is useful to view changes through the lens of discovery.

Not surprisingly, scholarship (and the training of scholars) in the United States is a mirror of our culture—it is ruggedly individualistic, draws its participants from all over the world, and is competitive in a market-driven sense. Scholars are rewarded very differently depending on their field of study and their accomplishments in areas deemed to be of a high priority. The scholarship of discovery remains at the top of the research university priority list, and, consequently, doctoral education focuses on giving students the skills required for the scholarship of discovery. No matter what the original motivation for entering a given discipline, the competitive environment that pervades the academy very quickly redirects the developing scholar from a prime directive of learning to a focus on prestige and marketability. This is not surprising—it is the (in)human condition we face in almost all pilgrimages through life.

One can make the argument that the professoriate's focus on prestige and personal material advancement has heightened, during the past decade, because of personal competition for jobs and institutional competition for funding and prestige among research universities. Additionally, increased financial opportunities for those few who succeed in applying the fruits of the scholarship of discovery in certain areas of high economic profile, such as the life sciences and information technology, have changed the focus of the academy. The market economy and the competition for research dollars involved in the scholarship of discovery are causing us to lose gifted scholars who do not want to play this game.

On the other hand, some of the same trends have led to rising interest in Boyer's scholarships of application, integration, and teaching. The length of time from a new scientific discovery to an actual, profitable application has shortened significantly in many fields. The Bayh-Dole Act of 1980 has allowed universities to own intellectual property derived from federally sponsored research, and has heightened interest in the possible monetary gains that come from technology-transfer agreements with the private sector. This has led trustees, senior university administrators, and many of our most gifted discovery scholars in some disciplines not only to accept but to strongly seek to engage in or encourage the "scholarship" of application. The rise in importance and number of technology-transfer offices, university-spawned spin-off companies, patents and licenses, and policies on intellectual property, as well as increased requirements associated with safeguards for human and animal subjects, are all symptoms of this evolutionary change. This general area is becoming a dominant consideration in the daily activities and priorities of the chief research office of a major university. The senior scholars of tomorrow, who are the graduate students of today, are immersed in this enticing environment, for better or for worse. It is a wonderful opportunity, but the danger of exploitation and muddying the learning environment require ongoing vigilance. Who will protect the university from becoming tainted or corrupted as a result of these opportunities? It will take a highly respected scholar with multiple talents and with sensitivity to the public good to keep us honest.

The ability to integrate knowledge drawn from diverse areas within a discipline or across disciplines has taken on a new premium, for several reasons. First, of course, many scholars who focus on discovery recognize that the frontiers of knowledge require individuals, and more often teams of individuals, who are sensitive to the power of a broad range of knowledge in order to make advances. The scholar who can integrate new knowledge in one area with new understandings in another has become more important as part of a discovery team. Second, discovery scholars working on applications in for-profit settings have learned this lesson well. The integrative scholar is a tremendous asset in the entrepreneurial environment that pervades many of those disciplines that are thriving in research universities. One note of caution I have heard expressed: We should not assume that a scholar educated in a multidisciplinary program would be more flexible, over a period of time, with regard to a different mix of disciplines, since it is possible to be narrow and multidisciplinary at the same time. A multidisciplinary program may be just a silo constructed on two adjoining pieces of property. When substantial personal profits are dangled in front of integrative scholars, what will they do? We need to reflect on the kind of education the next generation of scholars should experience, so that our kind of interdisciplinarity continues to evolve.

The scholarship of teaching has benefited significantly from leadership at the faculty and university levels, as well as from outstanding contributions by private foundations such as the Carnegie Foundation for the Advancement of Teaching. While there is much good news in this arena, one caution is worth mentioning. We wish for more legitimacy and a higher profile for those involved in the scholarship of teaching. But we could become victims of our own wishes. An imaginary scenario may illustrate my point. Imagine a future where universities feel a special need to legitimize (for fear of being sued or of adverse publicity) those scholars who are permitted to be in the classroom. Suppose an Institutional Review Board for Teaching (IRBT) is created that reviews teaching credentials and proposed materials before allowing a scholar into the classroom—much as our IRBs now screen proposals and scholars before permitting them to do their research. A prospective teacher's materials would, quite reasonably, reference well-known scholars who publish discoveries associated with the scholarship of teaching. We might well see the emergence of a cottage industry of marketable experts in this area, who publish in prestigious journals of discovery on the scholarship of teaching and who are well funded by grants. Now, suppose we asked if this new emphasis were really facilitating learning. Someone might answer, "Of course.

Many students are finishing their coursework, scholars doing discovery in the scholarship of teaching are highly paid and respected, there are new prestigious journals, and federal funding for these efforts has increased." Who would take the time to assess seriously the quality of learning in such a bull market for teaching? Do we do this assessment now for the quality of new knowledge associated with disciplinary discovery?

The next generation of scholars will have many difficult and wonderful choices. They need to be conscious of the implications of the decisions they make. It is they who will have the opportunity and responsibility for charting the course of scholarship in the university. They are in our classrooms now. What are we doing in our graduate programs to prepare these future stewards of their disciplines?

The Scholarship of Integration

David K. Scott

In *Scholarship Reconsidered,* Ernest Boyer (1990) proposed four dimensions of scholarship. Three were relatively familiar, representing, in a slightly different language, American higher education's traditional triple mission of research, service, and teaching. The fourth, integration, defined a new dimension of scholarship, which he described as the need for making connections across the disciplines and placing the disciplines in a larger context. In a subsequent study, *Scholarship Assessed,* Glassick et al. (1997) described this scholarship as overcoming the isolation and fragmentation of the disciplines, of making connections within and between them.

This approach to scholarship has gained momentum, during the past decade, as shown by the AAHE survey of chief academic officers reported in this volume (Chapter Twelve). Some 50 percent of respondents reported an increase in integrative scholarship at institutions where the leadership had identified this dimension as an important component of the mission and values. In contrast, for colleges and universities where the scholarship of integration was not so identified, only 16 percent reported an influence on faculty involvement. A full recognition of the scholarship of integration will occur only when it is placed in an overarching epistemology, rather than presented as simply more individual faculty activity. Boyer's work really anticipated a much larger movement toward transformation of the academy.

A significant part of this transformation related to Boyer's understanding of the interaction of the four forms of scholarship. We may think of teaching, research, and service as the axes of a Cartesian coordinate system (see Figure 2.1), an appropriate representation since the three are often viewed as orthogonal, with more of one implying less of the other two. *Scholarship Reconsidered* reminds us that the three components are mutually enhancing. By introducing new terminology for teaching, discovery, and application of knowledge, Boyer effectively transformed the three axes, through a rotation that shuffles the three independent variables. Thus the presentation of knowledge also involves discovery and is enriched by application, just as discovery has elements of presentation and application. However, the scholarship of integration is in a different category from the other three.

One interpretation of integration regards it as a vector in this three-dimensional space, with projections on the axes that vary over the academic career of an individual faculty member and among faculty members. Boyer's work promoted this dynamic among the components, making the integration of knowledge a function of the other three forms of scholarship. Over the past decade, this concept has led to a healthier, more vibrant life in the academy, as described by the Kellogg Commission study of the future of land-grant universities in the report "Returning to Our Roots: The Engaged Institution" (W. K. Kellogg Foundation, 1999).

The scholarship associated with teaching, research, and service is represented by the three orthogonal axes. Rotation of the axes,

FIGURE 2.1

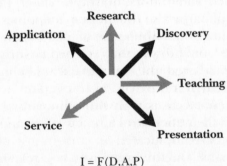

$$I = F(D,A,P)$$
$$= F[D(R_{TS}), A(S_{RT}), P(T_{SR})]$$

for example, by transforming scholarship to presentation (P), discovery (D), and application (A), makes each of the new dimensions a function of the original three. Then the integration (I) of knowledge is a function of D, A, and P, with D becoming a function of research but also of teaching and service, and so on.

Trying to envision the future of the scholarship of integration requires, first, reflecting on its history. The idea of integration in learning was introduced in 1855 by Herbert Spencer in *Principles of Psychology* (Knudsen, 1937). William James developed the idea, but used quotes around "integration," indicating that the word did not yet have current use in educational and psychological writing (Knudsen, 1937). By 1930, many articles on integration in education were appearing (Ciccorico, 1970), while by mid-century, Jean Gebser (1949) created a theoretical framework for integral thinking as the next stage of the evolution of consciousness.

It is worth emphasizing that integration and integral thought transcend the multidisciplinary and interdisciplinary approaches to knowledge that have been popular in the academy for decades and that led Clark Kerr (1982) to introduce the term "multiversity," to describe the modern university with its proliferation of centers, institutes, laboratories, and constituencies. However, these entities usually connect disciplines already closely allied. Perhaps "transdisciplinary" better describes the emerging forms of integrative scholarship.

Several educational theorists are credited with the concept of transdisciplinarity, including Piaget and Jantsch (Klein, 1996). It calls for a much deeper synthesis of disciplines. The work of Boyer, Rice, and their collaborators, however, contains the implicit idea that transdisciplinarity also describes new approaches to the scholarship of application. Gibbons et al. (1994) identified a fundamental change in the way that scientific, social, and cultural knowledge is produced, the elemental traits being complexity, hybridity, nonlinearity, reflexivity, heterogeneity, and transdisciplinarity. The new mode is transdisciplinary and integrative, in contributing to theoretical structure, research methods, and modes of practice that are not located on current disciplinary and interdisciplinary maps. One outcome is to replace and reform established institutions, practices, and policies. However, problem contexts are transient and problem solvers mobile. Emerging out of wide societal and cognitive pressures, knowledge is dynamic, stimulated by the continuous linking of influences across a dense communicative network with feedback loops.

Integrative approaches to learning are central to the work of many modern philosophers and theorists. For example, Geertz (1980) described the shift as a fundamental reconfiguration, "a phenomenon general enough and distinctive enough to suggest that what we are seeing is not just another redrawing of the cultural map—the moving of a few disputed borders, the making of some picturesque mountains, lakes—but an alteration of the principles of mapping. Something is happening to the way we think about the way we think" (p. 130).

In an article in the *Chronicle of Higher Education,* Connor (2003) predicted that the next few decades will witness an historic shift in the circumstances and conditions of the production of knowledge. Centers for advanced study will become primary loci for addressing new, especially transdisciplinary, questions and for the development of new paradigms. He speculates on the emergence of a third stage in the production of knowledge, the first stage originating in the 12th century with the appearance of universities, and the second in the 19th century with the development of research-oriented universities and the departmental and professional structures that went hand in hand with them. The third stage will deal more with questions that do not fit neatly into existing specialties: questions pointing to the growth of structures supporting integrative scholarship inside universities and outside, nationally and internationally. It will be crucial to recognize new forms of scholarship and faculty roles as these transformations occur.

We are now in a new period of convergence, but convergence to simplicity on the other side of complexity, as Oliver Wendell Holmes once said. As a result of the fragmentation of knowledge, the knowledge explosion, and the detailed understanding of all the disciplines, we are now able to see how to achieve a more complex level of integration—a knowledge implosion (Lewis, 1974). The result is a major transformation of our approach to knowledge, influenced greatly by the new ideas of scholarship, and particularly the scholarship of integration.

Higher education will not complete this transformation without a foundation of epistemological theory. This theory of integral and holistic thinking is now emerging, and the ability of many institutions to respond is greatly enhanced by the pioneering work of new approaches to the scholarship of integration and by *Scholarship Reconsidered,* as described in this volume. Boyer (1990) concluded his description of integration with the following prophetic words: "Today, interdisciplinary *and* integrative studies, long on the edges of academic life, are moving toward the center, responding both to new intellectual questions and to pressing human problems. As the boundaries of human knowledge are being dramatically reshaped, the academy surely must give increased attention to the *scholarship of integration*" (p. 28). This increased attention will help relieve the pain of disconnection and isolation experienced by many in the academy today. It will overcome the tension, and even the standing antagonisms, among the components of the triple mission of American higher education, the trilogy of American ingenuity in teaching, discovery, and application of knowledge. The scholarship of integration will also allow our institutions to become more vibrant by performing differently with fewer resources in the shifting context of funding for higher education.

References

Angelo, T. A., & Cross, P. (1993). *Classroom assessment techniques: A handbook for college teachers* (2nd ed.). San Francisco: Jossey-Bass.

Bass, R. (1999). The scholarship of teaching: What's the problem? *Inventio: Creative Thinking About Learning and Teaching, 1*(1). Retrieved March 15, 2003 from http://www.doiit.gmu.edu/Archives/feb98/randybass.htm

Becher, T., & Trowler, P. (2001). *Academic tribes and territories: Intellectual inquiry and cultures of the discipline* (2nd ed.). Buckingham, England: Open University Press.

Boyer, E. L. (1990). *Scholarship reconsidered: Priorities of the professoriate.* Princeton, NJ: Carnegie Foundation for the Advancement of Teaching.

Bransford, J., Brown, A., & Cocking, R. (1999). *How people learn: Brain, mind, experience, and school* (Committee on Developments in the Science of Learning, Commission on Behavioral and Social Sciences and Education, National Research Council). Washington, DC: National Academy Press.

Cambridge, B. (2002). Linking change initiatives: The Carnegie Academy for the Scholarship of Teaching and Learning in the company of other national projects. In D. Lieberman & C. Wehlburg (Eds.), *To improve the academy*, Vol. 20 (pp. 38–48). Bolton, MA: Anker.

Centra, J. (1993). *Reflective faculty evaluation: Enhancing teaching and determining faculty effectiveness.* San Francisco: Jossey-Bass.

Ciccorico, E. A. (1970, November-December). Integration in the curriculum. *Main Currents, 27:* 60.

Connor, R. W. (2003, January 17). Why we need independent centers for advanced study. *Chronicle of Higher Education*, p. B10.

Cooper, D. (2002, Spring). The making of a public scholar. *Campus Compact Reader, 3*(1): 1–3.

Cross, K., & Steadman, M. (1996). *Classroom research: Implementing the scholarship of teaching.* San Francisco: Jossey-Bass.

Donald, J. G. (2002). *Learning to think: Disciplinary perspectives.* San Francisco: Jossey-Bass.

Driscoll, A., & Lynton, E. (1999). *Making outreach visible: A guidebook to documenting professional service and outreach.* Washington, DC: American Association for Higher Education.

Edgerton, R. (1993). The re-examination of faculty priorities. *Change* 25(4): 10–17.

Edgerton, R., Hutchings, P., & Quinlan, K. (1991). *The teaching portfolio: Capturing the scholarship in teaching.* Washington, DC: American Association for Higher Education.

Gebser, J. (1949 [1985]). *The ever present origin.* N. Barstad & A. Mukunas (Trans.). Athens: Ohio University Press.

Geertz, C. (1980, Spring). Blurred genres: The refiguration of social thought. *American Scholar:* 165–166.

Gelmon, S., Holland, B., Driscoll, A., Spring, A., & Kerrigan, S. (2001). *Assessing service learning and civic engagement.* Providence, RI: National Campus Compact.

Gibbons, M., Nowotny, H., Limoges, C., Trono, M., Schwartzman, S., & Scott, P. (1994). *The new production of knowledge: The dynamics of science and research in contemporary societies.* London: Sage.

Glassick, C. E., Huber, M., & Maeroff, G. I. (1997). *Scholarship assessed: Evaluation of the professoriate.* San Francisco: Jossey-Bass.

Grossman, P. L., Wilson, S., & Shulman, L. (1989). Teachers of substance: Subject matter knowledge for teaching. In M. C. Reynolds (Ed.), *Knowledge base for the beginning teacher* (pp. 23–36). New York: Pergamon.

Gumport, P. J. (2002). *Academic pathfinders: Knowledge creation and feminist scholarship.* Westport, CT: Greenwood.

Healey, M. (2000). Developing the scholarship of teaching in higher education: A discipline-based approach. *Higher Education Research and Development, 19*(2): 169–189.

Huber, M. T. (2001). Balancing acts: Designing careers around the scholarship of teaching. *Change, 33*(4): 21–29.

Huber, M. T. (2002). Faculty evaluation and the development of academic careers. In C. L. Colbeck (Ed.), *Evaluating faculty performance* (pp. 73–83). New Directions for Institutional Research, no. 114. San Francisco: Jossey-Bass.

Huber, M. T., & Morreale, S. P. (2002). Situating the scholarship of teaching and learning: A cross-disciplinary conversation. In M. T. Huber & S. P. Morreale (Eds.), *Introduction to disciplinary styles in the scholarship of teaching and learning: Exploring common ground* (pp. 1–24). Washington, DC: American Association for Higher Education and the Carnegie Foundation for the Advancement of Teaching and Learning.

Hutchings, P. (1996). *Making teaching community property: A menu for peer collaboration and peer review.* Washington, DC: American Association for Higher Education.

Hutchings, P. (Ed.). (2000). *Opening lines: Approaches to the scholarship of teaching and learning.* Menlo Park, CA: Carnegie Foundation for the Advancement of Teaching.

Hutchings, P. (Ed.). (2002). *Ethics of inquiry: Issues in the scholarship of teaching and learning.* Menlo Park, CA: Carnegie Foundation for the Advancement of Teaching.

Hutchings, P., & Shulman, L. S. (1999). The scholarship of teaching: New elaborations, new developments. *Change, 31*(5): 11–15.

Kerr, C. (1982). *The uses of the university.* Cambridge, MA: Harvard University Press.

Klein, J. (1996). *Crossing borders: Knowledge, disciplinarities and interdisciplinarities.* Charlottesville: University Press of Virginia.

Knudsen, C. (1937, January). What do educators mean by integration? *Harvard Educational Review, 7:* 16.

Lazerson, M., Wagnener, U., & Shumanis, N. (2000). What makes a revolution? Teaching and learning in higher education, 1980–2000. *Change, 32*(3): 12–19.

Lewis, R. (1974, April). Implosions of knowledge. *Intellect:* 428.

Lyons, N., Hyland, A., & Ryan, N. (Eds.). (2002). *Advancing the scholarship of teaching and learning through a reflective portfolio process: The University College Cork experience.* Cork, Ireland: University College Cork.

Marchese, T. J. (1997). The new conversations about learning: Insights from neuroscience and anthropology, cognitive science and workplace studies. In T. J. Marchese, *Assessing impact: Evidence and action* (pp. 79–95). Washington, DC: American Association for Higher Education. Retrieved March 15, 2003 from http://www.aahe.org/pubs/TM-essay.htm

Martin, E., Benjamin, J., Prosser, M., & Trigwell, K. (1999). Scholarship of teaching: A study of the approaches of academic staff. In C. Rust (Ed.), *Improving student learning: Improving student learning outcomes* (pp. 326–331). Oxford: Oxford Centre for Staff and Learning Development, Oxford Brookes University.

Rice, R. E. (1991). Towards a broader conception of scholarship: The American context. In T. G. Whiston & R. L. Geiger (Eds.), *Research and higher education: The United Kingdom and the United States* (pp. 117–129). Milton Keynes, England: Open University Press.

Rice, R. E. (1996). *Making a place for the new American scholar.* Washington DC: American Association for Higher Education.

Sabin, P. (2002, Spring). Academe subverts young scholars' civic engagement. *Campus Compact Reader, 3*(1): 4–7.

Secor, B. (2002, Fall). Vice Provost Secor discusses the role and value of outreach in the university. In Outreach Communications (Eds.), *Faculty scholarship and the outreach imperative* (pp. 10–11). University Park: Pennsylvania State University.

Seldin, P. (1997). *The teaching portfolio: A practical guide to improved performance and promotion/tenure decisions.* Bolton, MA: Anker.

Shulman, L. S. (1987). Knowledge and teaching: Foundations of the new reform. *Harvard Educational Review, 57*(1): 1–22.

Shulman, L. S. (1993). Teaching as community property: Putting an end to pedagogical solitude. *Change, 25*(6): 6–7.

W. K. Kellogg Foundation. (1999). *Returning to our roots: The engaged institution* (Report of the Commission on the Future of State and Land-Grant Universities). Battle Creek, MI: Author.

CHAPTER THREE

ISSUES OF IMPLEMENTATION

Each author in this chapter was involved in initiatives that helped launch a movement for rethinking scholarly priorities across higher education. Also, each contributor's sphere of influence helped move the agenda ahead on a wide range of fronts and made *Scholarship Reconsidered* more than just another interesting foundation report to be read, acknowledged, and put aside.

In the chapter's first section, Robert M. Diamond examines the many barriers to change. He writes from his experience as the initiator of a national project based at Syracuse University on institutional priorities and faculty rewards; he also led a project focused on helping the disciplinary associations change their conceptions of scholarship. In the second section of the chapter, Kenneth J. Zahorski describes the process of redefinition at a small liberal arts college. Zahorski provided national leadership for liberal arts colleges as they struggled with institutionalizing a broader view of the scholarly work of faculty, beginning with his own institution, St. Norbert's College, and then working nationally through the Council of Independent Colleges. The third and final section of the chapter examines issues relating to professional socialization. Its author, Jerry G. Gaff, describes the hugely successful Preparing Future Faculty (PFF) program, which sought to introduce multiple forms of scholarship into the lives of faculty members at their most formative stage, at the very beginning of their careers.

—R.E.R.

Scholarship Reconsidered: Barriers to Change

Robert M. Diamond

The early 1990s witnessed an initiative that had the potential to transform American higher education. The publication of Ernest Boyer's *Scholarship Reconsidered* (1990) and subsequent work by the American Association for Higher Education (AAHE) led to national projects like "Institutional Priorities and Faculty Rewards," coordinated at Syracuse University, a study of faculty perceptions of institutional priorities and the conceptions of scholarship prevalent in disciplinary associations. Results of those studies suggested that many faculty perceived the reward structures at their institutions to be skewed toward research productivity, at the same time that institutional rhetoric made claims about the importance of teaching. Representatives of disciplinary associations spoke about narrow definitions of scholarship used for faculty recognition and rewards on most university campuses. Faculty reported that narrow definitions of scholarship were discouraging a rich variety of important work in the disciplines.

The hugely successful AAHE Forum on Faculty Roles and Rewards took up these issues, along with many others related to the changing roles of faculty. As the national conversation about scholarly work expanded, disciplinary groups and individual institutions drafted redefinitions of scholarship. Characteristics and criteria for scholarly activity were developed based on the works of Boyer and Rice, and on a monograph by Charles Glassick, Mary Taylor Huber, and Gene Maeroff, *Scholarship Assessed* (1997), as well as on my own *Field Guide to Academic Leadership* (Diamond, 2002).

In response to these efforts, institutions across the country have reconsidered their faculty reward systems and explored expanded definitions of scholarly and professional work. However, the many hours devoted to these activities, and large audiences at AAHE national meetings, have produced a disappointing impact on most campuses. Of the 25 disciplinary statements produced in my own "Defining Scholarly Work" project, most have not made an impact on the daily operations of teacher-scholars. Unquestionably, significant change in higher education is never easy, but these initiatives to reconsider scholarship have confronted a number of powerful barriers.

CHALLENGES TO CHANGE

Major change requires a clear institutional vision; leadership from the top; an agreed-upon, institution-specific mission statement; and sensitivity to the unique culture of the institution. Not only did many campuses lack clear mission and vision statements, but leadership and the campus committees that were formed often advocated a single approach that was not sensitive to the differences among the disciplines, faculty roles, or institutional structures and culture. In addition, many campuses experienced changes in key leadership, with new hires often unwilling to adopt the priorities and initiatives of their predecessors. Additionally, the initiative lost its major national spokesman with the death of Ernest Boyer.

Many faculty members in key leadership roles were comfortable with the status quo and were reluctant to change reward structures or definitions of scholarly work that had worked so well for them. Even where policies and procedures changed, many senior faculty members ignored the new definitions or criteria and did business as usual. Resistance carried over to national professional and disciplinary associations, whose leadership tends to be drawn from Research I universities (a Carnegie classification) and whose boards are rarely representative of the full membership. The constituency of such associations has been an important factor, since the biggest disconnects within reward structures at baccalaureate, master's, and doctoral institutions are between the professional schools, on one hand, and arts and sciences, on the other. The initiatives to review scholarship and to restructure the faculty reward system got caught up in the tenure debate. On both sides of the debate, many lost sight of the fact that whether or not they had tenure, they needed an appropriate and fair faculty reward system and definitions of scholarly work.

As the 1990s advanced, budget issues became paramount at a growing number of institutions. The new century has seen across-the-board budget cuts in many state institutions and in some private, forcing colleges and universities into a survival mode with change initiatives placed on hold. Budget flexibility has further declined over the past 10 years, as many major foundations and government funders began shifting away from the support of innovation in higher education.

Overcoming Potential Barriers: Advice for Academic Leaders

While some barriers and constraints, such as state budget allocations, are beyond the control of academic leaders, others are not. Academic leaders can take many actions early in an initiative that will circumvent potential problems. For example, if they wish to improve the quality of their faculty reward system, they could:

1. *Ensure top leadership support.* Every key campus leader must understand the importance of the project to the long-term health and vitality of the institution. One important incentive for leaders is to understand that a reward system supporting the mission of the institution can make their own jobs easier and more rewarding!
2. *Select the leaders of the initiative with care.* Those responsible for design and implementation must be credible and representative and have the necessary process skills.
3. *Institutionalize the process.* The goal should be to change policies, priorities, and procedures at all levels—department, school, college, and institution. Focusing on only one level will lead to unworkable policies and expectations.
4. *Reinforce new policies and procedures as they are approved.* Do not let the "old guard" maintain the status quo. At times this will not be easy, but it is essential. Do not start with a final structure and definition of scholarship in mind. Let it evolve from the faculty and the culture of the institution.

5. As the work evolves, *ensure that communications are open and that the entire faculty has the opportunity for input.* If there is a strong faculty senate or collective bargaining unit, make sure it is involved and has ownership from the beginning.

The past decade has not seen much investment in innovation in higher education. Unfortunately, the timing could not be worse. We need our best thinking across a variety of domains, to address increased competition among institutions and from for-profit competitors, as well as calls for greater accountability from external constituents such as state governments and community leaders. Research suggests that we can do a far better job of teaching our students. We can put disciplinary scholarship to good use in supporting our communities.

Social problems and technology challenges demand the attention of our best minds, and higher education can play a greater leadership role in the government and public policy arenas. The redefinition of scholarly work will open the doors of the academy and encourage young scholars to apply their energy and best thinking to issues and concerns of national interest and community need.

Redefining Scholarship: A Small Liberal Arts College's Journey

Kenneth J. Zahorski

When Ernest Boyer's *Scholarship Reconsidered* burst onto the national scene in 1990, St. Norbert College, like so many institutions of higher learning, responded to its compelling call to action. Although a campuswide conversation about what scholarship means and how it should be assessed had been going on at the college for nearly two decades, the dialogue had been sporadic, unfocused, and generally unproductive. The definition of scholarship, narrow and restrictive (in essence, "juried publications in the field"), prevented deserving candidates from attaining full professorship and, in fact, was simply an extrapolation from a rather sketchy list of promotion and tenure criteria. The time was right for redefining scholarship at St. Norbert College.

The impetus for redefining scholarship came from the then dean of the college, Robert L. Horn, who had been inspired by a keynote speech that R. Eugene Rice delivered at the fall 1988 Council of Independent Colleges (CIC) Dean's Institute. Horn then had his inspiration rekindled through the Boyer report. In April 1991, Horn appointed a faculty task force to develop a working definition of scholarship. That seven-member committee, which I chaired, immediately set to work on the first phase, which the dean wanted completed by November. The personnel committee would then spearhead the second phase, applying the new definition to the college's criteria for tenure and promotion.

While the dean empowered the task force to proceed autonomously, to do "what it felt best to get the job done," he strongly

ISSUES OF IMPLEMENTATION 61

urged a "collegial solution" that would significantly involve all members of the academic community, and a strategic approach that would use *Scholarship Reconsidered* as a core conceptual resource. The task force wholeheartedly endorsed both recommendations and plunged into its work.

From May through October 1991, task force members sought input from colleagues, through questionnaires, open fora, and perhaps most important, one-on-one office visits. In addition, they ordered three dozen copies of *Scholarship Reconsidered,* for systematic routing to all members of the faculty. Happily, we soon discovered that our colleagues were not only eager to share their views on scholarship but would even seek us out for second or third conversations. Hallways were soon abuzz. The published results, in late September, of the 22-item "Faculty Survey of Scholarship at SNC" generated even more corridor discussion. The collegial process was going well, but would the actual drafting process go as smoothly?

Armed with reams of recorded input, in late October the task force began the daunting task of drafting a new definition. About three weeks later, after considerable debate and several marathon sessions, members completed a four-page redefinition of scholarship, complete with accompanying rationale, and sent it to the dean. About three months later, after following the prescribed committee review system, the Faculty Assembly approved the new definition and made it policy. Shortly after, Dean Horn asked the personnel committee to apply the newly approved definition to the current criteria for tenure and promotion. After five meetings of intense discussion, the personnel committee sent its proposed modifications of the reward system to the Faculty Assembly (December 1, 1992), where, after brief discussion, the motion passed with only one vote against.

Making and approving policy is one thing; implementing it is quite another. Did St. Norbert College encounter implementation challenges after approving a new definition of scholarship? Of course. To begin with, promotion and tenure applicants needed to gain an even deeper understanding of the three newly identified types of scholarship, in order to make their applications as clear and compelling as possible. While the scholarship of discovery was a well-mapped and traveled realm, Boyer's scholarships of teaching, integration, and application represented relatively new territory. Thus, applicants had to become students of scholarship, not only studying the nuanced distinctions among the various types of scholarship but also learning how to concretely, and meaningfully, document achievement in these new areas. In addition, they had to carefully think through the matter of peer review, an aspect of assessment that took on even greater importance with our broadened definition of scholarship. Traditional evidence of scholarly accomplishment, such as juried publications, the coin of the realm in the scholarship of discovery, would not necessarily apply in the three other areas of scholarship. Applicants had other concerns as well, including whether the broadened definition implied the need for producing scholarship in all four areas, and how the personnel committee would interpret the new policy.

Perhaps the greatest challenges, however, confronted the personnel committee. For example, there was a need to break away from the mindset that only products of the scholarship of discovery constituted bona fide scholarship. New questions now appeared regularly during tenure and promotion deliberations. Exactly what constitutes the scholarship of teaching? What distinguishes Boyer's scholarship of application from the routine application of knowledge that most academics regularly practice? Is grant writing scholarship? How does one assess the quality of different types of peer evaluation? If scholarship is not only product but also process, how does one assess the value and quality of such activities as researching, learning, exploring, reflecting, and experimenting? What assessment guidelines exist for judging cross-disciplinary artistic creations and performances? These are but a few of the many interesting, provocative, and complex questions generated by the college's move to a broader definition of scholarship. And then there was always the grand, overarching question and concern: How does one broaden a definition enough to nurture the creative and varied talents of the faculty, but not so much as to compromise academic rigor and the integrity of the scholarly process? In short, how does one avoid the dilution effect?

As might be expected, we did not meet these challenges overnight. Attitudinal change comes slowly; learning takes time; change is sometimes resisted. However, semester by semester, year by year, with patience, resolve, and goodwill, we have made good progress. More than a decade has passed since the college undertook its journey. What have we learned? What have we gained? Following are some of the most important lessons learned and benefits accrued. First, the lessons learned.

- *Put faculty in charge of the process.* Policies governing scholarship and the reward system that are imposed from above often fail or, at the very least, weaken faculty morale. While administrative support, cooperation, and leadership are essential in any initiative to redefine scholarship, the actual deliberative and decision-making process should be placed in faculty hands.
- *Foster a spirit of shared ownership.* The leaders of any redefining initiative must vigorously and relentlessly seek faculty input. This is one corner that cannot be cut. Indeed, success depends upon achieving a strong sense of grassroots ownership: the entire academic community must be involved in the deliberative process from start to finish. In short, this must be a genuine exercise in collegiality and community, and it must be clear at the outset that the results of the process have not been predetermined. Where appropriate, students and student life colleagues should also be consulted.
- *Establish common ground for discussion.* A prerequisite for meaningful and productive dialogue about redefining scholarship is to find a common vocabulary and develop a collective familiarity with key tenets and concepts. "Scholarship" is an umbrella term that often means different things to different people. Consequently, a dialogue about scholarship can be more meaningful and productive if it builds on a solid referential foundation, such as *Scholarship Reconsidered.*
- *Make the process and product of redefinition congruent with your mission statement.* The one-size-fits-all approach to redefining scholarship probably will not produce the desired results. Studying the institutional mission statement (a valuable exercise at any time) should constitute an early step in any collegial conversation on redefining scholarship. Conclusions about redefinition should be reevaluated in terms of their congruency to mission statement tenets. In addition, the deliberative process itself should conform to the mission statement's expressed expectations regarding collegiality and community spirit.
- *Take a two-tiered approach.* Avoid the temptation of looking ahead at how a new definition of scholarship might affect reward

policy. In some ways, redefining scholarship is like drafting general education criteria. Both demand a two-tiered approach: that is, first engage in purely philosophical considerations, and then make practical applications. If we introduce reward-policy implications at the beginning of any definitional dialogue, we run the strong risk of compromising objectivity. It is prudent to divorce the definitional phase from the reward-policy phase. Even seemingly innocuous extrapolations about what a broadened definition might mean for existing promotion and tenure criteria can be distracting.

• *Prepare for heated debate and a broad spectrum of views.* Task forces charged with redefining scholarship soon find that discussing the issue in general terms is very different from setting down words that precisely and securely lock a definition into place. Further, they usually discover that a broad spectrum of views on scholarship exists, not only in the wider institutional community but among the task force members themselves. Discussion usually generates enough dialectical tension to make Hegel proud.

• *Work toward compromise.* Because the collegial dialogue on redefinition will likely represent both ends of the spectrum of opinion, and because some colleagues will be unwilling to relinquish certain philosophical ground, compromise is almost always necessary and should not be construed as failure. Indeed, not only can compromise conclude the debate but it often helps ensure that the definition is collegially inclusive, reflecting the strongly held philosophical beliefs of various institutional cohorts. Definitive consensus may be a "consummation devoutly to be wished," but is probably an unrealistic expectation.

• *Follow up redefinition with appropriate modification of the reward system.* This suggestion needs no explanation. Redefinition without subsequent modification of the reward system is like buying tickets without going to the game.

• *Prepare for an ongoing conversation, lingering questions, and tensions.* Just as the final chapter is never written on general education programs, so too the saga of redefining scholarship is continual. Once a definition becomes policy, an educative process among faculty and key committees must continue. Just because a broadened definition is approved does not put an end to questions about its application. Boyer's scholarship of teaching and scholarship of application, for example, can be particularly difficult for promotion and tenure committees to understand and apply, as contrasted with the much more familiar and conventional scholarship of discovery.

Is the exercise of redefining scholarship worth the time and effort? Without doubt. After a decade of operating under a broadened definition of scholarship, very similar in form and substance to the Boyer-Rice paradigm, and following a revised set of tenure and promotion guidelines, the St. Norbert College academic community has gained the following benefits: (1) reward guidelines are perceived as more just, equitable, and inclusive; (2) applications for the rank of professor have increased (along with an improved success rate); (3) there is more emphasis upon, and engagement in, interdisciplinary and collaborative scholarship; (4) there is a better understanding of, and interest in, classroom research; (5) there exists a greater sensitivity to the concept that regardless of the particular scholarly medium, dissemination and sharing are essential to the integrity of scholarship; (6) faculty have become better "reflective practitioners" of their craft; (7) the teaching-professional portfolio approach has taken on new credibility and importance; (8) morale has improved; and (9) the spirit of collegiality and community has been enhanced. Perhaps most notably, the community has gained a greater appreciation for what Boyer so felicitously termed the institutional "mosaic of talent."

In brief, redefining scholarship is a noble undertaking that holds promise of significant outcomes—if planned carefully and undertaken collegially. In this endeavor, along with so many others, process is key, and the old bromide that the journey is as important as the destination takes on fresh meaning.

Preparing Future Faculty and Multiple Forms of Scholarship

Jerry G. Gaff

The Preparing Future Faculty (PFF) program was launched more than a decade ago to develop alternative doctoral programs for preparing graduate students to do the kind of work expected of faculty at most colleges and universities, namely, to teach and advise students; conduct and evaluate research; and perform service to the department, institution, and community (Gaff, Pruitt-Logan, & Weibl, 2000). More than 4,000 doctoral students participated in PFF, a collaboration between the Association of American Colleges and Universities and the Council of Graduate Schools, before the program ended in 2002, after a decade of fruitful work. Two grants from the Pew Charitable Trusts supported creation of campuswide PFF programs at 23 doctoral-producing universities; grants from the National Science Foundation and Atlantic Philanthropies supported partnering with 11 disciplinary societies in the natural sciences, mathematics, social sciences, and humanities (Gaff, Pruitt-Logan, Sims, & Denecke, 2003). Each society awarded grants to departments in its discipline to develop model PFF programs and highlighted the work of PFF in its meetings, publications, and other activities, as leaders advocated these new approaches. Through these programs, 44 departments established PFF programs, each of which included a cluster of diverse institutions. (For more information, see www.preparing-faculty.org.)

A central feature of PFF programs was that they brought together the "producers" of doctorates (about 150 research universities) with the "consumers" (the approximately 3,500 colleges and universities that hire new faculty), which have quite different missions, student bodies, and expectations for faculty. Thus, each PFF program involved a "cluster" of institutions with diverse missions, such as a private liberal arts college, a public comprehensive university, and a community college. Faculty members and administrators from the "partner institutions" and their colleagues in graduate education discussed what they needed in new faculty, and the answers always included effective teaching and the ability to work well with the kinds of students they enrolled. The partner institutions gave graduate students an opportunity to work with a "teaching mentor" and to teach part of a course, attend faculty or committee meetings, meet with undergraduate students—and then to reflect on the meaning of these experiences. In short, doctoral students learned to teach, gain perspectives on faculty life, and envision careers in institutions other than research universities.

The cumulative experience and assessments of PFF programs have been very positive (Pruitt-Logan, Gaff, & Jentoft, 2002). Almost all participants queried have responded that they would recommend PFF to others. Graduate students and alumni have cited a number of benefits, such as learning to teach diverse students, understanding faculty roles in different institutions, and deciding on a career and finding a position that is a "good fit" with their goals. Most credit involvement in PFF as a key factor in securing their first faculty position.

From the outset, PFF was intertwined with the initiative to promote multiple forms of scholarship. R. Eugene Rice served on the original advisory committee that oversaw the launch of PFF, and he made presentations on the broader definitions of scholarship and changing roles of faculty members to enthusiastic graduate students and faculty members at the early working conferences. Leaders at PFF clusters frequently included ideas about multiple forms of scholarship in their new programs.

In my experience, innovative faculty members are drawn to and make good use of a variety of innovations in their academic work. So it was no surprise that PFF was cross-fertilized with the initiative that is the subject of this book. Every PFF program emphasized the scholarship of teaching and learning, whether or not it was called that. Some PFF programs included courses on general aspects of teaching and learning, such as setting learning goals, designing a course, choosing instructional methods that engage students, creating an inclusive climate, understanding student learning styles and developmental stages, and assessment and grading. Other programs included courses focused on teaching in a discipline. These discipline-specific courses also included discussion of how to deal with common challenges in teaching a particular subject.

Some programs also offered an opportunity to teach with supervision and feedback, be mentored by a faculty member, and prepare a teaching portfolio. An alumna of the PPF program at Duke University spoke for many when she said, "My participation in PFF broadened my education at Duke beyond focused lab experiments and classes by providing a forum to discuss education beyond basic research. PFF enabled me to cultivate skills that may not have developed within the framework of the traditional graduate school experience."

Of course, research is central to any doctoral program, and PFF students gained opportunities to observe the kinds of research done at the various institutions in their clusters. For example, they discovered that undergraduates were frequently involved in research, that some faculty studied community problems and tried to find solutions, and that others derived satisfaction from connecting ideas across fields in interdisciplinary research and teaching. In short, PFF students saw for themselves that faculty members were engaging in multiple forms of scholarship and finding satisfaction in doing so.

Let me end by reflecting on four questions:

1. *How does the new generation of faculty react to multiple forms of scholarship?* My impression is that the "new" generation is more similar to the "old" than different. Yes, it has more women, and faces some difficult working conditions, including fewer tenure-track jobs, higher expectations for success, and more limited resources. But as with previous generations, individuals are eager to learn about the profession they seek to enter, want to determine where they might best "fit," and are ready to do all they can to prepare themselves. Like many current faculty members, future faculty have wide-ranging intellectual interests, and their agile minds are un-

comfortable about limiting their curiosity to micro-specializations and research agendas defined by old-fashioned ideas about the scholarship of discovery. Many are excited about seeing their interests in the scholarship of engagement, integration, and teaching validated.

2. *How did PFF and multiple forms of scholarship affect individuals from underrepresented groups?* Anecdotal evidence suggests that both were more congenial to underrepresented groups than traditional approaches. For example, Julio Rojas, a psychology graduate student at the University of Georgia, was not attracted to a career in the academy, which he thought was primarily concerned with intellectual abstractions far removed from his community. He wanted to find a career enabling him to "give back" to his community, as many Hispanic and other minorities do. His professor encouraged him to participate in PFF, where he learned that through service-learning and community-based learning he could advance both good education and community development. To cite another example, in 2002, the Howard University mathematics department awarded four doctorates to African American women, two of whom had been directly involved in PFF. During the previous year, only six such degrees were awarded to African American women in the entire country. Further, nearly all PFF programs included components on teaching for an inclusive classroom. Both PFF and broader definitions of scholarship seem to have been more encouraging of and attractive to minority students.

3. *How can the concept of multiple forms of scholarship further penetrate the academy?* One of the best ways is to include it in doctoral programs that prepare future faculty. When graduate students are forming their ideas about research and scholarship and developing their professional identities, it is important that they take a broad view of scholarship. They must see the intellectual value of connecting ideas across academic disciplines, applying abstract ideas to real-world problems, and gaining theoretical insights from practice. They should also learn about the mysteries of communicating their specialty to nonspecialists, which is to say, to teach the subject so that others can learn. And they should understand the range of scholarship that can lead to discoveries and can be

done within the constraints of different kinds of institutions. By understanding the breadth of the intellectual terrain, graduate students can find their own niche, where they can contribute to teaching and research and derive satisfaction in their own careers.

4. *Will institutions support and reward multiple forms of scholarship if the new faculty come with such expectations and capacities?* This, I fear, is the crux of the matter, and the jury is still deliberating. My impression is that there are crosscurrents but no clear trends. For example, I know of several research universities that point proudly to faculty members who gained tenure based not on their research but on their teaching or technological prowess, but those individuals are still few in number. On the other hand, some liberal arts colleges have raised the bar for research in order to get tenure. And leaders at a comprehensive university I visited that had recently done a great deal of new hiring were enthusiastic about their ability to recruit researchers from top-rated departments, but when they launched a review of their undergraduate general education program, they realized that the new faculty were neither prepared to help nor interested.

Both faculties and administrations are responsible for the systems to support and reward faculty, and either or both can be swept away with visions of research and publications glory defined in old and narrow terms. Conditions can change with the appearance of a new president, a new provost, or a new strategic plan.

We can only hope that the current generation of academic leaders will find the wisdom and courage to forge support and reward systems that provide incentives for faculty members to pursue their ideas, wherever they may lead. If they do, we can be optimistic that the next generation of professors will be able to learn about the breadth and complexity of modern scholarship in their formative years, so that they can contribute to multiple forms of scholarship and gain satisfaction in doing so throughout their academic careers. But I fear that success will come only because academic leaders create a more effective reward structure, one institution at a time. This promises to be a long, hard process. We have no time to delay.

References

Boyer, E. L. (1990). *Scholarship reconsidered: Priorities of the professoriate.* Princeton, NJ: Carnegie Foundation for the Advancement of Teaching.

Diamond, R. M. (2002). *Field guide to academic leadership.* San Francisco: Jossey-Bass.

Gaff, J. G., Pruitt-Logan, A. S., Sims, L., & Denecke, D. (2003). *Preparing future faculty in the social sciences and humanities.* Washington, DC: Council of Graduate Schools and Association of American Colleges and Universities.

Gaff, J. G., Pruitt-Logan, A. S., & Weibl, R. (2000). *Building the faculty we need: Colleges and universities working together.* Washington, DC: Association of American Colleges and Universities and Council of Graduate Schools.

Glassick, C. E., Huber, M. T., & Maeroff, G. I. (1997). *Scholarship assessed: Evaluation of the professoriate.* San Francisco: Jossey-Bass.

Pruitt-Logan, A. S., Gaff, J. G., & Jentoft, J. E. (2002). *Preparing future faculty in the sciences and mathematics.* Washington, DC: Council of Graduate Schools and Association of American Colleges and Universities.

PART TWO

LESSONS LEARNED FROM CAMPUS STUDIES

CHAPTER FOUR

A QUESTION OF MISSION
Redefining Scholarship at Franklin College
David G. Brailow

INSTITUTIONAL HISTORY AND CONTEXT

Historically a Baptist college founded in 1834, Franklin College of Indiana emphasizes a "values-focused, career-sensitive liberal arts" program designed to prepare students for lives of "leadership and service." Its Carnegie classification as a liberal arts college was recently changed to general baccalaureate as the number of majors in preprofessional programs, journalism, teacher education, and business exceeded those in liberal arts. The college placed 21st among Midwest regional colleges in the 2002 *U.S. News and World Report* rankings. Franklin enrolls just over 1,000 students, 70 percent of whom reside on campus, and employs 61 full-time faculty, including some with limited teaching duties. The college requires all students to take an extensive set of general education courses and offers 34 majors, including 11 in the National Council for the Accreditation of Teacher Education (NCATE) teacher education program.

Franklin's motto is "For Leaders, For Life," and it takes the leadership theme seriously. The college requires every student to take a leadership course, usually during the January term of the

The author acknowledges the substantial contributions of the faculty at Franklin College who conducted research and assisted with the project: Alice Heikens, Steven Browder, Paul Johnson, Jayne Marek, and James Williams.

first year, and to participate in a Professional Development Program, which includes a portfolio, a professional development course, and a senior-year experience involving professionally related activities, such as an internship.

Considering the relatively small number of full-time faculty, there are many demands on faculty time and energy—the implementation of the leadership and professional development programs, heavy teaching loads imposed by the general education program, recent changes in the teacher education program, the requirements of the assessment plan, the need to cover courses and advise students, and committee work at the administrative level. The budget has tightened, due to diminishing returns on the endowment and higher tuition discounts, and this prevents the college from hiring more full-time faculty. At the same time, the student body has grown from 880 in 1990 to 1,048 in 2002. Since 1993, the proportion of classes with 17 or fewer students has decreased from 62 to 53 percent, while that of classes with 18 to 32 students has risen from 34 to 43 percent. Advising loads can be as high as 40 students within some departments. Though classes of more than 32 students remain at only 4.5 percent, and most faculty members have fewer than 20 advisees, faculty perceive that their workloads have increased markedly over the past decade.

The chief responsibility of the faculty, in accord with the mission of the college, is teaching and advising students, followed by scholarship and service. Inevitably, faculty tend to defer scholarship in its traditional guises—primary research, publication in refereed journals, and refereed presentations at national conferences—even though some form of professional activity has always been a criterion for promotion and tenure. Expanding the definition of scholarship used for promotion and tenure became a way for Franklin to acknowledge existing faculty scholarly contributions, as well as to press faculty to become involved in different forms of scholarship during their careers. In 1997, Franklin officially changed the language in its faculty handbook to incorporate Boyer's four categories of scholarship as defined in *Scholarship Reconsidered: Priorities of the Professoriate* (1990); a second revision expanding and clarifying the definitions took place in 2001. In response, some fundamental disagreements about the role of faculty scholarship in relation to the mission of the college have surfaced. I led a team of faculty who undertook a campus study of the change process, its impact on faculty roles and rewards, and the shape of the faculty debate over scholarship at Franklin College. Shortly before beginning the study, I assumed my current position as vice president for academic affairs (VPAA).

LOOKING IN THE MIRROR FIVE YEARS LATER

Our study examined how changes in the definition of scholarship used in promotion and tenure affected institutional culture and individual faculty behavior. In particular, it attempted to uncover whether the original aims of the revision—to clarify the expectations regarding scholarship, place greater emphasis on faculty scholarship in the promotion and tenure process, and accord greater recognition to scholarly efforts of all kinds—had been achieved and to what extent. In addition, it sought to describe faculty attitudes toward scholarship generally and Boyer's categories in particular. The results were also intended to guide Franklin's promotion and tenure committee in evaluating all four kinds of scholarship. The study aligned with the agenda of the VPAA, which is to help shape a culture that nurtures and supports faculty scholarship. Campus leaders wanted to promote a wider conversation among the faculty about what scholarship is and ought to be at Franklin College.

The following questions framed the campus study:

1. What are the prevailing attitudes toward faculty scholarship, five years after the change?
2. Has the change affected faculty participation in scholarly activity?
3. Do older and younger generations of faculty differ in attitudes and behaviors?
4. Do the systems of evaluation, incentive, and reward support the original aims of the revision?

In addition to the VPAA, the campus study committee consisted of three members of the faculty promotion and tenure committee, a former chair of the faculty steering committee, and a former chair of the curricular assessment and planning committee. The faculty represented three of the six academic divisions and four departments. Two committee members compiled a history of revisions to the faculty handbook with respect to scholarship, drawing on their own knowledge of events, minutes of appropriate committees, and the expertise of other faculty. Committee members elicited and compiled responses to a faculty survey and conducted follow-up interviews with individual faculty members. Of Franklin's 61 full-time faculty, 51 percent responded to the initial survey, and committee members conducted follow-up interviews with approximately half of the faculty who completed the survey.

A NEW VICE PRESIDENT AND A NEW VISION

Prior to 1997, Franklin's rewards system in both policy and practice required little formal scholarship. In policy, the handbook contained no language that specifically defined scholarship. However, criteria in the section titled "Ranks and Criteria for Promotion and Tenure" (Franklin College, 1996) presupposed academic and intellectual preparation for all ranks, which included "intellectual competence, curiosity, and independence." The criteria for assistant professor also included engagement with one's discipline and active enlargement of one's own liberal education. The criteria for ranks above instructor read, "Other considerations may include membership and service in professional organizations, writing and publication, and other activities which make the College available and of service to the larger community." The criteria for senior ranks included "intellectual productivity beyond the requirement of one's teaching assignments," "sustained service to one's field, beyond its expression at Franklin College," and "the ability to make original contributions to one's field and the ability to relate one's field to other fields." Finally, the handbook's criteria for tenure specified that "tenure should be awarded on the basis of . . . demonstrated excellence in teaching effectiveness, as well as in intellectual and professional development" (Franklin College, 1996, II, p. 25).

In practice, faculty reported that, for the most part, traditional forms of scholarship were not required, particularly encouraged, or rewarded before 1997. The tradition of the promotion and tenure committee reflected the prevailing culture, which held classroom teaching as the primary responsibility and traditional

scholarship as, at best, ancillary to the faculty's "real" work. There were limited funds for faculty travel to conferences and virtually none for sustained research. Even the terminal degree was regarded as unnecessary. Despite this, some faculty did pursue traditional forms of scholarship, including publication and presentation, and many more engaged in activities that would fall into Boyer's scholarships of teaching, integration, and application. While faculty did not discourage these activities, they and those who served on the promotion and tenure committee did not see them as crucial to the promotion and tenure process. Faculty members who engaged in research projects saw them as labors of love, with little expectation that they would be supported or rewarded. In such a context, even as recently as 1996, new faculty members with doctorates received mixed messages from the faculty handbook and from the culture about the expectations for scholarly activity.

Clearly, faculty could not find a concise and understandable description of the college's expectations for scholarly activity in the faculty handbook, filled as it was with ambiguity. This problem was compounded by the fact that in the period between 1989 and 1996, five appointments filled the position of VPAA, the chief academic officer responsible for meeting with the promotion and tenure committee and making recommendations to the president regarding promotion and tenure. Continual turnover in the VPAA's office and lack of guidance by the faculty handbook left faculty members, especially newer ones, uncertain about the expectations for scholarly activity. Some thought there was an expectation of traditional scholarly output, while others saw scholarship as relatively unimportant. Promotion and tenure committee members who served during the same period commented that, owing to the "revolving door" of VPAAs and the lack of clarity in the faculty handbook, scholarship was rarely considered in faculty evaluations.

Franklin College suffered several problems as a result. First, the lack of clear expectations for scholarship placed additional stress on junior faculty and caused confusion throughout the ranks. Second, the college did not benefit from the prestige of a national reputation for scholarly excellence. Third, individual faculty careers did not benefit from the prestige of a reputation within their disciplines. Finally, the North Central Association, an accrediting body, expressed concern about a lack of emphasis on scholarship in its re-accreditation report in 1992. Though many faculty acknowledged the problem of confusion over the definition of scholarship, lack of prestige or reputation was not necessarily perceived as a problem at the time.

In spring 1997, a new VPAA, Allen Berger, urged the faculty to adopt specific language about scholarly activity for inclusion in the faculty handbook. The handbook, he suggested, should clearly describe the faculty role as having three parts, teaching, service, and scholarship. He noted that five years earlier, the North Central Association had criticized Franklin's traditions and expectations for overemphasizing the first two elements to the detriment of the third. He was "pleased to discover" that the college's promotion standards contained a response to North Central's criticism, yet he "was also concerned with how poorly we defined the range of contributions that might qualify as scholarship. . . . More often than not, scholarship is simply equated with the number of jargon-ridden, refereed articles accepted for publication in esoteric journals [that] are read only by a handful of colleagues. . . . Surely our profession can do better. And surely Franklin College can do better" (Berger, 1997). Berger saw the writings of Ernest Boyer as a tool for demonstrating that scholarship mattered at Franklin. Referring to Boyer's four categories as a worthy effort to restore "some sanity" to the debate about scholarship, Berger wrote that "in a sense" the Franklin faculty already knew that "the true scholar is one who is intellectually vital and who continues to grow." The essence of scholarship was "the life of the mind," as expressed and measured in many ways, not simply articles in refereed journals. Boyer's language would enable Franklin's faculty to make that clear in the handbook (Berger, 1997).

Berger pushed the faculty to include Boyer's definition of scholarship in the handbook in order to address three critical needs: (1) responding to North Central's concerns, (2) increasing scholarly activity among the faculty, and (3) gaining clarity in the guidelines for promotion and tenure decisions.

Berger brought the proposal through the curricular allocations and priorities (CAP) committee, rather than the promotion and tenure committee. The CAP members were already working to simplify language in the handbook regarding faculty workload, and added a statement about scholarship at the end of the section outlining faculty responsibilities. Under "Scholarship," the addendum stated that faculty members are expected to stay current and vital in their areas of scholarly interest and expertise. This scholarship may take many forms. The statement then described Boyer's four types of scholarship.

Minutes of the CAP indicate that members spent considerable time discussing the workload formula but very little discussing the accompanying language about scholarship. Conversations with those involved reveal that members were far more concerned with the complexities and the potential for conflict involved in workload adjustments; they were less concerned with something they perceived as primarily a clarification rather than a substantive change in promotion and tenure criteria. In fact, this tendency to view Boyer's language as little more than a description of what already existed at the college persists to this day in the attitudes of many of the faculty members who were involved in the process. One might speculate that Berger encouraged this view to facilitate what might otherwise have seemed a threatening development. The proposal came to the faculty in April 1997, was passed by a two-thirds voice vote the following month, and won approval by the board of trustees in October 1997. Minutes of the faculty and board meetings contain virtually no discussion of this addition to the handbook. It is clear that the change was not perceived as controversial, either by the faculty or the board.

ROLES OF THE FACULTY

In fall 2000, the promotion and tenure committee sought to add clarity and detail to all three areas of the faculty role, starting with teaching. Then the committee turned to scholarship, with the goal of making the definitions complete and consistent yet flexible enough to respond to individual talents and activities. Committee members hoped that the language would encourage faculty to engage in different forms of scholarly activity, but as they revised the language referring to scholarship they avoided emphasizing scholarship over service, and they added the statement that teaching faculty "must show evidence of both scholarship and service, but the balance between those two areas may vary." They argued that a faculty member's career could move in a number of different directions, and that the college ought not to impose any quantified requirement for scholarship. While distinguishing between institutional service and the scholarship of application, committee members thought that the lines dividing scholarship and service had become, appropriately in their view, less sharp. Their goal was to create a framework that would allow faculty members to engage in and receive credit for meaningful activities. However, it is possible that as a result some faculty developed a view that Boyer's definition broke down distinctions between scholarship and other important faculty functions.

Another addition specifically protected faculty who do not publish or present at conferences: scholarly activities, "which may involve acquiring knowledge as well as generating knowledge, may take many forms. While a faculty member might not engage in all areas of scholarship and professional development . . . each of these areas is of equal value." The committee added the phrase "acquiring knowledge" to cover cases where a faculty member might attend a symposium without necessarily making a presentation. Additionally, the language covered faculty who needed to complete continuing professional education in order to maintain professional licenses. Committee members wanted to make scholarship more inclusive by ensuring that no form, particularly publication or presentation, was valued over others. Here again, the committee interpreted Boyer's categories broadly enough to validate the kinds of activities already practiced by the faculty. Also important, the tendency to affirm existing practices tempered the VPAA's intent to encourage more faculty involvement in scholarly work. This conflict between the desire to preserve a student-centered teaching focus and the need to situate the college within the larger academic world, here evident in the divergence of the committee's work from the VPAA's vision of a redefined scholarship, manifested itself in various ways throughout the change process.

As the promotion and tenure committee turned its attention to each of the four areas of scholarship, it continued to broaden, rather than to narrow, the categories. The committee widened the definition of "scholarship of discovery" to "scholarship of discovery or creativity" and added specific reference to artistic endeavor. The section on scholarship of application was revised to recognize work to obtain or maintain professional certification, even though such a standard would seem to conflict with Boyer's intentions. The committee also recognized the importance of the scholarship of integration in a liberal arts setting, expanding that definition to lay particular stress on interdisciplinary work.

In the attempt to modify the section on the scholarship of teaching, a split developed between the VPAA's approach and the committee's views. While the VPAA insisted that anything labeled "scholarship of teaching" had to be externally peer reviewed, the committee's preference for the prevailing faculty view, that it should include activities such as course development, ran counter to the standard of external peer review and dissemination. The definition was later broadened to state that a scholarship of teaching "seeks to improve teaching, learning, and advising" but does not require a professional public audience.

THE PROPOSAL PASSES

In May 2000, the departure of Allen Berger and the appointment of an interim VPAA changed the dynamics of the process. Each definition of scholarship, under Berger's direction, had included wording about "presentation to appropriate professional audiences." Although the promotion and tenure committee interpreted the phrase broadly, they did not feel confident that other key individuals, including the new VPAA, would do so. After extensive deliberation, the committee removed the language, believing it would be used to require faculty to publish in a journal or present at a conference. The committee members believed that publication or presentation was not necessary to legitimize a scholarly activity. In the end, they gave responsibility for evaluating faculty scholarship to college peer reviewers, whose role was expanded in the overall revamping of teaching, service, and scholarship.

The committee finalized its recommendations and presented them to faculty. The college requires two readings for any proposals for changes in the faculty handbook. The first review and discussion took place in March 2001; the second came one month later. Most of the April discussion of the revised definitions of scholarship centered, again, on the issue of presentation to professional audiences. A faculty member who supported the original language proposed changing "required" to "encouraged," so that the statement would read, "Faculty members . . . are *encouraged* to present their work to appropriate professional audiences."

After significant debate, the amendment passed by majority voice vote. Immediately following, the faculty broke out into more discussion, and someone motioned to remove the just-passed amendment. That motion passed by majority voice vote as well. Clearly, the faculty had considerable ambivalence toward this standard; many argued that even the milder language of the amendment could be used to force faculty members to undertake traditional forms of scholarship. Finally, by unanimous vote, the faculty passed language on scholarship that did not include "presentation to appropriate professional audiences." The board subsequently approved it, and the revised definitions of scholarship currently appear in the faculty handbook. Although VPAA Berger's push for a standard of presentation had failed, the goals of clarity and acknowledgment of a broader range of faculty activity as scholarship had been achieved.

INITIAL IMPLEMENTATION

After the revised definitions of scholarship became part of the faculty handbook, in fall 2000, the promotion and tenure committee moved to the next part of its job, educating the faculty about the changes they had passed the previous spring. The fact that the faculty had read and approved the modifications was no guarantee that they understood or would respond to them. The committee ran promotion and tenure workshops for faculty members under review and for faculty members who would be acting as classroom visitors and peer reviewers.

These workshops had actually begun two years earlier, in 1999, when the promotion and tenure committee realized it was going to be redefining not only scholarship but teaching (in 1999) and service (in 2001). The workshops were a new experience: none of the veteran faculty interviewed could recall such a formal and complete discussion of promotion and tenure matters. Workshops enabled the committee to educate the faculty on basic issues, before turning attention to the specifics of the scholarship issue. One long-standing faculty concern was that promotion and tenure decisions were "black box" processes. Throughout the change process in all three areas of faculty work—teaching, service, and scholarship—the committee had to state clearly that it wanted to lower faculty anxiety about promotion and tenure. The group stressed that all the changes were designed to make the process transparent and allow faculty to have as much control as possible.

Younger faculty members were usually more familiar with Boyer's definitions and more receptive to the redesigned system, whereas mere mention of a "portfolio" would upset many veteran faculty members. Workshop coordinators tried to communicate to all that the redesigned system was more open but placed greater responsibility upon those being evaluated as well as upon classroom observers and peer reviewers. The meetings that dealt primarily with scholarship issues were held in September 2001. After the preliminary discussion about faculty control and anxiety reduction, the workshops for promotion and tenure candidates stressed the revised definitions of scholarship, the thinking behind them, and how candidates could best present their own cases.

Faculty responded positively to these workshops, and, according to committee members, the quality of submissions for promotion and tenure improved markedly. They took greater care to document their claims of having met required standards of teaching, scholarship, and service; the quality of peer reviewers' submissions also reportedly improved. As a result, the promotion and tenure committee felt capable of making more informed decisions about scholarly work.

SCHOLARSHIP REDEFINED: WHAT CHANGED AND WHAT DID NOT

In spring 2002, our team conducted a survey and follow-up interviews to determine the effects of the handbook change on faculty attitudes and actions. The study revealed that faculty at all career stages considered Boyer's categories appropriate for a college with Franklin's mission. At the same time, the results showed that the revisions of the faculty handbook had not changed, and probably would not change, the extent and variety of faculty participation in scholarly activity. Those who, before the revisions, were inclined to see peer-reviewed publication and presentation as the appropriate mode of scholarship continue to do so and continue to produce that kind of work. Those who put their energies into pedagogy and service continue to do so, and those who were relatively inactive before continue to be so. Nearly all think that the handbook changes will mean greater recognition and affirmation of the variety of activities that Franklin faculty have always performed. As one senior faculty member stated in a follow-up interview, "I believe that the change to the Boyer criteria is not so much a way of facilitating more of the traditional varieties of scholarship so much as a way of acknowledging the great variety of intellectual gifts persons have and the diverse ways in which they share those gifts. What is happening is not new activity, but a new acknowledgment of the value that that activity has had all along."

Some junior faculty members said that one factor in their decision to come to Franklin College was the chance to work within Boyer's categories. They felt particularly empowered by the broader definition of scholarship. When asked about rewards and incentives, more than half of faculty surveyed said that the change signaled a new emphasis on a broad definition of scholarship and a movement away from what many viewed as an excessive emphasis on service (in the form of committee and other administrative work). Despite the reservations of some and the indifference of others, the data overwhelmingly show that faculty members across disciplines and at varying stages of their careers approve of the change, find it appropriate for the mission of the institution, and see it as potentially or actually enhancing the quality of work life. Faculty believe that their work will be more valued and better rewarded.

A GENERATIONAL DIVIDE?

An analysis of responses also reveals a division in thinking about what constitutes appropriate scholarship for a faculty charged with carrying out the mission of a small student-centered institution. Roughly half of the junior faculty expressed concern that a broadening of the definition of scholarship might devalue or discourage more traditional forms and possibly encourage continued inactivity by those who have done little scholarship of any kind. Said one highly active young scholar, "Faculty activities will seem to increase as work that had been done in the past will now be recognized. . . . However, I would be inclined to believe that in certain kinds of scholarship (publication, for instance) it will have the opposite effect, as the need to perform in those areas will be seen as less great." Another junior faculty member said, "I am concerned that there may be a small number of faculty members who mistakenly think Boyer gives them an excuse to do nothing but teach classes, toss out some ideas at committee meetings, and go to an occasional workshop." A junior faculty member who publishes regularly was even harsher: "Some things that other people are calling scholarship are pretty weak. Basically, if I can do what some of my colleagues are doing and are calling scholarship without any previous training in their fields, then how can they (how dare they) call what they are doing scholarship? . . . I don't prefer calling 'anything' scholarship. That doesn't help anyone, it only serves to dilute the meaning of the term."

Approximately 25 percent of respondents expressed the opposite fear: that the handbook's new language reflects a new emphasis on scholarship that might cause scholarship to replace teaching as the most important criterion for evaluating faculty. These faculty members seem unconvinced that Boyer's categories might actually help reduce such pressure by including as scholarship some activities usually thought of as part of teaching or service responsibilities.

Thus, faculty opinion about the proper role of scholarship in relation to the teaching mission of the college appears polarized, with approximately one-quarter of the surveyed faculty believing that more emphasis on scholarship is needed, a comparable proportion believing that too much emphasis on any form of scholarship is inappropriate, and the rest distributed in between.

A QUESTION OF RIGOR

Those who fear the move away from traditional forms of scholarship ask a very reasonable question about the evaluation process. In traditional research, refereed journals, academic publishers, and national conventions provide standards of rigor. How can that same rigor be established in the scholarship of teaching, integration, and application? Our team posed this question to faculty members from various disciplines and career stages. Three of our team who were also members of the promotion and tenure committee conducted "self-interviews" on this question.

To put these responses into the proper context, it is important to understand the review process itself. Faculty members undergo a review every year for the first four years of their probationary period; during the sixth year (the year of the tenure decision); and every five years after receiving tenure. Promotion reviews are generally done at the same time as either the tenure review or, later, the five-year review. A faculty member must provide a portfolio of material amassed during the period between the previous review and the current review. The portfolio materials must demonstrate an appropriate level of achievement in teaching, scholarship, and service. In addition, the committee requires student evaluations, classroom visitation reports from the VPAA and one colleague, department chair evaluations (during the first three annual reviews), two to five peer evaluations (depending on the type of review), and a self-evaluation. No off-campus evaluation is required. This omission makes me uneasy, as VPAA, because it could foster complacency among faculty who would look only to on-campus peers for appraisal.

Promotion and tenure committee members have argued that rigor should be determined by on-campus peer evaluators. VPAA Berger tried to insist on external audiences for most forms of scholarly activity, but the faculty rejected this plan. Standards for scholarship are internally determined, which led me to ask what those standards are and how one would know someone has met them. Nearly all of the senior faculty respondents were untroubled by this question. They felt it was appropriate for the standards to be set by their Franklin peers or even themselves. One senior faculty member stated, "Surely that is what professionalism is—the self-definition and self-criticism by the discipline itself. I have internalized professional standards. I do not feel bound by juries of any kind—or even the opinion of [the promotion and tenure committee] for that matter. . . . However, I shall probably be harder on myself than any external examiner."

A junior faculty member who shared this view noted, "Boyer's definitions put more of a burden on faculty than mere publishing does." But nearly everyone, when pressed, acknowledged that measuring outcomes in the scholarship of teaching or of application is very difficult. They didn't say, "We'll know it when we see it," but that seemed to be the prevailing spirit. This may be liberating for the faculty member, but how can the institution be accountable for the actions it takes on promotion and tenure? Our team found that the faculty has not fully grappled with this question.

As the VPAA, I am concerned that faculty have not yet discovered ways to evaluate scholarship through forms that are externally peer reviewed or at least placed before an external professional audience. The promotion and tenure committee fears placing too much emphasis on traditional forms of scholarship, but, like approximately one-half of the junior faculty, I fear that a lack of objective standards may allow faculty who do not wish to engage in any form of scholarship to escape evaluation and consequences. Arbitrary or nonexplicit standards could also contribute to an atmosphere in which promotion and tenure decisions are politicized and personalized rather than based on more objective assessments of accomplishment.

Several of the more traditionally active scholars on the faculty responded quite vehemently that too much second-rate work is accepted without question at Franklin College. For example, one faculty member stated:

> Rigor, to me, means (a) clear evidence of good critical thinking, shown in part by solid readable writing, logical thought, and appropriate reference to sources; (b) clear evidence of knowing and using recent work in a field as well as "classic" ideas in a field, so that it's evident how the faculty member's work is part of the progress of ideas; (c) clear evidence of some kind that the faculty member's contributions are part of the discussions in the field, such as responses from off-campus peers, which might mean inclusion on a panel at a professional conference, publication in peer-reviewed journals, consultation with other professionals or publishers, etc.; and (d) extent—that is, professional work should be long enough to show sustained thinking and achievement. I think this last criterion is necessary but hard for many people at Franklin College to achieve, in part due to time constraints, Franklin College's climate of half-heartedness, and other factors. A final, obvious criterion is that a faculty member's work should be appropriate to her or his field of expertise, the field in which s/he was hired and is teaching. Relying on casual, tangential, or hobby-like skills would not constitute academic rigor. Nor would "service" as many here define it. Boyer is pretty clear about what

the scholarship of application means; it requires one's expert academic components being directly addressed to community issues, not helping out at a bake sale.

However, for about half of the faculty interviewed (most of the senior faculty interviewed plus some 40 percent of the junior faculty interviewed), the teaching mission of the college trumps any further need for establishing measures of rigor in scholarly activity. Not everyone was equally sanguine about the promotion and tenure committee's ability to assess the scholarships of integration, application, and teaching. Nor was everyone confident that either the committee or the faculty at large would be able to decide how much scholarship in any area is appropriate to warrant tenure and promotion. However, most seem satisfied that the peer and self-evaluation systems are right for the college at this point.

One group of senior faculty presented a thoughtful response to the question of how to measure rigor. Academic rigor, they argued, cannot be defined only by juried publication or presentation, and the college (and especially the promotion and tenure committee) "should view scholarly activity through the lens of the concept of student benefit." Faculty should be able to demonstrate a tangible benefit to their students or the college. Furthermore, while the institution ought to "create a climate . . . where scholarship is embraced and supported," it should be "appropriate scholarship" and not "selfish scholarship." Selfish scholarship "is conducted only for the personal or professional benefit of the faculty member involved," while appropriate scholarship is "student centered."

This formulation helps shift the debate away from a discussion of "half-heartedness" versus rigor and toward a more altruistic discussion about the aims of scholarship. The concept of selfish scholarship is questionable, of course. If faculty members engage in scholarship that deepens their understanding of a subject area and contributes significantly to a discipline, there would presumably be a tangible benefit for students. If such scholarship enhances the reputation of faculty members and thus the college, a tangible benefit would again accrue to students. One wonders, then, under what circumstances scholarship conducted "for the personal or professional benefit of the faculty member" would be deemed selfish rather than appropriate.

Still, this group of faculty is seeking an objective standard for evaluating scholarship, particularly one that would take into account the primacy of teaching. They have reservations about the pursuit of scholarly reputation at the expense of one's responsibility to students. Others, however, including me, do not believe that a conscientious teacher-scholar has to sacrifice fidelity to good teaching and caring for students in order to pursue serious scholarship of all kinds. If the tangible-benefit standard were to be defined as limiting appropriate scholarship to the areas of teaching, application, and integration, for example, then it would actually run afoul of current faculty handbook language, which stresses the legitimacy of all four types of scholarship.

One example of how this conflict tends to manifest itself involves integration. Nearly all faculty members responding to the campus survey understood the new definition of scholarship provided in the handbook, but confusion persists about the meaning of the "scholarship of integration." In interviews, some faculty members seemed to view integration as involving mostly reviews of the work of others (and indeed some integration scholarship consists of that kind of work). Others saw preparing and teaching interdisciplinary courses or curricular work on general education as scholarship of integration. Those in favor of raising the bar see these categories as valuable but not always matching their (or Boyer's) meaning of the scholarship of integration. Yet, such activities are appropriate to the college mission, and the faculty who do much of this work—and at least 30 percent of our faculty engage in one or another form of integration—see the adoption of Boyer as validating what they do. There is no question that the scholarship of integration could be and to some extent already is a vital aspect of the intellectual life of the college, but the question remains how to decide when the work itself takes place at a level or in a context that can be defined as scholarly. The lack of faculty consensus on this point reflects the larger discussion about scholarship at Franklin College, and it also reflects the larger national conversation about the nature of the scholarship of integration.

This difference of opinion regarding scholarship and its relationship to the mission of the college does not break cleanly along generational lines. At the same time, a larger group of senior faculty strongly resist a shift toward greater rigor in the evaluation of scholarship of all kinds, while many junior faculty would like to see more emphasis placed on more rigorously and in some cases more traditionally defined scholarship. Nor is this primarily a self-interested debate between those who "produce" and those who don't. A more meaningful way to view the conflict is to think of a struggle between those who would like to see the college improve its intellectual climate and move up in academic reputation and those who fear that the character and mission of the college might be lost in the effort to achieve those aims. The move to Boyer's definition of scholarship and the present campus study have brought this debate into sharper view, so that a meaningful and, one hopes, productive discussion can take place.

REMAINING BARRIERS

No such discussion can ignore the obstacles faced by faculty who wish to do serious scholarship of any kind at Franklin College. Faculty members were united in identifying time constraints as the most intractable and defeating obstacle to increased participation in scholarly activity. With numerous faculty members serving as department chairs and six more serving as division heads under a new reorganization, and with 16 standing and several more ad hoc committees, the faculty has considerable governance work. Faculty reviews, program reviews, and various accreditation processes absorb additional time. Students at Franklin, as at most small colleges, are accustomed to personal attention, and since that is a key advantage over the competition, the faculty and staff put great emphasis on making themselves available. Scholarship, however it is placed in the faculty handbook, is pushed aside during the regular academic year.

Faculty members also described the limitations of the library and the current uses of faculty development funding as constraints. While few thought that the amount of money available for development was an issue, some questioned whether the money allotted for development was being used wisely to encourage, support, and reward faculty scholarship. For example, since time and workload considerations are such pressing issues, should more money be spent for release time to allow faculty to complete scholarly projects? Are there other ways to relieve the time burden? Could professional staff assist faculty with projects?

The rewards, incentives, and supports for scholarship are within the realm of decisions the VPAA can make independently. My office has acted on several recommendations that emerged from the current campus study: (1) it raised the limits on small grants from two endowed funds used to supplement travel and support scholarly effort, (2) instituted a policy of using the Rinker Faculty Excellence fund to pay for release time, (3) announced an annual competition for a $5,000 grant to support scholarly endeavors, and (4) announced that the college will confer a faculty scholarship award at commencement each year, alongside existing awards in teaching and service. Finally, it announced a pilot program for faculty who develop and team-teach interdisciplinary courses. This pilot program will compensate each faculty member on the team for full credit, as opposed to the current practice of splitting the credit hours between the two faculty or assigning slightly more than half credit to each faculty member. This will help promote integrative work, which is perceived by many to be an important type of scholarship for faculty at liberal arts institutions.

My office has also initiated discussion of curricular changes that might reduce the faculty workload. We have suggested that the faculty investigate reducing the total number of hours required for graduation (they made this change in 2003) and the total number of hours required in the general education program. Additionally, we suggested moving toward a standard teaching load of three, rather than four, courses per semester. This initiative will require a great deal of time, effort, and consensus building, and there is no guarantee that it will succeed. However, it would help address the time constraints that continue to pose the greatest challenge to faculty engaging in scholarship.

SCHOLARSHIP AND THE MISSION

Our study team encountered many faculty who perceived the shift to Boyer's framework as legitimizing the work they already perform, especially in the areas of teaching, curricular development, and service. Some regretted the expansive definition and felt that it would lead to less effort being put into traditional forms of scholarship. Still others said that the recognition and rewarding of various faculty talents and accomplishments was overdue. It is important to remember, however, that the faculty had to *react* to a change that was handed down from the administration. As mentioned earlier, the impetus for change came from the then VPAA and his wish to encourage greater scholarly activity by all faculty members. Whenever change comes from the top, it can be more difficult to secure buy-in and achieve the objectives. Indeed, this study reveals that Franklin's faculty, as a whole, must still reach consensus on the need for, and importance of, the change in the definition and importance of scholarship.

At Franklin College, scholarly activity as defined by Boyer has not significantly increased or decreased as a result of the revisions to the faculty handbook. However, the implementation of rewards and incentives geared toward a wider spectrum of activity has sharpened the perception that scholarly activity is supported and rewarded by the college. The college is fortunate to have relatively strong faculty development and rewards programs, supported by several endowed funds. The potential clearly exists for making progress toward wider faculty participation in scholarly endeavors of all kinds.

Two major obstacles remain: time constraints and a culture that tends to place scholarship and teaching at odds with one another, despite the use of Boyer's four categories. My office is initiating reforms that should ease the first problem, and a vigorous discussion is emerging about how much and what kind of scholarship is "appropriate" to the mission of Franklin College. One of the primary lessons from our experience is that, in a liberal arts college, change undertaken without full and broadly based consideration of its implications vis-à-vis the mission will encounter difficulty. On the other hand, change also offers an opportunity for the college to reexamine its mission and how best to implement it in a rapidly changing educational climate. Such discussion and debate are essential to the vitality of the liberal arts college.

References

Berger, A. (1997, March 13). *Address to the faculty*. Franklin, IN: Franklin College.

Boyer, E. L. (1990). *Scholarship reconsidered: Priorities of the professoriate*. Princeton, NJ: Carnegie Foundation for the Advancement of Teaching.

Franklin College. (1996). *Franklin College handbook: Information, policies and procedures for faculty and academic administration*. Franklin, IN: Author.

CHAPTER FIVE

REDEFINING THE CULTURE OF SCHOLARSHIP
Madonna University
Dennis Bozyk

Independent universities face their own special challenges and opportunities regarding the culture of scholarship. The great majority of colleges and universities in the United States are independent liberal arts institutions, which tend to be much smaller than public institutions in terms of enrollment and faculty. Size and mission affect the ethos of these institutions in all areas, including the culture of scholarship.

This campus study of Madonna University explores the recent efforts of a medium-sized, independent, liberal arts university to redefine its culture of scholarship in order to encourage and reward faculty for scholarly accomplishments related to its mission. Specifically, the study analyzes the effects of a mandate issued by the university's Task Force on Scholarship. Based on extensive interviews, it illustrates faculty attitudes and intentions toward scholarship and relates them to the past work of the task force and the mission and daily work of the university. Faculty interviews indicate there has been a "soft revolution" in the culture of scholarship at Madonna University, and this study explores the dynamics surrounding this change as well as possible consequences for the near future.

A college's culture of scholarship should be examined in the context of the larger institutional culture, particularly at schools with a strong emphasis on mission. This campus study of Madonna

University may be particularly helpful to other independent liberal arts universities with similar mission-driven cultures.

INSTITUTIONAL HISTORY

Madonna University is an independent, coeducational, Catholic, liberal arts university, sponsored by the Felician sisters. The university began its institutional life in 1939 as Presentation Junior College, founded for the education of Felician sisters. In 1947, Presentation Junior College became Madonna College, a four-year liberal arts college offering preprofessional programs in teaching, medical technology, and social welfare to sisters and lay women. In 1954, the college was approved by the Michigan Board of Education to recommend graduates for teaching certificates, and in 1959, Madonna College received its initial accreditation by the North Central Association of Colleges and Schools.

During the 1960s, the college began a four-year degree program in nursing that the State of Michigan Board of Nursing approved in 1967. By 1973, Madonna College had added several new majors, including business administration and criminal justice, and had become coeducational. The college added a Master of Science in Administration, with specialties in business and nursing, to the curriculum in 1982, followed by master's degrees in business, education, and nursing and health. In 1991, Madonna College became Madonna University and was reorganized into five entities: the College of Arts and Humanities, the School of Business, the College of Nursing and Health, the College of Science and Mathematics, and the College of Social Sciences. The College of Continuing and Professional Studies was soon added. In 1996, Madonna University became the first institution in the United States to offer a graduate certificate and a master's of science in hospice.

Throughout this progression, Madonna University's mission played a central role in the functioning of the institution. The present-day mission, found in the university's bulletin, is to instill "Christian humanistic values" in students, along with "intellectual inquiry, a respect for diversity, and a commitment to serving others through a liberal arts education, integrated with career preparation and based on the truths and principles recognized within the Catholic tradition." Informing the mission are Franciscan values such as "a reverence for the dignity of each person; a love of God translated into assisting all peoples, especially the poor, minority groups, and individuals challenged with disabilities; an appreciation of nature and all creation; and a conviction that the liberal arts and sciences develop the intellect so as to prepare the individual to render more effective service to humanity" (Madonna University, 2002, p. 6).

From its modest beginnings to the present day, Madonna University has been organized around service to its students and, through them, to the community. The commitment and values of the sponsoring body of Felician sisters imparted a very real and concrete meaning to the words *mission, vocation,* and *service,* which deeply affected the traditions and culture of the university. An exploration of the culture of scholarship must include consideration of the university's commitment to the values and mission of the Felician sisters, who provided the dedication, resources, and models that made the university and its successes possible.

Madonna University serves nearly 4,000 students in southeastern Michigan. Categorized as a Master's (Comprehensive) University within the Carnegie classifications, the university offers associate and baccalaureate degrees in the traditional liberal arts disciplines and baccalaureate and master's degrees in the professional areas of business, education, and nursing and health. The teaching faculty consists of 108 full-time and 205 adjunct members. All baccalaureate degree programs include a strong liberal arts, general education component.

For philosophical and practical reasons, independent liberal arts universities such as Madonna University designate the education of their students as their primary mission. Madonna University's goal is to provide a strong liberal arts education, combined with excellent career preparation, within a Christian humanistic perspective. The curriculum and the teaching-learning process are central to the achievement of this mission. All of the administrative, faculty, and staff roles are defined with respect to this priority. Additionally, independent colleges and universities, which do not receive significant public funding, depend upon tuition as their main source of revenue. Attracting and retaining students depends on satisfying their needs through quality instruction. The entire community, including the faculty, recognizes that teaching is the clear priority. Therefore, any discussion of scholarship and its im-plications for faculty roles and recognition occurs within the con-text of the priority of teaching. Human, fiscal, and physical resources of the university are dedicated first to the excellent de-livery of the curriculum to students. Other priorities closely related to the delivery of quality teaching, such as advising and committee work, are also important faculty responsibilities.

What, then, is the role of scholarship at independent liberal arts universities such as Madonna University? What are the expec-tations of these universities in the area of scholarship? What do in-dividual faculty members hope and expect to accomplish in the area of scholarship? How might such universities encourage and support more scholarship, consistent with the priorities established by their accepted mission?

THE CHALLENGE

In 1991, Madonna College became Madonna University. For some, this was primarily a name change, to coincide with the addition of graduate programs and changes in the number and kinds of bac-calaureate degrees. For others, something more significant was happening regarding the role of the institution and the role of fac-ulty: the word *university* connoted an institution of higher learning that included a strong commitment to the creation of new knowl-edge. Some felt that faculty roles would change according to this new commitment, in that faculty would be expected to accomplish more scholarship.

Since its beginning, Madonna University has been an educa-tional community dedicated to teaching and service. These goals were central to the original mission of the Felician sisters and to those who joined them in the rapid and successful growth of the university. However, the change to university status implied that this mission was being expanded to include a larger responsibility for producing scholarship. In this study's interviews, several faculty members who were at Madonna University during the change ex-pressed concerns that new requirements for scholarship might compromise their primary roles as teachers. Faculty members hired after 1991 expected the university to include scholarship among the significant responsibilities of the faculty, and they were disappointed to discover that there was no allocation for scholarship in the faculty workload. In some cases, according to deans and department heads, faculty candidates turned down positions because they preferred universities that would offer more support for traditional disciplinary scholarship. In the 1990s, some of Madonna's faculty members wondered how their professional lives would be affected, specifically in terms of what responsibilities would be included in their evolving job descriptions and how these expectations would be supported, assessed, and rewarded. Would there be a responsibility for scholarship? What kinds of scholarship would be included? How might newly defined scholarship responsibilities correlate with the traditional priorities of teaching and service, which already demanded the full attention and resources of the university and its faculty? These questions quickly became important for the larger community.

With these concerns in mind, and informed by Ernest Boyer's (1990) *Scholarship Reconsidered: Priorities of the Professoriate,* the vice president for academic administration (VPAA) in 1998 invited the faculty to form a yearlong Task Force on the Definition of Scholarship. The VPAA challenged the task force to explore questions related to scholarship and to propose a definition that would be meaningful to Madonna's academic community. He also asked them to encourage a broad discussion about the role of scholarship at Madonna University and to propose plans for actualizing faculty decisions about scholarship.

Sixteen faculty and administrators from various parts of the university community formed the task force. The group included members who were leaders in research and publishing and representation from the College of Nursing and Health, which led campus efforts in scholarship and publishing at the time. The members of the task force divided into two groups. A smaller number of members became active participants who read, discussed, proposed, and critiqued ideas and practices related to scholarship. The remainder of the group approved the work of the others with little direct participation. It is possible that the smaller number of active participants facilitated a clearer focus and made possible the accomplishment of the group's goals within the mandated timeline of one academic year. Although the committee members considered a broad range of ideas related to scholarship, much of their time was devoted to a rigorous study and assessment of Boyer's (1990) framework for scholarship. In the end, the committee succeeded in preparing a new definition of scholarship, based on Boyer's ideas. The definition stated:

> Scholarship is the disciplined quest for knowledge through discovery, integration, application, and teaching that transforms individuals and communities. Discovery is the research process of revealing new knowledge that in turn contributes to humanity's collective knowledge. Integration is the process of developing cognitive connections that illuminate ideas in new ways. Application is the process of using abstract and/or theoretical knowledge to affect real problems or situations, resulting in new intellectual understandings that emerge through conscious analysis and synthesis of the experience. Teaching is the dynamic process of engaging students, others, and ourselves in active learning. (Brenner, 1999, p. 1)

This was presented to the faculty and approved as the operational definition of scholarship.

In its final report, the task force recommended an organized, institution-wide follow-up to this portion of their work. The members suggested another task force, with different members, that would help the campus operationalize the definition by clarifying faculty roles and responsibilities, workload, institutional support (time and money), professional development training, recognition, and rewards. As an alternative to this option, the task force recommended that the Faculty Affairs Committee assume these responsibilities. However, other university priorities delayed this follow-up—with predictable results.

According to interviews conducted in 2002–2003, few faculty members remember that the Task Force on Defining Scholarship ever existed. Very few remember that the task force proposed a definition of scholarship based on the ideas of Ernest Boyer, and that the faculty approved it as the operational definition of scholarship. Had all of the task force's efforts, like so many similar initiatives in academia, been in vain? This campus study sponsored by the American Association for Higher Education (AAHE) provided some surprising, hopeful, and positive findings about the emerging culture of scholarship at Madonna University in the years following the work of the task force.

THE CAMPUS STUDY

The campus study findings are based on extensive interviews with 51 full-time faculty members and administrators. The goal was to understand faculty views about the emerging culture of scholarship, four years after the work of the task force and the subsequent adoption of the new definition. The study analyzes faculty responses to several questions: What do faculty members mean by "scholarship"? How important is faculty scholarship to Madonna University? How important is scholarship to the faculty's individual professional lives? What obstacles to conducting scholarship exist at the university? How might the university encourage and support scholarship? How were faculty affected by the definition of scholarship that emerged from the 1998–1999 scholarship task force? What kinds of scholarship would the faculty be interested in pursuing in the near future?

Faculty responses to these questions provide Madonna University and similar institutions with insight into the dynamics surrounding scholarship within their academic communities. They also provide ideas from faculty about how to maximize an expanded definition of scholarship in relation to mission and resources.

The interviews were qualitative, investigative, and Socratic. All of the interviews were conducted one on one and focused on a set of fundamental questions. Faculty responses to the questions did not vary greatly *early* in each interview—comments about scholarship assumed a definition related to traditional, highly specialized, disciplinary research. The respondents changed their attitudes about scholarship markedly after they were reminded of the work of the task force and the expanded definitions of scholarship that had been approved by the faculty. Although the responses varied greatly by college, department, and individual, they shared several themes.

Soon after the study commenced and news about the interview process became more widely known at the university, many faculty asked to be interviewed. Several had strong opinions about scholarship and wanted their views represented in the study. Almost every respondent concluded the interview by expressing a heightened awareness of the opportunities for different kinds of scholarship at Madonna University and an increased determination to participate in the culture of scholarship. Thus, in addition to its original goals, the interview process informed faculty about institutional policies related to multiple forms of scholarship and motivated them to take advantage of the increased opportunities for meaningful research offered through them.

FINDINGS

UNIVERSITY EXPECTATIONS OF SCHOLARSHIP

At the beginning of the interview, participants were asked for their views about the relative priority given to scholarship by the university and, specifically, by administrators and supervisors. An overwhelming consensus emerged. Faculty acknowledged the clear priority of several other responsibilities—including teaching, advising, curriculum development, committee work, and professional development—over any form of scholarship. They said that scholarship was valued in words by the administration, and they acknowledged that it was supported by summer stipends and sabbaticals. However, most respondents said other responsibilities expended the university's human and fiscal resources and their own time and energy, and scholarship was neither demanded nor expected. They perceived that the university was reluctant to have faculty spend time on activities that might detract from higher priorities, and that little time and money could be allocated to support faculty scholarship at the institutional level. Faculty members said they appreciated the recognition (for example, public announcements and congratulations) that the university provided to those faculty members who were able to eke out different forms of scholarship under difficult conditions. They also appreciated that the lack of scholarship would not affect their performance reviews and applications for promotion, particularly if they contributed positively to the university's priorities.

All of the deans interviewed claimed to react very positively to the scholarly efforts of the faculty, and two said that they demanded evidence of scholarship in faculty reviews. However, the faculty from these two colleges said these same deans were very understanding of their workloads as related to other university priorities, and would not penalize them for lack of scholarly activity. The College of Nursing and Health was the only area in which both the dean and the faculty agreed that scholarship was a serious criterion in the faculty review process and might affect the professional assessment of the faculty member. Faculty participants were impressed by the scholarly accomplishments of some of their colleagues, as much for the difficult context in which they were achieved as for the quality of the work. Participants noted that while some students respected faculty for their scholarly activity, most were unaware of such activities and did not consider scholarship in rating the faculty.

The Priority of Scholarship to Faculty Members

Many faculty believed the university did not prioritize scholarship, but almost all of them said that conducting scholarship was important to their personal and professional lives. Respondents were interested in all roles related to the profession, and their self-image as university professors, their graduate training, and their professional relationships to larger disciplinary communities had inculcated in them the importance of being scholars. Many reported wanting to contribute to a larger community of learning by producing scholarship. They said that external colleagues expected scholarly accomplishments from them as peers, and they believed that such achievements would increase the prestige of the university and their departments. Scholarly activity would demonstrate—to themselves and to others—their continued professional growth.

The interviewees, without exception, strongly supported the university priorities of teaching, advising, curriculum development, and service, but a large majority clearly wanted space in their professional lives for the voluntary accomplishment of scholarship. Not all were confident that they would successfully make use of such opportunities if provided by the university, but they were clear that such space should be given to faculty members, particularly those strongly motivated toward scholarship. Respondents did not favor a publication requirement for retention and promotion but welcomed release time, financial support, and university recognition for scholarship.

The responses outlined so far suggest a tension between faculty interest in producing scholarship and a perceived lack of university support, based on allocation of scarce resources and rewards. This tension is the opposite of the tension found in large research universities, where many faculty members question the unbending demand for scholarly publication, often accompanied by a diminution of their teaching and advising roles.

OBSTACLES TO THE ACCOMPLISHMENT OF SCHOLARSHIP

When faculty participants were asked to identify obstacles to the accomplishment of their own scholarship and that of their colleagues, they responded, not surprisingly, that there was little time or money allocated to scholarship. It is clear that scarce resources are dedicated to the areas of teaching, advising, curriculum development, retention, and recruitment. From the faculty point of view, there is little encouragement to engage in scholarly endeavors and virtually no tangible reward for the successful accomplishment of quality scholarship. The respondents said that neither the university nor the Faculty Professional Development Committee made a sufficient effort to motivate or support faculty to conduct scholarship. Several respondents said that their supervisors were concerned that individual scholarly efforts, based on intrinsic motivation, might distract faculty members from the higher priorities of the university, college, and department. These faculty members said that they felt they needed to defend their scholarly efforts by demonstrating excellence in the higher priorities of teaching and advising.

Even so, since the general perception was that much more needed to be done in the areas of highest priority, how could faculty members justify time and effort on disciplinary research and publication? Lack of time for scholarship as an allocated part of the faculty workload was reported to be the greatest obstacle to scholarly accomplishment. Respondents did not view the workload issue simply as a matter of values. They also connected the issue to financial resources, as some faculty would need to be remunerated for assuming responsibilities of those given release time for scholarship.

ENCOURAGING AND SUPPORTING SCHOLARSHIP

When asked how the university might encourage and support more scholarship, faculty respondents said they could not offer solutions. The scarcity of human and fiscal resources, the priority of other roles, and the attitude that scholarship would distract faculty from higher university priorities seemed to militate against finding ways to encourage and support more scholarship. Only a few interviewees felt that faculty should simply be held responsible for scholarship in addition to their other responsibilities in order to achieve positive faculty reviews for retention and promotion. Several others argued that such demands, without support, would be unfair, unsuccessful, and likely to create stress, negativity, and a drop in morale without a commensurate increase in quality scholarship. The VPAA who had asked the faculty to reconsider the definition and place of scholarship four years earlier stated that he would not favor increased scholarship demands on faculty. Several faculty members specifically opposed rigid requirements in the area of published research for retention and promotion. Based on the assumption that "scholarship" meant highly specialized disciplinary research, the interviewees saw little possibility of finding ways to encourage and support more of it.

REDEFINING SCHOLARSHIP

At this point in the interview, the author asked faculty members a pivotal question: What do you mean by scholarship? Almost all respondents initially defined scholarship in terms of traditional research; that is, the discovery of new knowledge in a discipline, based upon the discipline's content boundaries, epistemology, and methodology. The author then asked respondents if they recalled the 1998–1999 task force on scholarship, the group that had proposed an alternative understanding of scholarship based on Boyer's framework. The author also reminded them that the faculty had unanimously approved the group's expanded definition. Very few of the interviewees were aware of the task force or the faculty approval of the new definition of scholarship. They were informed that the new definition was being used in faculty reviews for retention and promotion. The VPAA had also begun to recognize a broader set of scholarly activities reported to him by the faculty. These activities did not necessarily meet the narrow criteria of traditional disciplinary research, but they did meet the criteria of quality scholarship outlined in Boyer's framework.

At this point in the interview, several faculty members asked questions about the new definition and what it meant for their work. There was a noticeable increase in interest about scholarship among almost all of the participants during the ensuing discussion of the four components of Boyer's schema. This also prompted many faculty members to return to earlier questions, in order to explore them in terms of the expanded definition of scholarship.

However, several interviewees were reluctant to equate the value of the scholarships of discovery, integration, application, and teaching. While they were willing to recognize broad scholarly accomplishments, they gave more weight to the scholarship of discovery, which for them most closely conformed to the traditional view of scholarship as specialized disciplinary research. They were convinced that university peers would respect such research more deeply and that such research was the best evidence of accomplishment by faculty members, departments, and universities. One dean clearly prized the scholarship of discovery, accepted for publication by leading professional journals and publishers. She said that scholarship related to integration, application, and teaching would be welcome in faculty portfolios, but stressed that the scholarship of discovery was the type most respected by accrediting bodies, professional organizations, and peers—and thus was most likely to enhance the professional reputation and recognition of her college. This dean's review of faculty members included high expectations for publication in the most prestigious journals related to her college's disciplines. Other deans also reported valuing the scholarship of discovery, but they placed less explicit demands on faculty for publication in journal articles and books. They also reported being more accepting of the scholarships of integration, application, and teaching on par with the scholarship of discovery.

Considering the new definition of scholarship, several faculty members said they felt that the university would place greater value on scholarship if it related more directly to existing priorities within the university's mission. Respondents said that the scholarships of application, integration, and teaching would more likely reinforce teaching and service, rather than distract from them, and thus university support for these activities seemed more likely.

At this point in many of the discussions, the interviewees became more specific with regard to the role of scholarship in their own professional careers at Madonna University. Their earlier, generalized "wish" to do more research became increasingly more concrete as they considered possible opportunities for scholarship under the new definition. Individually, several interviewees valued scholarship that related more directly to teaching and to the development of programs, particularly through service to the community. They worked at Madonna University because of their commitment to teaching and service, and believed that their professional lives would be enhanced in identifiable ways by their participation in the scholarships of application, integration, and teaching. One indicated that she had begun her professional career with the credentials provided by her graduate studies in her discipline, but that other career accomplishments and professional growth had gone unrecognized. She believed that validation of the scholarships of teaching and application would allow recognition of her professional development and broad contributions to the university. More than one-half of the interviewees described projects that they had not previously considered to be scholarship under the traditional definition. They expressed firm intentions to produce more scholarship under the expanded definition.

For these reasons, almost all of the interviewees believed that philosophical, institutional, and structural obstacles to scholarship would be reduced with the new definition of scholarship, and that opportunities for scholarship related directly to their highest professional interests and concerns would increase. They then began to brainstorm ways in which the university might support these new forms of scholarship.

SUPPORTING SCHOLARSHIP, REVISITED

The new definition of scholarship reinvigorated the discussion about ways that Madonna University might support and encourage increased scholarship within the limits of scarce resources and consistent with the priorities of teaching and service. During the interviews, several faculty members mentioned the advantages of "teaming," specifically with leaders of important support offices at the university. Faculty respondents expressed interest in working with individuals in service-learning, international studies, disability resources, multicultural affairs, instructional technology, and the library to explore scholarship opportunities in the areas of application, integration, and teaching. To expand the community of scholars in this way is significant, because representatives of these support areas are not usually included in academic scholarship. In the interviews, the administrators who were the leaders of these offices expressed great interest in participating in such scholarship, although they worried about time and resource constraints. However, faculty members in the academic and professional areas were convinced that meaningful, cutting-edge scholarship related to teaching, integration, and application would result from collaborations with these offices.

Since the interviews, the director of service-learning has formed a university-wide working group of faculty members interested in scholarship related to service-learning. All four forms of scholarship represented in the new definition will be included in this collective enterprise. In the past, faculty who participated in service-learning often completed the experience and moved on without reflection and without writing methodologically sound accounts of what they learned and accomplished. Now, under the director's leadership, participating faculty are intent upon exploring these experiences as examples of the scholarship of application, and publishing their findings for the benefit of future faculty participants. The new definition of scholarship will help Madonna University become a "learning organization" that reflects upon its experiences and produces sound scholarship for use in future projects.

Some senior faculty members expressed concern that they had not accomplished scholarship of any kind for many years. They proposed teaming across disciplinary and departmental lines in order to work with faculty members with more experience in scholarly activities. This may facilitate more scholarship of integration as well as other forms of scholarship. The senior faculty members argued that this strategy would provide them with expertise, encouragement, and insight into the process, and would increase the number of experienced faculty returning to long-neglected participation in scholarship.

Following an interview, the chair of the Faculty Professional Development Committee asked that the new definition of scholarship be presented to the committee for response. This presentation resulted in a decision by the committee to include support for scholarship in future agendas and activities. The committee also explicitly added scholarship objectives to the plans for Madonna University's new Faculty Professional Development Center. Since the campus study, the committee has committed itself to supporting the scholarships of discovery, integration, application, and teaching and to finding ways to substitute approved research projects for teaching load requirements. This affirmation is likely to result in additional resources and moral support for new forms of scholarship.

Interviewees also connected the scholarship of integration to the recent development of collaborative studies in the curriculum. The university is intent upon making collaborative studies an integral part of first-year student programs. In collaborative studies, a group of students are enrolled in a block of courses where enrollment is limited to that group. The faculty members leading these courses also work together to help the students integrate their studies. It is hoped that such collaboration will foster a community of learning and help students and faculty integrate the general education curriculum. Faculty participants in collaborative studies expressed an interest in studying the dynamics and effectiveness of this curricular innovation, thereby incorporating the scholarships of integration and teaching into their professional goals and responsibilities.

Several faculty members mentioned that they would value assistance from the director of research for the university, who also serves as the dean of graduate studies. Many faculty members respect the director for the quality of her own research and for her ability to provide effective support to researchers. In her interview, the director expressed a willingness to help and a concern that her present responsibilities might prevent her from doing as much as she would like. Participants hoped that the university would increase resources to her office so that her guidance would be available as a resource to them.

As stated earlier, many faculty respondents ended their interviews optimistic about expanded opportunities for scholarship. It became clear that a "soft revolution" was in progress. Faculty intentions to increase scholarship did not depend upon threats or intimidation related to reviews for retention and promotion, nor did they depend on a substantive increase in time or money. These hopes were not predicated on major changes in the priorities of teaching and service in the university's mission. The new definition, if the positive attitudes developed over the course of the interviews are given credence, validates forms of scholarship that are close to faculty hearts and minds and that can directly contribute to the achievement of the faculty's daily responsibilities and professional goals. Four years after the task force on scholarship had accomplished its limited task of redefining scholarship for the university community, its work was beginning to make a difference.

CONCLUSIONS AND IMPLICATIONS

For professional and practical reasons, medium-sized independent liberal arts universities are likely to place the excellent delivery of quality teaching at the center of their missions—a priority strongly supported by the Madonna University faculty. The faculty members interviewed for this study agreed that the human and fiscal resources of the university should support the teaching mission above other goals, including scholarship.

In response to an academic leader's challenge, the task force on scholarship proposed a new definition of scholarship, based upon the Boyer model of multiple forms of scholarship. This definition legitimized changing scholarly practices among the faculty but did not immediately stimulate a marked increase in either traditional or new forms of scholarship. The interviews revealed that many faculty members would like to accomplish more scholarship, particularly within the expanded framework provided by the new definition of scholarship. The Boyer model of multiple forms of scholarship is recognized as *supporting* university and faculty priorities rather than diverging from them. It allows for scholarship related to teaching and service that is consistent with the university's mission, in addition to the development of disciplinary knowledge.

Faculty members explored several ways that the university could support scholarship, consistent with the weight given to teaching and with due attention to scarce resources of time and money. In addition to expanding the *definition* of scholarship, the interviewees agreed that the *community of scholarship* should become more inclusive. Teaming with leaders of support offices can bring opportunities, expertise, and resources to scholarship efforts. Many faculty members observed that these offices offered opportunities for cutting-edge work in the scholarships of application and teaching related to their disciplines.

The opportunity to study the culture of scholarship at Madonna University became more than a process of static description. The interviews often resulted in dialogues in which fundamental assumptions and attitudes about scholarship were challenged and reconsidered. The process of the study became an occasion for critical discussions about the Boyer framework for scholarship and a force for assessment and change regarding the place of scholarship. Faculty leaders collaborating with service-learning and other student support offices are exploring ways to participate in multiple forms of scholarship. Many of these efforts were made possible by the work of the 1999 task force on scholarship and were stimulated by the interviews from the 2002–2003 campus study. What began in 1998 as a simple challenge to faculty to reconsider the definition of scholarship has resulted in the likelihood of substantive changes in the practice and place of scholarship.

References

Boyer, E. L. (1990). *Scholarship reconsidered: Priorities of the professoriate.* Princeton, NJ: Carnegie Foundation for the Advancement of Teaching.

Brenner, P. (1999). *Year end report from the task force on defining scholarship.* Unpublished report. Madonna University, Livonia, MI.

Madonna University. (2002). *Undergraduate bulletin 2002–2004.* Livonia, MI: Author.

CHAPTER SIX

ENCOURAGING MULTIPLE FORMS OF SCHOLARLY EXCELLENCE AT ALBANY STATE UNIVERSITY

Barbara DeVeaux Holmes

This chapter describes a historically black college and university (HBCU) that faces the challenge and crisis of enhancing faculty scholarship during a time of declining enrollment and increasing retention and persistence issues. Albany State University has a faculty body with an excellent teacher record and strong commitment to students but little documented scholarship as traditionally defined. In 2000, the University System of Georgia (USG) notified Albany State that it would lose funding for developmental studies in 2002. This loss would seriously hurt enrollment, decrease student retention and persistence, and leave many students without critical academic support. Given the faculty's proven commitment to serving the university's at-risk student population, and the extra work needed to recruit and retain students, it would seem impossible to raise faculty standards for scholarship under such circumstances.

Yet this is what university leaders accomplished. They redefined scholarship to include teaching effectiveness, the scholarship of discovery and application, and the integration of knowledge gained by faculty to enhance student achievement and skills. They developed programs to boost faculty skills and involve faculty members in scholarship that addresses institutional priorities and fun-

damental student learning needs in the areas of preparation, retention, and persistence. This chapter includes examples of these
programs, describes the uphill battle of supporting faculty scholarship with minimal support services, and presents lessons learned
as a result of expanding a traditional definition of scholarship.

INSTITUTIONAL HISTORY AND CONTEXT

Albany State University, located in southwest Georgia, is a comprehensive, coeducational HBCU that offers undergraduate and graduate curricula that build on a strong liberal arts foundation. A
regional institution of higher learning, Albany State is one of 34
units in the Georgia system, with a range of offerings including the
liberal arts, sciences, education, and some preprofessional programs. Albany State provides innovative instructional and professional programs through its four academic colleges (Arts and
Sciences, Business, Education, and Health Professions) and through
its graduate school. Combined, these schools offer nearly 50 graduate and undergraduate degrees.

Albany State is the primary higher education provider in southwest Georgia, a rural and economically depressed area. Through
its teaching, research, creative expression, and service, the university seeks to promote the growth and development of southwest
Georgia, the state, and the nation. Albany State proudly serves its
historical role of improving the quality of life of African American
students while also serving the needs of an increasingly underprepared, diverse, and at-risk student population. The university's
2002 fall semester enrollment was 3,525 students, of whom 92 percent were African Americans and the majority were first-generation
college students.

RETENTION AND PERSISTENCE:
ALBANY STATE'S SPECIAL MISSION

Helping students persist in higher education has been an institutional priority since the university was founded: its special mission
is to serve underprepared, first-generation college students who
are at risk for not persisting in higher education owing to a myriad

of socioeconomic factors. Albany State has a strong commitment to support students who generally cannot pursue other avenues of higher education.

Because Albany State students tend to be underprepared from their secondary school experience, they typically gain conditional admission to the university. As of 2000, the USG Board of Regents required first-year students to have a combined Scholastic Aptitude Test (SAT) score of 830. In 1999, the average SAT score for first-year students at Albany State was 707. Students are seriously deficient in reading and mathematics preparation, resulting in a significant number enrolling in developmental studies and other learning support programs in order to attain full admission status. Such academic deficiencies prevent many students from persisting through the first year, as the rigors of college life exceed their expectations and preparation.

In fall 2002, the USG Board of Regents eliminated funding for developmental studies in all 16 constituent institutions; this seemed likely to cause a catastrophic drop in enrollment for Albany State University. The university is still trying to grapple with this challenge and what it will mean for its historic mission of access, retention, and persistence for students. A priority for the university is to find ways to serve those who need developmental studies and retain them in the university's learning community.

FACULTY ROLES AND REWARDS: A LOOK BACK

Albany State's teaching faculty consists of 184 highly qualified, diverse individuals, more than 70 percent of whom hold doctoral degrees; the instructor-to-student ratio is 1 to 19. In the recent past, a typical faculty workload might have included four class preparations each semester, an advisee load of 50 or more students, assignment to two or more college committees, and involvement in community service. Faculty were encouraged to write grants to seek external funding for departmental and college initiatives. Funding of a grant proposal usually entitled a faculty member to receive release time equal to one or two courses. The heavy workload kept most faculty members from engaging in research or other scholarly pursuits, however, or pursuing publishing opportunities.

In 1996, the USG Board of Regents gave Albany State status as a university, a change bringing a concomitant expectation that faculty would embrace more traditional forms of scholarship and publish more frequently. The change in expectations was not accompanied by a change in teaching or advising loads and was a challenge for many faculty, whose expertise through the years had been in working with undergraduates and preservice teachers and preparing them for the world of practice. A review by the National Council for the Accreditation of Teacher Education (NCATE) Board of Examiners Accreditation Team in 1998 commented extensively on the faculty's scholarship in its report to the institution (NCATE, 1998). After noting that the change to university status had been accompanied by an emphasis on faculty research as integral to the processes of evaluation, promotion, and tenure, the examiners cited "a lack of recent research and recent publication by faculty members." Most of the faculty's research-related activities consisted of professional presentations at state and national conferences, with a few members "actively involved" in writing grants and publishing in refereed scholarly journals and monographs and collections of essays. The NCATE report noted that the majority of faculty involved in teaching courses in advanced programs have not been involved in scholarly activities other than conference presentations since the last NCATE visit in 1992.

The report offered an objective perspective on the status of scholarship and helped focus faculty and administrative attention on this vital area. The transition from college to university status was essentially not being reflected in the work and actions at the heart of the university—its faculty. Given that Albany State was founded as a normal school to prepare teachers, the clash between historical mission and current expectations indicated by university status was perhaps inevitable. Thus, the institution faced trying to increase and improve faculty scholarly activity while increasing faculty involvement with students because of board-mandated cuts in developmental programs and higher entrance requirements.

The Magnitude of the Problem

Meyer (1998) introduced the term "mission confusion" (p. 4) to describe the precarious position in which faculty are placed regarding their teaching, research, service, and other responsibilities.

Mission confusion occurs when faculty are placed in a tenure, promotion, and reward system that values research over teaching, even though this emphasis may compromise student learning opportunities and experiences. Meyer cites statistics by Astin that demonstrate a negative correlation between faculty research orientation and factors such as student orientation, hours per week spent teaching and advising, and commitment to student development. Faculty members at Albany State find it difficult to ascertain what the institution values more: work with students or research and scholarship. Meyer urged institutions to address mission confusion by defining the skills and knowledge graduates should possess upon graduation, clarifying curricula and mission, using technology, understanding the market, realigning rewards for teaching and research, focusing on student learning, and restructuring (Meyer, 1998, p. 4).

Broad questions surrounding faculty productivity are not new, and they tend to be similar across institutions. At the same time, there are specific concerns regarding scholarship for faculty who are diverse in terms of race, gender, and institutional location. According to Elizabeth Creamer (1998), the amount of scholarly publishing is commonly used as a measure of prestige for a department or institution and "is strongly associated with an individual faculty member's reputation, visibility, and advancement in the academic reward structure, particularly at research institutions" (p. 1). One view of why women and minority groups have not moved quickly up the academic reward ladder focuses on their lower rate of scholarly publication, which may also explain why they are promoted "at slower and lower rates than majority, male academics; and why they are concentrated in less prestigious institutions." Academic administrators who understand the interrelationships among publishing, gender, and race, and how they are "insinuated in traditional criteria" can better define methods of "shaping institutional reward structures in ways that advance the careers of a heterogeneous faculty" (Creamer, 1998, p. 1).

Because Albany State is an HBCU, it is critical that minority faculty voices be a part of the larger discussion about issues that affect learning in the disciplines. Significant teaching loads mean that faculty members at state universities and HBCUs must work harder to find time for scholarship. Albany State is still struggling to delineate faculty responsibilities in a manner more balanced across teaching, scholarship, and service.

CRISIS AND OPPORTUNITY

Several internal and external factors during the past eight years have impelled Albany State to reexamine and redefine scholarship and to strategize about nurturing multiple forms of scholarly talent. Internal factors included shrinking enrollments, the elimination of developmental studies programs, low pass rates on exit examinations, and the shift from college to university status. External factors included both the USG Board of Regents and the local community calling for greater university accountability and increased student achievement. While the board focused on higher admissions standards, the community decried the quality of Albany State graduates. As mentioned earlier, the board eliminated funding for developmental studies—programs used by 60 percent of students.

At the same time, local newspapers reported that teacher education graduates were failing state teacher examinations and nursing students were failing state board examinations. Students were admitted who did not meet minimum SAT scores for admission, and faculty were promoted and tenured with little, if any, documented scholarship of the traditional sort. The call for accountability from the board and pressure from the community forced the university to explore the question: What does our status or mission as a "university" mean given these factors and these conditions?

To help build a case for change, Albany State's Office of Institutional Research analyzed data from the university's First-Time Freshman Profile. The analysis revealed three programmatic themes that influenced student persistence problems. Freshman students were not persisting because (1) they were not academically prepared to handle college-level classes, (2) their personal expectations did not match college reality, and (3) they entered college with significant deficiencies in mathematics and reading. Armed with this information, a new president would forge a path to reshape scholarship and increase scholarly activity, while staying true to the university's historic mission.

A NEW PRESIDENT RESHAPES SCHOLARSHIP

A critical event was the appointment in 1996 of a new president, Portia Shields, whose experience was grounded in research institutions. The president faced a serious dilemma of how to enable faculty to strengthen their teaching and service to help achieve student success and at the same time raise the standards for scholarship. Both areas were crucial to the vitality of the institution and its success in serving students.

The new president communicated a clear and compelling expectation that faculty scholarship would be at the center of the university's work, calling upon faculty to contribute to the knowledge base in ways that aligned with the university's mission, including conducting action research to address the many challenges facing the university. "No one is knocking down the door to serve the students that [Albany State] serves," she reminded the faculty (Shields, 2000). Indeed, it took a special kind of commitment and dedicated service to work with an at-risk student population. Faculty needed to invest time and effort to determine student learning styles, study habits, and skill deficits; understand the impact of socioeconomic conditions; and become experts in the preparation of African American students.

At this point, the president encouraged faculty to "study what you know"—to engage in action research on student needs and to use the findings to improve instruction and, ultimately, student achievement. It was imperative, she argued, that HBCUs embrace the task, because few other institutions were interested in serving this population. She also requested that faculty document the process of how HBCUs work with underprepared African American students and assist them in becoming high achievers. This story of student transformation, she believed, should be told.

In 1999, the president appointed a committee to review the evaluation and reward system for faculty. Part of this process involved a campus study of faculty perceptions of scholarship, and the committee also reviewed the faculty evaluation system, including the four performance criteria: teaching effectiveness, research and scholarship, service, and professional development.

Following the change to university status in 1996, campus leaders believed the faculty would want to reduce an emphasis on teaching and increase an emphasis on research and scholarship. Just the opposite happened. Prior to 1996, teaching effectiveness was 40 percent of a faculty evaluation and research and scholarship 20 percent. In 2000, the faculty recommended that teaching effectiveness be 50 percent of the evaluation and research and scholarship 15 percent. The administrators and deans were surprised by the decreased emphasis on research and scholarship being suggested by the faculty, at a time when university status would suggest increased activity in these areas.

Senior-level administrators knew, by 2001, that they needed to encourage extended discussion around these issues. They wanted faculty to discuss their reluctance to place more emphasis on scholarly activity. The committee charged with reviewing evaluation and rewards interviewed faculty and discovered that one major reason for their reluctance involved faculty members who felt ill prepared for, and uncomfortable with, traditional research and writing. A second reason was that many older faculty members were uncomfortable using technology, inside and outside of the classroom. Albany State's president realized the university needed a new definition of scholarship, as well as strategies to help faculty members engage in different forms of scholarship.

After exploring these issues with faculty, Albany State decided to use Ernest Boyer's (1990) framework to broaden definitions of scholarship for the institution and encourage faculty involvement in all forms of scholarly activity. Since 2001, faculty have recognized the wide range of options available to them. Albany State has experienced significant improvement in the levels of scholarly activity of all kinds.

A Multifaceted Response Agenda

The university has sponsored several initiatives to help reach the goal of becoming a more scholarly institution. One of the first was to add a workshop on faculty scholarship to the Annual Faculty Fall Conference, which all faculty are required to attend. A visible symbol of the centrality of faculty scholarship in the work of the university, the workshop provides an opportunity for faculty members to openly discuss impediments to scholarship and feel assured that they are heard by the administration. It also provides a forum for faculty across disciplines to share information and identify common concerns regarding scholarly production.

Another strategic response involved the creation of a Center for Excellence in Teaching and Learning (CETL) in 2000. One of the center's major functions is to implement a professional development program that will assist faculty in gaining the skills needed to engage in the scholarship of teaching and learning. Several faculty members have used the center to initiate a research agenda. A husband-and-wife team in the sciences developed WebCT workshops for faculty and then studied how faculty used this technology in creating Web-supported courses. Other faculty members have created workshops focused on portfolio development and preparation for post-tenure review. Faculty members have also received assistance in identifying grant opportunities and preparing grant proposals. The center provides staff and clerical resources to support faculty in these initiatives.

Using data from a technology survey, the center implemented a professional development series offering faculty training in essential technology skills. The scholarship associated with this effort had university-wide impact, given that faculty from all disciplines participated and ultimately integrated technology into instruction.

As an institution founded as a teacher-training school, Albany State promotes the continual refinement of teaching and pedagogy. The university encourages the faculty to examine their own pedagogical practices as a way to initiate scholarly activity. Faculty in the College of Education, for example, are encouraged to write a reflective essay on their teaching effectiveness and submit this essay as a part of the annual evaluation process. In the college's meetings and seminars, faculty members are encouraged to share their reflections so that the group can work collaboratively to improve teaching. Following is a characteristic excerpt of a reflection on teaching from a senior faculty member in education:

> As a person who reflects often on my life and my duties, reflection on my teaching effectiveness is a constant for me. At the end of every class, I go back over the high points and low points of the session. Did the candidates ask questions? Did I see any yawns or sleepy eyes? Were most of the candidates not only on task but also eager to participate in learning? When I grade tests or papers, es-

pecially in the latter part of the semester, I spend time analyzing what the candidate missed and I try to decide if I did a poor job of teaching the material or of designing a test that accurately measures what the candidate knows and has learned.

Faculty members who participate in this form of scholarly reflection and analysis are viewed positively by their colleagues and favorably on the "teaching effectiveness" criterion of the annual evaluation. The annual reflections are included in portfolios that faculty develop for the promotion, tenure, and post-tenure review process, to demonstrate the record of analyzing pedagogical effectiveness over time.

Faculty members across the university are encouraged to conduct action research in their classes. Based on the definition of action research by Johnson (1995), faculty in the mathematics department embraced the notion of "learning from one's own work or behavior by critically examining it" (p. 92). For example, the department recognized that there was a very high failure rate in college algebra, at times 75 percent. Instructors developed a survey examining variables that might affect student performance, such as age, gender, major, mathematics taken in high school, years since last mathematics class, study habits, knowledge of graphic calculators, and knowledge of geometry. The survey revealed that the average age of college algebra students at Albany State was 27, and that it had been four years or more since they had last taken a mathematics class. Knowledge gained from the survey enabled the department to begin changing the way college algebra is taught.

Faculty are also encouraged to work with students outside of the classroom. The university's strategic plan emphasizes work-based learning paradigms, where faculty partner with local industries so that students apply new skills and knowledge in work settings. Faculty who develop these innovative instructional partnerships are recognized at the annual fall conference and provided with tangible rewards, including stipends up to $1,000, release time equivalent to one course, upgraded computer support, and laptop computers.

The university has also prioritized students' entrance into, and persistence in, academic programs. It encourages faculty to develop innovative models and strategies that assure support for first-year students entering into majors, greater persistence into sophomore year, and better preparation for success at that level. Several faculty members have also produced manuals to help students prepare for and pass Praxis and other exit examinations. These manuals are well received by students and are used extensively to support classroom instruction.

Another institutional priority is the integration of technology into instruction. Campus leaders have noted that increased technology skills help faculty to engage in scholarly activity. Faculty members who complete 50 hours of technology training in the state-approved InTech Program receive certification and recognition in their evaluation. This training is recognized at the state level as proof of technology proficiency and may be used to support "Clear and Renewable" teaching certifications. Similarly, faculty who incorporate at least four technology-connected lessons into their instruction earn merit consideration at evaluation time.

Encouraging the Scholarship of Discovery

The performance of Albany State students on exit examinations commanded faculty attention in fall 2001. The USG Board of Regents presented statistics on test scores for Georgia students on the Praxis I test, which measures basic proficiencies in reading, writing, and mathematics. Georgia institutions of higher education that prepare teachers are required to have 80 percent of test-takers pass the test.

Albany State faculty were shocked to see the wide gaps in achievement between black and white students, particularly given the large percentage of Albany State students who are African American. All Albany State students are required to take regents tests of basic proficiency in reading, mathematics, and writing after completing 45 credit hours at the university. Education students are required to take and pass the Praxis I examination to satisfy the criteria for admission to the teacher education program. Because overall pass rates on these examinations were less than acceptable in many cases, the university encouraged the faculty to look "behind the tests" to see if they could determine root causes of poor performance.

As a result of this serious institutional problem, several faculty members began disaggregating the data and reviewing the areas of deficiency. This analysis led one faculty member to develop a manual for the Praxis examination in early childhood education—a scholarly effort well received by students and faculty and very helpful in preparing students to take the test.

Another initiative that grew out of this discovery was the development and implementation of a supplemental instruction program. Led by faculty, this program applies the new knowledge about student performance to help increase student achievement. Through supplemental instruction, faculty members are encouraged to reteach difficult content to students and assess the effectiveness of working in an extended learning format. They receive stipends for this work. The university now offers instructor-led supplemental instruction sessions in college algebra, biology, zoology, computer science, and writing composition.

The involvement of faculty members from the College of Arts and Sciences and the College of Education in supplemental instruction has led to new research interests and the development of a paper, "Supplemental Instruction: A Multi-Faceted Model for Student Persistence" (Okonkwo & Holmes, 2003). This paper has been widely disseminated and is now housed on the NCATE Web site. Research focused on student success and persistence and on evaluating programs aimed at improving these areas has increased at Albany State, strengthening institutional effectiveness.

Getting faculty members to devote time to their own professional development establishes a strong foundation upon which to build scholarly pursuits. An adage says, "How you spend your time determines what you value." Campus leaders believe that faculty members need to spend considerably more time thinking about their own skills gaps and discovering creative ways to address them through scholarly activities.

ENCOURAGING THE SCHOLARSHIP OF APPLICATION AND INTEGRATION

Faculty members are encouraged to keep current in their disciplines and to present papers at conferences about how they are applying new knowledge, skills, and technology in their academic work. Professional development and graduate initiative funds help them improve their programs and explore ways to link scholarly talents to community concerns.

Related to the scholarship of integration, stronger connections between the College of Education and College of Arts and Sciences have been encouraged so that there is shared responsibility for the preparation of preservice teachers and school leaders. The faculty is encouraged to develop paired courses and share instructional responsibility for learning outcomes. Faculty members who participate in these collaborative efforts are supported to travel to conferences on innovative instructional practices and are recognized during the annual faculty development conference.

Recently, faculty members in the College of Arts and Sciences and the College of Education developed a course entitled "Mastery Learning" that focuses on helping students analyze and understand individual learning styles and learn course content. This course is team taught by faculty members from both colleges who are focusing their scholarship on how students learn. They were encouraged and supported to work together by a university that is working hard to create the conditions that facilitate the scholarship of integration.

Faculty Rewards

Faculty at HBCUs know intuitively that their work may be harder and more intense than at many other colleges and universities. Their work lives involve significant teaching loads, large numbers of advisees, intense advising sessions, direct participation in registration, many course preparations, and frequent and extended outside-of-class contact with students. As formidable as these challenges are, faculty at HBCUs willingly undertake them as expressions of their personal and professional commitment to make a difference in the lives of students who would otherwise remain underserved and uneducated. These activities form the basis of the "normal" faculty workload at an HBCU.

As noted earlier, Albany State recently revised its institutional reward system, policies, and procedures to better recognize faculty action research, applied knowledge projects, and cross-discipline collaboration. Campus leaders hope that these efforts will further stimulate scholarship. Faculty members have already welcomed other changes regarding scholarship. For example, every semester, each college is required to submit a Faculty Accomplishments Report to the vice president for academic affairs. This report details the actions of the faculty in advancing scholarship within the university and the community. The president developed a special bimonthly newsletter, *ShortTakes—A Publication For and About Albany State University Employees,* and the university created *Albany State University Research Review;* both publications recognize and publicize faculty research and scholarship. The Graduate School provides funding of $35,000 annually to each college to support graduate faculty scholarship, and developed a new publication, *Academia,* which highlights research efforts. The university has created new recognition categories for Researcher of the Year and Teacher of the Year. Criteria for these awards include documentation of the answers to the president's question: What have we come to know and how are we applying that knowledge? Faculty members who show evidence of scholarly efforts to help retain students are recognized for these activities. The university has also developed two annual conferences (on technology and on leadership) at which faculty and students present their scholarship on how technology affects learning. University-wide recognition is at the heart of the changes that have been made to focus attention on scholarship and its high value.

THE CAMPUS STUDY: RESEARCH QUESTION AND METHODS

In order to better understand the three-year impact of campuswide initiatives designed to encourage multiple forms of scholarship, Albany State initiated a campus study in 2001. A central question of the study was, "Do faculty feel that they have the support that they need to engage in any or all forms of scholarship?" During 2001–2002, I interviewed 20 faculty members about the culture and climate surrounding scholarship as part of faculty life.

Most faculty members interviewed agreed that in order to increase faculty scholarship, several aspects of the university's academic culture would need to be improved. They identified several factors that impact—and sometimes impede—scholarly activity.

IMPEDIMENTS TO SCHOLARLY ACTIVITY

Insufficient Time to Conduct Research

Foremost among faculty concerns is lack of time. With an average teaching load of 12 hours per semester, faculty members claimed to lack time for serious research. In addition to teaching responsibilities, they listed other responsibilities: student advising; registration; departmental, college, and university committee work; participation in graduation; attendance at Honors Day and other university events; and community involvement. Interviewees perceived a disconnect between the university's expressed expectations regarding faculty scholarship and the inadequate allocation of resources dedicated to this effort, including time.

Lack of Secretarial Support

With the distribution of computers to individual faculty members, the university expected that faculty would do their own typing and word processing. Typically, the college dean and the department chair each have a secretary, but rarely is there a secretary assigned for faculty members, who view secretarial resources as essential to their work. Across the university, faculty members consider the lack of secretarial support to be a major barrier in conducting research.

Insufficient Support in Researching, Preparing, and Transmitting Grants

Faculty members generally are unfamiliar with the many sources of grant monies that would help support scholarship. Interviewees indicated they would like more assistance with identifying grant opportunities and help in writing them. Because the grant support office at the university consists of just two staff people, it cannot provide one-on-one assistance in grant preparation in any significant way. Many faculty are unaware of the institutional process of transmitting grants out of the institution. Consequently, they do not build enough time into the process for the grant to be reviewed by internal offices. Faculty members find the transmittal process time consuming, energy draining, and frustrating, and believe that a secretary would best handle the process.

Inadequate Computer Equipment and Training

While all faculty have computers in their offices, they are frustrated by a lack of institution-wide computer support. The university has no systematic plan for upgrading faculty equipment, leaving many with outmoded machines. Computer training is offered regularly through the Center for Excellence in Teaching and Learning and the Educational Technology Training Center, but teaching schedules often conflict with course offerings, and faculty members report that they do not have time to take the classes. This leaves faculty unskilled in many software applications that are used to catalog and analyze data. Very few faculty members feel that they have the skills to handle data analysis tasks associated with research endeavors.

Inadequate Library Materials

Interviewees described the library holdings in their respective fields as less than adequate, and they disliked interlibrary loan because of the inordinate amount of time it takes for materials to be retrieved. They must then rely on the Internet to support their research efforts, yet this poses a problem for a great many faculty who do not yet have the technological skills to use the Web.

Low Faculty Morale Caused by Inability to Get Promoted

Faculty who fail in obtaining promotion or tenure because of insufficient scholarship perceive that they have been treated unfairly. They believe that an institutional bias against teaching thwarts their professional growth, given that teaching is not rewarded to any significant degree in promotion and tenure decisions. For a faculty member who is an excellent teacher, advisor, and committee member, the chances of getting promoted or tenured on this record alone are remote. In spite of very explicit institutional messages about the value of multiple forms of scholarship, some faculty continue to apply for promotion without a strong scholarship record in discovery, pedagogy, integration, or application. This creates a problem not only for the individual faculty member but also for the institution as a whole.

The Shifting Paradigm

Survey results indicate that many faculty members still equate scholarship with research, and have yet to internalize the expanded definitions of scholarly activity as put forth in Boyer's (1990) framework. This is likely to be reinforced by promotion and tenure committees, which often see the path to full professor as including significant research. The lack of time was a concern expressed repeatedly by faculty, whether regarding class loads, service, or scholarship, and it continues to impede the fulfillment of faculty responsibilities. Faculty who had served on promotion and tenure committees noted that the required forms used to evaluate applicants do not address any form of scholarship other than research. The university will have to revise these rating forms to reflect the breadth of activity that now constitutes scholarship.

Faculty who embraced scholarly activity as part of their participation in the academic community said that the university provides the conditions for their continued success; they felt rewarded and respected as scholars of note in this learning community, and in many instances had three or four years to go before they engaged the promotion and tenure systems. The university is encouraging these active scholars to support and nurture their colleagues so that the community can engage in mutual learning and continue to grow professionally.

Administrators are aware of the changes that need to be made and have encouraged broad discussions about how to achieve the richness that being a university entails. Albany State University celebrated its 100th birthday in 2003. As a part of the yearlong celebration, the university invited campus and community leaders to share their thoughts about what must be done in the next 100 years to position the university as a premier provider of education in Georgia and beyond.

Implications

Supporting faculty through the redefinition of scholarship is a national issue in higher education. Meyer (1998) noted:

> One way to create a more heterogeneous faculty is to recognize a broad range of scholarly activities as making a contribution to the

production and communication of knowledge. Diversifying the faculty in the United States requires diversifying the criteria used to judge their work performance. Traditional measures of impact or utility of publications, such as citations, must be expanded to recognize that academics are just one of many communities that are impacted by the production of new knowledge. New, convenient methods are needed to assess the impact of a variety of forms of scholarly communication, such as through unpublished works, conference presentations, speeches, and the ever-expanding electronic venues of communication. (p. 6)

Albany State's president has noted that working at one HBCU is just like working at another. Most HBCUs are challenged by (1) limited resources, (2) the expectation that one should always do more with less, (3) students who are often at risk and underprepared, (4) faculty who are committed but unhappy with working conditions, (5) a lack of money, and (6) a lack of scholarly activity. We have developed "Five Habits for Managing HBCU Scholarship Endeavors," to share with other institutions attempting to increase scholarship productivity. These habits are as follows:

1. *Communicate the scholarship vision.* Having an institutional vision and an individual vision of scholarship are core values of the university. At Albany State, the president, vice president for academic affairs, deans, and all academic leaders communicate the scholarship vision at the annual fall conference and in departmental faculty meetings.

2. *The scholarship messages must be clear, consistent, and frequent.* Marketing experts know that product messages must be clear, consistent, and repeated frequently. Albany State has adopted this strategy. The university communicates a clear expectation that all faculty members must be involved in scholarship. This message is included in print materials, annual reports, and presidential addresses; it is also communicated during an individual's annual goal-setting process, and in some colleges faculty must post two office hours per week devoted to scholarly endeavors.

3. *Find and fund the risk takers.* Faculty members who publish and write funded grants are provided with release time, new equipment, laptops, monetary stipends, and other incentives that enable

them to continue to be successful. They are supported to attend conferences and seminars to share their work with others.

4. *Reward productive behavior.* A well-known behavior modification technique is to reward desired behavior so that it is repeated. Faculty who engage in scholarly activities are institutional heroes; they receive preferential consideration during evaluation and merit processes.

5. *Recognize and celebrate the trailblazers.* Recognition is a valuable motivator. The university has created the Researcher of the Year award and presents it annually at the fall faculty conference. Recently, the president created an additional Presidential Award for Faculty Excellence, designed to publicly recognize those who achieve excellence over the four performance criteria areas: teaching excellence, research and scholarship, service, and professional development.

Campus leaders have just begun the very complex work of identifying and recognizing expanded definitions of scholarship. They are making progress. Their actions are beginning to yield positive results, as faculty members in various colleges work together on projects and in ways not envisioned 10 years ago. The faculty's understanding of scholarship has expanded beyond the boundary of writing a book or an article. The university and faculty value and reward action research conducted on the issues facing the campus. The university's leaders see new forms of scholarship and significant collaboration, yet they remain concerned that faculty productivity overall has not increased more significantly. Continued progress will require everyone to stay focused on scholarship as an institutional priority, and to find new ways to reward and celebrate excellence in this area. The university remains committed to this end.

References

Boyer, E. L. (1990). *Scholarship reconsidered: Priorities of the professoriate.* Princeton, NJ: Carnegie Foundation for the Advancement of Teaching.

Creamer, E. G. (1998). *Assessing faculty publication productivity: Issues of equity* (Report No. 26). Washington, DC: George Washington University, Graduate School of Education and Human Development. (ERIC Document Reproduction Service No. ED420242)

Johnson, B. (1995). Why conduct action research? *Teaching and Change, 3*(2): 90–104.

Meyer, K. A. (1998). *Faculty workload studies: Perspectives, needs, and future directions*. ASHE-ERIC Higher Education Report Vol. 26, No. 1. Washington, DC: George Washington University, Graduate School of Education and Human Development.

National Council for the Accreditation of Teacher Education [NCATE]. (1998). Board of Examiners Accreditation Team, National Council for the Accreditation of Teacher Education. Unpublished report.

Okonkwo, Z., & Holmes, B. (2003). Supplemental instruction for enhancement of student success. *International Journal of Educational Studies, 2*(1): 13–26.

Shields, P. (2000, August). Faculty fall convocation speech. Unpublished speech. Albany State University, Albany, GA.

CHAPTER SEVEN

FACULTY SCHOLARSHIP IN A NONTRADITIONAL UNIVERSITY

The University of Phoenix

Catherine Garner, William Pepicello, and Craig Swenson

Recently, U.S. higher education has undergone a paradigm shift from an emphasis on teaching to an emphasis on learning, focusing on the student rather than the teacher or the classroom (Barr & Tagg, 1995; Tagg, 2003). In January 1997, Palomar College sponsored a national conference, The Learning Paradigm, to discuss this change in philosophical outlook and to stimulate further discussion. The dialogue has included all aspects of traditional higher education, including teaching strategies, faculty roles, and scholarship.

This campus study addresses how the role of scholarship is evolving on one campus as a result of the paradigm shift from teaching to learning. More specifically, the study examines the place and value of scholarship within nontraditional, adult higher education, using Ernest Boyer's (1990) framework, through which the work of faculty is both recognized and valued within the mission of the institution.

DRIVERS OF CHANGE

One of the factors driving the shift from teaching to learning is the changing demographics of students. As the average age of students attending college rises and the proportion of working adult students increases, many basic assumptions about serving students have changed. Studies conducted under the auspices of the College Board (Aslanian, 2001; Aslanian & Brickell, 1980; Brickell, 1995), for example, indicate that older students seek out curricula that are not only content-rich but also directly applicable to the workplace.

Part of this larger shift involves a shift in the role of faculty in the teaching-learning process. In a traditional "instruction paradigm," as described by Barr and Tagg (1995), faculty members serve as content experts and encourage teacher-to-student (vertical) interactions. In contrast, in a "learning paradigm," faculty members partner with students in a collaborative, team-based environment. Faculty members remain content experts, but they also serve as learning facilitators, encouraging peer (horizontal) as well as teacher-to-student (vertical) interactions and the application of the discipline to the workplace.

As the faculty role of researcher-lecturer evolved to include practitioner, colleges and universities recognized the value of including working professionals in faculty ranks. With academic qualifications that underwrite mastery of content, working professionals comprise a portion of adjunct and part-time faculty on many campuses. At the University of Phoenix, the recognition of this constituency has produced a model wherein practitioner and full-time academic faculty collaborate to meet the needs of working adults.

Notably, this model has existed for 25 years at the University of Phoenix. The university serves primarily nontraditional students through various modes of delivery, including online courses and courses that combine online and classroom learning experiences. In this model, faculty members are no longer primarily creators and purveyors of information. Rather, they are facilitators, accountable for "managing" student learning and for the relevance and applicability of the curriculum (Boyatzis, Cowen, & Kolb, 1994).

An Evolutionary Model

The University of Phoenix has evolved in response to the needs of its adult learners and the paradigm shift from teaching to learning. This evolution is reflected in its current mission statement, where the university strives "to educate working adults to develop the knowledge and skills that will enable them to achieve their professional goals, improve the productivity of their organizations, and provide leadership and service to their communities" (www.uofphx.info).

In addition, the university's infrastructure has changed to embody a student-centered approach to academics and student service. To be convenient for full-time professionals, the university offers courses in the evening that meet weekly for five or six weeks. It is also typical for students to enroll in only one course per semester. Instructors are practitioner faculty who work in their fields of expertise. Faculty members facilitate learning rather than lecture, enabling students to be active partners in the process. Achievement is measured through outcomes assessment rather than recorded seat time, and students are assessed for content knowledge and for additional competencies such as written and oral communication, group skills, and critical thinking. Students work in learning teams outside of class and are assessed on both group and individual work. Academic content is directly related to the workplace and personal lives of students, and students are expected to add value to courses as well as to take away useful information.

As embodied in the mission statement and pedagogical mode, the University of Phoenix's learning paradigm dictates a new definition of faculty and, in turn, a reexamination of faculty roles and responsibilities. Paramount in the model and in the life of the university is the role of scholarship. This campus study of the University of Phoenix highlights the salient issues related to faculty roles and scholarship in the context of a learning-centered educational paradigm.

The Emerging Role of Faculty

The University of Phoenix employs more than 250 core full-time faculty members and more than 17,000 professional "practitioner-scholars," with the full-time faculty overseeing the curriculum, quality assurance, and training. While the use of part-time faculty is a matter of convenience or economic necessity at many institutions, at the University of Phoenix it is a conscious choice to help achieve the mission of providing education responsive to the needs of working adult students.

Practitioner-scholars are recruited from many occupations and sectors outside the university. They include experienced managers and other professionals from major corporations, government agencies, and educational institutions, as well as scholars and researchers in private practice. Their experiences in the field often result in the generation of new knowledge and theoretical models that traditional researchers can then begin to study.

Pracademics

Practitioner-scholars undergo a rigorous selection, training, and mentoring process, and they participate in regular, ongoing staff development. The University of Phoenix practitioner-scholar model redefines and extends the role of the adjunct faculty beyond that customarily found in higher education. Rather than merely serving as surrogate instructors, practitioner-scholars more closely approximate full-time faculty. They are involved in curriculum, governance, and professional development activities; they serve, for example, as area chairs and members of academic councils at the campus level, members of academic program councils at the college level, and representatives on the university's academic cabinet. This commitment to involving practitioner-scholars in the central work of the university results in a high degree of faculty loyalty and retention.

The university has been successful in implementing this practitioner-scholar model primarily due to its ability to "unbundle" the traditional functions of the faculty. The roles and responsibilities of full-time faculty at most institutions include research, curriculum development, course preparation, instruction, student advisement, and service to the community. At the University of Phoenix, the same responsibilities exist. However, they are not necessarily expected to reside with one person: roles are realigned through disaggregation and specialization.

For example, academic program councils consisting of deans, full-time faculty, and practitioner-scholars assume responsibility for the content and coherence of specific academic programs. Under their direction, smaller teams of faculty experts, aided by instructional designers and curriculum development project managers, create curriculum outlines for each course within a program. These outlines provide a structure for practitioner-scholars who might not have the time or expertise for preparing courses. Consisting of course objectives, activities, and assignments, the outlines are enhanced by individual instructors who bring additional resources and professional experience into the course.

Academic counselors, specifically trained for each program, handle the advising through classes averaging 14 students. These counselors provide students with significant exposure to faculty members practicing in fields in which students work. Students thus have access to a variety of content experts in their courses but maintain a single point of contact for the administrative aspects of their program.

All faculty members have the option to participate in academic governance, and practitioner-scholars who serve as representatives are compensated separately for this involvement. Since most practitioner-scholars do not have administrative duties, they can focus on activities that relate more directly to student learning. The university maintains instructional quality through the aforementioned curriculum outlines, faculty assessment and development processes, and regular and periodic peer and administrative reviews.

This "pracademician" faculty model has served the university well. The unbundling of faculty roles has allowed for rapid expansion into new geographic and program areas. Faculty recruitment has never been an impediment to the growth of new programs or geographic areas. With the exception of periodic increases in pay, the basic structure of roles and rewards for faculty has not changed substantially.

This model has not always met with favor in the traditional academic community, in part because many individuals lack a deep understanding of the model. The university has weathered several ostensibly hostile reviews by state and accreditation agencies, only to have reviewers finish the process with positive recommendations. An almost constant need to prove the model is successful has had a positive result, however, in that there is extensive evidence regarding the process and the outcomes of student learning.

As part of several reviews, university leaders aggregated curriculum vitae of faculty from various programs, but they had no systematic, ongoing database for this information. The university developed a faculty database for two reasons: (1) to increase the internal efficiency of processing and updating faculty files, and (2) to capture faculty academic activity in a systematic fashion to use in regulatory and accreditation reviews and for broadcast to internal and external stakeholders.

THE CAMPUS STUDY

In spring 2002, the university began the process of automating faculty files. Faculty members were asked to update their vitae in a revised electronic format. This automated system allowed the investigators for this study to aggregate and analyze the faculty's academic and professional activities and also provided examples of the scholarship of discovery. The initial report indicated that the faculty produced significant ongoing scholarship, in all the dimensions described by Boyer. Research questions that guided the campus study and analysis of this data included

1. What is the depth of the faculty's scholarly activity?
2. How can the institution best communicate this activity to a variety of stakeholders, including accrediting bodies?
3. How should the university support the various forms of scholarship produced by practitioner-scholars?

To explore these questions, the researchers analyzed 5,622 profiles belonging to 32 percent of the 17,544 active practitioner-scholars who had completed the automated vitae by the time the study was conducted. The scholarly contributions of these faculty members reflect the diversity of an institution of higher learning, with heavy emphasis in the areas represented by the six colleges: business, health sciences and nursing, information systems and technology, behavioral and social sciences, education, and general studies.

FINDINGS: DOCUMENTATION OF FACULTY SCHOLARSHIP
THE SCHOLARSHIP OF DISCOVERY

Although discovery-based research is not the primary mission of the university, most faculty actively engage in this activity, both as principal investigators and as senior team members. The study found that, since 1992, faculty members participated in more than 415 funded research initiatives as principal or co-principal investigators. These initiatives represent more than $150 million in research funding, predominately in the areas of engineering, technology and biotechnology, education, and health care. Numerous national foundations and government agencies, including the State Department, National Institutes of Health, and Department of Defense, provided funding.

With regard to publications, the faculty authored or coauthored more than 400 academic texts, and 450 faculty members received academic recognition, including awards, from groups outside the university. Faculty members also authored 248 original software programs, with the primary source of funding coming from private companies and with the content ranging from educational software to advanced technology applications in health care, telecommunications, and microprocessing industries. This work in software development boosted the number of patents filed by individual faculty to more than 90.

The study also found a strong record of publishing within the arts, though the university would not claim to have a liberal arts focus. Faculty members published 47 original works of poetry, five plays, three musicals, two motion picture screenplays, and several television documentaries. With shows at major galleries, faculty members contributed to the arts through painting, sculpture, and photography. Four produced significant musical compositions that received critical acclaim.

THE SCHOLARSHIP OF TEACHING AND LEARNING

By far, faculty members were most prolific in writing about learning models and education. They reported more than 900 research publications about teaching and learning, more than 700 works related to course development (for audiences outside the university), and more than 40 postdoctoral fellowships. One hundred ninety-one research studies centered on education or teaching and learning outcomes in both traditional and nontraditional academic settings. Faculty members conducted 11 major research studies on the university distance-learning model alone, adding to a core of knowledge in this area for the university and, increasingly, for other institutions moving into distance education and Web-based learning options.

THE SCHOLARSHIP OF INTEGRATION

Faculty members actively worked at disseminating new knowledge and presenting new data, models, and theories in 1,943 presentations since 1998. These presentations represented diverse interests and occurred in a range of professional organizations. Faculty members with expertise in areas such as international business, information technology, and health care presented papers in Brazil, Canada, China, Germany, Honduras, Japan, Korea, Russia, the United Kingdom, and 20 other countries.

In addition to presenting in academic forums, faculty members were primary authors of 743 journal articles and contributing authors of an additional 366. They also authored 127 book chapters for academic texts focusing on all aspects of learning. The vast array of topics provided the impetus for the deans and the doctoral programs steering committee to assemble faculty within a "virtual community of scholars," described following.

Although most institutions expect the faculty to serve on professional and editorial boards, the University of Phoenix does not have this expectation. It was therefore notable that faculty members served as editorial board members of 53 professional journals and reviewers for an additional 98, representing major publications in business, education, health sciences and nursing, information technology, counseling, and criminal justice. This was affirmation that the university's practitioner-scholars are recognized as scholars within their fields, despite not having full-time academic credentials.

As would be expected of professionals who maintain high-profile positions in industry, faculty members testified 112 times before various state legislative committees and commissions since 1998. In addition, they testified before 61 federal panels and congressional committees, including the Federal Trade Commission, the Federal Energy Regulatory Agency, the U.S. Postal Commission, and the Office of Management and Budget. Topics ranged from economic policy and business regulation to health service delivery and issues in education. Recognized by influential policymakers, these practitioner-scholars bring expertise to the teaching of adults in baccalaureate and master's programs.

THE SCHOLARSHIP OF ENGAGEMENT

The emerging profile of a University of Phoenix practitioner-scholar is that of a business leader involved in the teaching of others and engaged in the pursuit of new knowledge. This scholar also actively uses professional expertise to partner with communities and solve problems of public interest. More than 91 percent of interviewees reported involvement in at least one, and very often two or more, of the following areas: appointments to community boards, committees, and associations; voluntary service on community boards and associations; service to professional associations; professional letters to the editor; community presentations; and service awards. Clearly, academic expertise combined with practical experience is being used to benefit not only students but also the community at large. The breadth of involvement was surprising to many campus leaders, even those who have been very involved with the faculty. The challenge to administrators at this point is to maximize the benefits of this involvement within the university's own academic community, for students and prospective students, as well as within the larger community.

IMPLICATIONS FOR CONSTITUENTS INSIDE AND OUTSIDE THE UNIVERSITY

This study served to validate the scholarly pursuits of the University of Phoenix faculty in a language that is becoming familiar to traditional academic communities, as well as provide an excellent communication vehicle for use with accrediting organizations. Communication of this information to accreditation agencies and regulators will continue to be important to the university as it continues expansion into other states and regional markets.

The expertise of the faculty in adult education and distance education is significant to the larger academic community, as higher education evolves into a system for lifelong learning and as increasing numbers of institutions embrace distance-learning modalities. The amount of educational research conducted with faculty has helped administrators formalize this as an area for further encouragement and enhancement. For example, the results of this study prompted an internal leadership council to begin to formalize a university-wide research agenda related to distance education. A two-day retreat resulted in a preliminary internal research plan for soliciting interest from internal and external researchers. The results of this study also assisted administrators in prioritizing requests from external researchers who approach the university for access to students and faculty.

There are plans to further analyze the faculty files, specifically the links between scholarship outside the classroom and student satisfaction, faculty peer evaluation, and other measures of learning outcomes. The present study will serve as a platform for continued study of associations between subsets of Boyer's classifications and learning outcomes. In addition, the full-time faculty will be compared to practitioner-scholars in coming years.

While one of the goals of this study was to examine the relationship between student learning outcomes and the level of faculty involvement in scholarship, this proved beyond the scope of the actual study. The challenges of constructing this research design were compounded by the vast array of faculty activities. However, the university hopes to ascertain the influence of faculty involvement in various forms of scholarship on student learning outcomes. Several internal discussions have focused on identifying the key dependent and independent variables; it appears that several smaller studies are necessary to properly address this question. Researchers must consider both the faculty profile variations and the many variables in the adult learners themselves, an effort that continues as a result of the preliminary results reported here.

RAISING THE PROFILE OF SCHOLARSHIP WITHIN THE UNIVERSITY

The authors presented this data to the full-time faculty at the annual Academic Meeting in August 2002, and the presentation generated pride and excitement about the accomplishments of the practitioner-scholars. The information also impressed the deans and the campus directors of academic affairs, who plan to use it to identify faculty for advisory committees as well as curriculum and faculty development training. This is the first time that the entire faculty database is available across the university.

The study provided further support for a new position, the director of scholarship, responsible for garnering corporate recognition of University of Phoenix scholarship. Residing in the new School for Advanced Studies, which houses the university's four doctoral programs, this office will coordinate the university's internal research agenda and develop a formal structure that supports faculty development in the areas of research and publishing.

SUPPORT FOR FACULTY SCHOLARSHIP

A pilot initiative, the university's Virtual Community of Scholars, is being formalized for rollout to all faculty. This online community is designed to foster exchange of research ideas and resources among faculty and doctoral students. Chat rooms will allow faculty to converse about interdisciplinary trends and best practices both in education and in application to industry. An expanded Web site is planned to provide a forum for presentation and dissemination of original research and new knowledge. During the pilot phase, more than 200 faculty members participated in forming eight key research initiative groups. Doctoral students are now using the community to consult with faculty and find mentors and dissertation advisors. The Institutional Review Board has used the community to identify ad hoc reviewers for specific topics. There are also preliminary plans to link the faculty database to the community so that additions to each faculty member's curriculum vitae can be posted for university-wide recognition.

A committee will develop the community's resource section beyond current links to alerts for grants and funding, information on publication review, and resources on editing. University leaders see this forum as an international network that provides internal resources and also identifies research needs in the workplace that can be addressed through scholarly discourse and study.

THE ROLE OF FULL-TIME FACULTY

The university remains committed to the practitioner-scholar model for the reasons cited, but committee members have focused on whether this model, which has served students well at the baccalaureate and master's level, is suitable for doctoral-level students. University leaders understand that an increase in the number of doctoral programs will require developing a culture within the new School of Advanced Studies that focuses more on discovery-based scholarship. In recognition of this, administrators are creating faculty structures within the school that place more emphasis on original research. The school's core full-time faculty members, who will serve as primary mentors for doctoral students regarding research and advisement, will be individuals who have demonstrated proficiency in traditional research. At the same time, practitioner-scholars with training at the doctoral level will still teach courses and serve on doctoral committees. This will help maintain the university's emphasis on the practical application of knowledge to students' professional lives. The addition of "scholar-practitioners" to the "practitioner-scholars" who are the bulk of the faculty will allow the university to broaden its scholarly mission but retain its applied, professional focus.

Lessons to Share

The university learned several lessons through this study that are worth sharing with others. First, it is helpful for campus leaders to examine faculty contributions to all areas of scholarship that relate to the institution's mission. In the case of the University of Phoenix, the primary mission is teaching. Formalizing Boyer's criteria allowed the authors to generate a rich description of the faculty, including its expertise, academic pursuits, accomplishments, and commitment to the community. Administrators received a detailed picture of the faculty and a way to validate whether its values and experiences matched the goals the university had for its graduates.

Second, this study helped the institution target areas of strengths and weaknesses. This is significant when prioritizing resources for faculty scholarship and identifying areas of expertise that need to be encouraged. For example, as campus leaders discovered the extent to which faculty members were experts in and researchers of distance learning, they recognized the leadership role the campus could take in this area and worked to harness faculty capabilities to do so.

The university must still find ways to link faculty scholarly activity and talents to student outcomes. It remains to be seen whether breadth and depth of scholarship, as defined by Boyer, will be a good predictor of student learning. While the intuitive response is yes, only extensive, well-controlled studies will provide definitive answers.

The University of Phoenix is working to address the correct mix of faculty scholarships for doctoral programs. This is particularly important because students have chosen doctoral programs at the University of Phoenix to enhance their contributions to the workplace rather than to pursue the role of full-time academic researcher. As stated previously, this will require different support structures for the faculty in these programs. Administrators and faculty have held a series of work groups to address these issues, in an ongoing process that affords another opportunity for campus study.

SUMMARY

The experience of the University of Phoenix suggests that making the shift from teaching to learning requires new ways of viewing faculty roles. The model of scholarship outlined by Boyer is consonant with the needs of adult learners. Scholarship must be viewed globally, rather than as one component of the traditional triad of teaching, research, and service. Further, an institution's approach to scholarship should be driven by, and congruent with, its mission and purposes. Scholarship at the University of Phoenix permeates all areas of the institution and shapes internal and external enterprises. Given the mission and history of the university, the Boyer model works well in framing the scholarly endeavors at the institution.

The challenge now is to recognize, codify, and provide active support for this broad array of activities, to inculcate scholarship even more throughout the university and nurture it as a vital force in the daily work of the faculty.

References
Aslanian, C. B. (2001). *Adult students today*. New York: College Board.
Aslanian, C., & Brickell, H. (1980). *Americans in transition: Life changes as reasons for adult learning*. New York: College Entrance Examination Board.

Barr, R., & Tagg, J. (1995). From teaching to learning: A new paradigm for undergraduate education. *Change, 27*(6): 13–25.

Boyatzis, R., Cowen, S., & Kolb, D. (1994). *Innovation in professional education: Steps on a journey from teaching to learning: The story of change and invention at the Weatherhead School of Business.* San Francisco: Jossey-Bass.

Boyer, E. L. (1990). *Scholarship reconsidered: Priorities of the professoriate.* Princeton, NJ: Carnegie Foundation for the Advancement of Teaching.

Brickell, H. (1995). *Adults in the classroom.* New York: College Entrance Examination Board.

Tagg, J. (2003). *The learning paradigm college.* Bolton, MA: Anker.

CHAPTER EIGHT

ENSURING EQUITY ACROSS THE MISSIONS OF A LAND-GRANT UNIVERSITY

South Dakota State University

Carol J. Peterson and Diane Kayongo-Male

South Dakota State University (SDSU) was established in 1881 under the Morrill Land Grant Act. Originally known as South Dakota State College, the institution received university status in 1964. Today, this comprehensive university delivers its teaching, research, and service missions through the colleges of Agriculture and Biological Science, Arts and Science, Education and Counseling, Engineering, Family and Consumer Sciences, Nursing, Pharmacy, and General Studies and Outreach Programs, and the Graduate School.

The history of SDSU faculty roles and rewards, as related to scholarship, has been strongly influenced by the institution's governance system. SDSU is governed by the South Dakota Board of Regents (BOR), within a highly unified higher education system that includes five other public universities. South Dakota State is the largest and most complex institution in the system, and it currently serves approximately 10,000 undergraduate and graduate students. All basic personnel policies are established and negotiated between the BOR and the Council on Higher Education (COHE), which has represented the system faculty in collective bargaining since the late 1970s.

The collective bargaining agreement addresses general standards and processes for awarding rank, promotion, and tenure. Since 1992, the agreement has included a general appendix that speaks to faculty roles and expected activities within those roles. Within this context, SDSU has long had teaching as its priority. However, many campus constituents hold traditional expectations for scholarship as research. This is due primarily to the university's traditional role in agriculture and biological sciences research through the Agriculture Experiment Station. As early as 1987, the vice president for academic affairs became concerned about the imposition of standards from the physical and biological sciences on other disciplines during the promotion and tenure process, and by 1990 she had established the Task Force on Faculty Standards.

In June 1992, the BOR awarded the Office of Academic Affairs at SDSU a grant to develop a model "Integrated Faculty Role Description and Evaluation System." This model was an effort to incorporate Ernest Boyer's (1990) framework on scholarship into a statement of faculty expectations based on the BOR-COHE agreement—before alternative views of scholarship were imposed from outside SDSU. In addition, this generic system was to be a model for all departments within SDSU to develop their own standards documents. The faculty standards task force worked to develop the generic model in the form of a university standards document.

A study done in 2001–2002 evaluated this decade-long process and its impact. This chapter explores the history of SDSU's efforts to ensure equity across its missions, analyzes the outcomes of these efforts, and discusses implications of these efforts for institutions considering similar changes in faculty roles and rewards.

History: Developing the Model and Departmental Documents

Key Factors Precipitating Change

Several factors prompted the development of a university standards document that would incorporate Boyer's concepts of scholarship. First, there was an internal leadership change in 1987, when the university appointed the current vice president for academic affairs. One of her responsibilities was to chair the university's promotion and tenure committee. Through this role, she became aware of the very narrow view of scholarship used to make promotion and tenure decisions. Despite SDSU's primary teaching mission and diversity of disciplines, the promotion and tenure committee looked primarily at accomplishments in traditional research. The vice president for academic affairs began to use the term "scholarship" also to mean work outside of traditional research. As more literature became available on the topic, she shared this new view of scholarship with the promotion and tenure committee and campus leaders.

Second, in the early 1990s, the BOR applied external pressure in the form of an appendix to the collective bargaining agreement, entitled "Statement Concerning Faculty Activities" (South Dakota Board of Regents and Council on Higher Education, 1992). This appendix included representative activities under teaching, scholarship and creativity, and service at a system level. The BOR indicated that each university in the system should select those activities consistent with its mission that could be used to evaluate faculty performance and make promotion and tenure decisions. Each university was charged, in 1992, with developing its own statement of expectations to implement this appendix document.

Because of SDSU's leadership role in the public system of higher education, the vice president for academic affairs was invited to submit a proposal to the BOR for financial assistance in developing a standards document. The BOR awarded SDSU's Office of Academic Affairs $18,000 to conduct the project, which essentially provided for the creation of the first edition of the university standards paper. The project "Development of an Integrated Faculty Role Description and Evaluation System" began in June 1992. Its purpose was to develop, pilot, and evaluate integrated position descriptions with associated role expectations, and create an evaluation system demonstrating how the BOR statement would be used in the process. The processes, materials, and findings would be available at the system level for demonstration purposes. The conceptual model proposed at the time is described following.

The assumptions underlying the model were (1) faculty positions include assignments in teaching, scholarship, and/or service; (2) relative emphasis on the three roles depends on institutional missions and specific assignments; (3) excellence in teaching, scholarship, and service can be described at the institutional level; (4) expectations can be defined in terms of quality and quantity; and (5) position descriptions and role expectations can be linked to annual evaluations, evaluation for promotion and tenure, and discretionary salary decisions.

Although the initial point of this project was to meet a BOR mandate, it evolved into a comprehensive project that used the Boyer model to develop a university-wide standards paper. Describing different forms of scholarship became an integral part of this effort. These two factors, occurring during the same time period, prompted campus leaders to convene a standards task force charged with developing a university standards document.

THE STANDARDS TASK FORCE

A task force consisting of two faculty members (one representing the Academic Senate), three deans (Arts and Sciences, Agricultural and Biological Sciences, and Pharmacy), and two department heads developed the first university standards document. Task force members received a copy of *Scholarship Reconsidered: Priorities of the Professoriate*. Another key resource was Elman and Marx Smock, *Professional Service and Faculty Rewards* (1985). These readings became the foundation upon which the members built their discussion on scholarship and, subsequently, two versions of the university standards document.

One of the unique qualities of SDSU is its tremendously complex faculty role structure—there are many variations in percentages for research, teaching, and outreach in faculty appointments. One of the foundational principles of the development of the SDSU approach to rewards and standards was the assumption that diverse faculty role combinations had to be treated equitably in the formulation of the university standards document.

PURPOSE OF THE GENERIC DOCUMENT

The task force solicited ideas from heads of departments and engaged in reading and discussion of critical works on scholarship. It then prepared the first generic university standards document, "Achieving Excellence in Faculty Roles," which was distributed to department and unit heads, who were asked to work with their faculty to develop departmental standards (South Dakota State University, 1995). These departmental standards were expected to reflect the best disciplinary standards while generally adhering to the generic university document. The assumption was that these departmental documents would be used in promotion and tenure decisions, merit pay decisions, post-tenure review, and annual faculty evaluations. Once the department standards documents were submitted to the Office of the Vice President for Academic Affairs, the task force reviewed them to determine the extent to which departments had developed a document that met expectations.

The second version of the standards document, "Achieving Excellence in Faculty Roles," was developed during 2000–2002 (South Dakota State University, 2002). The vice president for academic affairs again headed the task force, which also included one faculty member, two deans, one department head, and one associate dean.

The first two sections of the revised standards documents discuss the tripartite mission of SDSU: teaching, research, and service. This mission has been redefined more specifically in the past few years, in terms of what are called "lead forward land-grant goals" (that students become socially responsible, globally informed, flexible, and skilled in communication). The third and fourth sections define scholarship and discuss the relevance of this definition to the various faculty role combinations. The fifth section, the largest and most detailed part of the document, covers standards of performance for the areas of teaching and advising, research and creative activity, professional outreach, and general service. The last section explains how the standards relate to BOR policy, the BOR-COHE agreement, annual evaluations, rank, and promotion and tenure.

MEANING OF SCHOLARSHIP

Boyer's four forms of scholarship have served as the foundation for both editions of the faculty standards document. Diagrams used to illustrate the various types of faculty role combinations were modified so as to more clearly indicate that scholarship is expected as part of one or more role assignments.

Although the university used this external framework, there are two areas—advising and public scholarship—that may distinguish the institution from others of similar type. South Dakota State places a much heavier emphasis on the quality of advising, in terms of strategic planning and the heavy advising load of most faculty members, than land-grant universities of comparable size. Public scholarship at SDSU, very similar in meaning to the term "engaged research," refers specifically to scholarship that addresses the expressed needs of local communities and directly results in an improved quality of life for those communities. Public scholarship is one way land-grant universities can "return to their roots," rather than merely serving large corporate interests.

COMMUNICATION, FEEDBACK, AND MODIFICATIONS

The development of both versions of the standards document involved frequent meetings among task force members, interviews with deans and other administrators, and open forums for faculty members and others to voice opinions or ask questions. The document was also made available online to facilitate feedback before completion.

The most difficult part of the process was reaching agreement on terminology for performance. One concern of the task force members and heads of departments was the lack of agreement among the terms used in three key documents: the university standards document, the BOR-COHE collective bargaining agreement, and the annual evaluation form. South Dakota State had control over the first document, but the remaining two were defined by the university system. While the new terms fit somewhat better with the annual evaluation form, problems remain, such as linking the standards document to the language of the BOR-COHE agreement and the assessment of performance relative to merit pay.

Departments had until October 2001 to update their standards document based on the revised university standards document (South Dakota Board of Regents and Council on Higher Education, 2000). Department documents were a product of discussions among faculty members and with the department head. Once the department agreed on the statement or document, the departmental standards statement was sent to the task force for critique and feedback. The task force then gave each department a composite critique (evaluation) sheet with a deadline for submission of the final departmental document to the vice president for academic affairs. The task force asked each department to revise its document based on the composite rating and task force comments and suggestions.

THE CAMPUS STUDY

In spring 2001, the vice president for academic affairs applied to the American Association for Higher Education (AAHE) for a grant to study the impact of SDSU's university and departmental standards documents on faculty roles and rewards. The basic question underlying the 2001–2002 campus study was, "Did SDSU's faculty reward system change as a result of the university-wide effort to develop standards documents?" The authors were as interested in the usefulness of the process as in the outcomes derived from using the documents, and further wondered whether

1. Faculty believed that the process for defining departmental standards had invited their participation,
2. The process improved faculty understanding of Boyer's view about multiple forms of scholarship,
3. The documents were actually being used by promotion and tenure committees or by candidates,
4. Administrators (deans, department heads) and faculty members could identify additional barriers to broadening the definition of scholarship in policy and practice, and
5. Benefits had accrued to faculty, departments, and the university from the process of creating institutional and departmental standards documents.

The data the authors collected for the study consisted of 10 years of documentary evidence on the development of the standards documents, the reports of two individuals who had been part of the process since 1990, and responses from focus groups and surveys of deans, department heads, and faculty completed during the 2001–2002 academic year. The documentary evidence included memos from the vice president to deans and other administrators, minutes from the standards task force meetings, the two drafts of the university standards document, two versions of 40 departmental standards documents, and summary evaluations of the most recent departmental documents. In addition, the authors designed and administered three questionnaires in April 2002. Questionnaires for deans and department heads were completed during university management meetings, while the faculty completed their survey online. All nine college deans, 38 out of 42 department heads, and 81 out of 450 faculty members completed surveys.

Of the faculty respondents to the survey, 25 percent had been at SDSU for fewer than five years, 21 percent from five to nine years, and 54 percent for more than 10 years (with the longest term of 36 years). Of the colleges represented, 46 percent of the respondents were from Agriculture and Biological Sciences, 22 percent from Arts and Science, and 6–8 percent from the remaining colleges—Family and Consumer Science, Engineering, Nursing, Education and Counseling, Pharmacy, and General Studies and Outreach. Just over half of respondents had tenure, and 41 percent were full professors; 17 percent were associate professors, 33 percent were assistant professors, and 9 percent were instructors.

We conducted two focus groups with a total of nine individuals, including faculty, department heads, and a dean. The participants were members of the university promotion and tenure committee from 1996 to 2002, the years following the inclusion of departmental standards documents in the process. The groups reported on the use of departmental standards documents in promotion and tenure decision making as well as changes in the work of the committee over the seven-year period. A third focus group consisted of members of the standards task force, who reported on changes members had observed in promotion and tenure decision making during the previous decade.

Outcomes

This section is divided into five subsections corresponding to the questions framing the campus study.

Was the Process Inclusive and Effective?

More than one-half of the faculty members who completed the survey said that colleagues in their department had drafted the departmental document as a group with their department head, and another 36 percent said the document resulted from work by a department subcommittee. One-half of the faculty members reported that they were very active in developing their departmental standards document, 36 percent reported a very passive role, and 14 percent reported no role. It is probable that this fairly high participation level increased the likelihood that the faculty would "own" their departmental documents and understand and support a broader definition of scholarship.

Did Faculty Better Understand and Accept a Broader Definition of Scholarship?

The faculty survey included questions that addressed attitudes toward scholarship, particularly related to Boyer's expanded framework. While 98 percent of the surveyed faculty agreed that the more traditional "discovery of knowledge" indeed constituted scholarship, nearly as high percentages—82 and 89 percent—agreed that "transmission of knowledge" and "application of knowledge" also constituted forms of scholarship. The campus culture surrounding scholarship is clearly in line with Boyer's expanded framework, with more than 80 percent of the faculty agreeing that transmission and application of knowledge were valid forms of scholarship. However, the study also revealed that 25 percent of the respondents still did not clearly understand the fine points of Boyer's expanded view of scholarship. These faculty members continued to associate scholarship with research, and, though familiar with Boyer's framework, either did not understand it or resisted it.

With regard to the specific criteria participants believed determined scholarship, the study revealed two things. First, 80 percent of faculty members in the study were still using traditional criteria—such as being "informed by current knowledge in one's discipline," "published in peer-reviewed journals," and "evaluated by disciplinary peers"—to assess scholarship. However, 90 percent selected the criterion of "dissemination of results of scholarly activity by means other than peer-reviewed journals" as an indication of legitimate scholarship, and another 69 percent felt that the "results of scholarly activity should be evaluated by consumers of knowledge"—both indicators of change in institutional culture.

Surprisingly, 85 percent of faculty in the study said that their discipline did not have a similar process in place for redefining standards for research, teaching, and service. There are two possible interpretations of this finding. One is that specific disciplines are lagging behind the campuswide (and national) movement toward redefining scholarship. Another is that most faculty members are simply not well informed about changes in their discipline's view of scholarship.

Department heads were asked to respond to the same questions regarding faculty understanding of Boyer's expanded framework for scholarship. Of the total number in the study, 82 percent either agreed or strongly agreed that in their departments, many aspects of college teaching were defined as scholarship. Only 3 percent strongly disagreed with this broader interpretation of teaching as scholarship. Another 89 percent felt that in their departments, there was general agreement that integrating and synthesizing existing bodies of knowledge in interdisciplinary research could be considered scholarship. Another 75 percent considered public scholarship to be a legitimate form as well. Since the survey respondents answered the questions anonymously, and almost all department heads responded to the survey, it is clear that this group strongly supported an expanded view of scholarship.

However, there were problems identified as well. One department head wrote an extensive comment about misunderstandings with regard to Boyer's work:

> Faculty and administrators commonly misunderstand Boyer's work. Teaching and the activities included therein do not, in and of themselves, constitute scholarship in Boyer's view. He argues instead that publications and research *based on* teaching and related activities should be considered scholarship. If a faculty member integrates a certain body of knowledge in the discipline into a course in a novel or creative manner that serves to increase learning, then the faculty member should write about that and publish that. Furthermore, the faculty member could compare the outcomes associated with this new method with the outcomes received using

traditional methods and publish those results. Simply performing an extensive literature review to improve the class reading list is *not* scholarly work in Boyer's opinion. This is widely misinterpreted.

While this department head was referring to faculty in his department, comments by other department heads and several deans confirmed this misinterpretation was more widespread. It is difficult to generalize about the extent of the misunderstanding on campus, since there were no survey questions about this issue and many faculty and department heads did seem to understand Boyer's conceptualization of scholarship. The finding that there was some misunderstanding of Boyer's framework suggests that the campus should hold workshops on new forms of scholarship, and that departmental documents that correctly interpret Boyer's perspective should be made available to the campus community.

DO FACULTY AND PROMOTION AND TENURE COMMITTEES USE THESE DOCUMENTS?

In terms of quality, 67 percent of faculty members rated their departmental standards document as good, 26 percent as excellent, and only 7 percent as poor. When we compared the second edition of the departmental standards with the first edition, we identified areas of progress. Generally, the department papers were more distinctive relative to their own discipline and drew more indirectly from the university standards paper. In the second edition, more of the departments addressed levels of advising performance. Some of the departments independently began to develop sections on documentation to address how the various levels of performance could be observed and evaluated. Overall, the 2001–2002 versions of the department standards papers were significantly improved from the 1995 versions, and some of the most impressive elements from updated department papers were then incorporated into the university paper.

A variety of behavioral outcomes could demonstrate the extent to which the effort to recognize multiple forms of scholarship through the standards documents has succeeded. These would include faculty members (1) obtaining a copy of the standards document, (2) reading the document, (3) participating in the development or revision of the document, and (4) using the document to prepare a tenure dossier or annual performance summary. Ninety percent of the faculty in the study said that they had a copy of their departmental standards document; 61 percent said that they had downloaded their own copy of the university standards document. When asked how carefully they had read the university standards document, 35 percent reported very carefully, 51 percent in a cursory fashion, and only 15 percent not at all. Members of the university promotion and tenure committee indicated that, in the past five years, more faculty had begun to use the departmental standards document in preparing their portfolios for promotion and tenure.

We asked deans whether they thought that, with regard to evaluation, specific faculty activities counted for more or less today than 10 years ago. The most significant change identified was the recognition of other, nontraditional forms of research as scholarship. Six of the nine deans responded that teaching as scholarship was still not fully accepted at SDSU. Campus leaders could use one-day workshops to familiarize faculty and administrators even more with this topic and broader views of scholarship generally. They could also widely disseminate examples of documentation, such as portfolios, relevant to the scholarship of teaching.

Since a major impetus for developing the standards documents was a desire to make the reward system and missions more consistent, a crucial outcome would be a change in the reward system. When asked how the departmental standards document was used, 59 percent of the faculty reported that it had been used for professional staff evaluations (PSEs), 23 percent reported for merit pay decisions, and 18 percent for promotion and tenure decisions. Since most faculty members have never been on the promotion and tenure committee, their responses provide a picture of general perceptions versus a more accurate assessment of the use of the document.

Those individuals who sit on the promotion and tenure committees are the most knowledgeable about the actual use—either by the candidates for promotion or tenure or by the committee—of departmental standards documents. The promotion and tenure focus group spoke of two factors that determined the extent to which the documents were used—individual variations among faculty members and departmental climate. The group said some faculty members copied the departmental document "almost to a fault," others completely ignored the document, and still others effectively used the document in preparing for review. Faculty from particular departments had much higher quality "packets" or portfolios. This suggests that these departments had taken the idea of a broader view of scholarship more seriously, spent more time educating faculty on the use of the document, or provided a more supportive environment for faculty to "own" the departmental document.

Focus group members from the promotion and tenure committee said that departmental standards documents affected decisions about promotion and tenure in several concrete ways. The departmental standards document was most likely to be used in borderline cases, where there was some contention about the case or some discrepancy in the faculty member's application. Additionally, since the introduction of the departmental standards documents, promotion and tenure committee members reported being less likely to "rubber stamp" decisions made by other individuals or committees prior to their review of a candidate's eligibility.

If all of the materials and letters submitted by the candidate were strong, there was less use of the departmental document. On the other hand, it was more likely that the departmental document would be used to resolve the discrepancy if there were disagreements between the recommendations of the head of department and dean, or a poor résumé with strong recommendations. Focus group members from the promotion and tenure committee reported strong agreement about the standards in the departmental documents. Once the document was in place, they did not feel it was their role to judge or evaluate it. Several indicated that they were instructed to take the departmental documents at face value, but they suggested that, in the future, it would be fair to compare SDSU's department documents with comparable department documents from other universities. This comparison would be outside the activities or purview of the promotion and tenure committee. As the documents stood, they protected faculty in cases where a faculty member adhered to the standards enumerated therein, and they disadvantaged faculty whose letters of recommendation misrepresented them or whose work did not reflect excellence as elaborated upon in the appropriate departmental document.

Focus group members were asked how their decision making differed before and after the introduction of the departmental documents into the process. They noted that it was much easier to overturn decisions by department heads and deans after the standards documents were incorporated into the process, as they provided documentation clearly outlining performance standards. Previously, the standards were more ambiguous and open to interpretation.

What Barriers Impede Use of the Standards Documents?

Asked about barriers to encouraging multiple forms of scholarship, the deans identified the extremely heavy teaching load of four courses per semester as significant. Even if the *idea* of the scholarship of teaching was strongly supported, there was inadequate time for faculty members to conduct research on teaching and learning or to write articles related to teaching for peer-reviewed journals. Many deans also reported that faculty members were being urged to excel in all areas of work simultaneously, with pressure coming from a continuing focus on traditional research in some disciplines, and from heavy teaching and advising loads. In addition, many deans reported that department heads had insufficient understanding of, or training in, new forms of scholarship.

What Benefits Have Accrued From the Process or From Use of the Documents?

Almost all of the faculty in the study felt that one or more of the following benefits resulted from having a departmental standards document: (1) a clearer idea of what criteria are used for evaluating faculty, (2) a record of what the department considers to be high-quality work, and (3) a faculty discussion of standards for teaching, research, and service. Within the study, 80 percent of faculty members reported using the departmental standards document to prepare goals for their PSEs, to document fulfillment of goals, or to plan long-term career goals.

Lessons Learned, Implications, Reflections

Departments Need Flexibility and Time to Apply Standards to Disciplines

One of the key lessons learned from developing two university standards documents and 40 departmental documents over a decade is that departments need sufficient time, flexibility, and freedom to develop a standards document that closely matches their disciplinary standards. While some effort was made to ensure comparable quality of documents across departments, there was concern at the outset that departments not be forced into inappropriate molds from other disciplines. Departments need time to make sure they integrate disciplinary norms and institutional norms effectively in their final documents.

Deadlines Are Important

When campuses attempt to make a permanent significant change in their reward system, they must establish deadlines for all phases of the process. The standards task force had internal deadlines for various objectives related to the creation and revision of the standards document. Departments had reasonable deadlines for the preparation of their standards documents. There were deadlines for faculty beginning to use the departmental document as well. Setting deadlines also communicates to constituents that adherence to new standards is required rather than optional. Additionally, clarifying deadlines for goal setting in the next cycle and for use of the standards in evaluating performance ensures that faculty are not held accountable to standards that came after their goal setting in the previous cycle.

Parties Must Agree on Terminology Regarding High Performance

The most difficult part of developing the university standards document was the lack of agreement on performance terminology. We found disagreement over what terms should be used in the documents to describe the highest level of performance of faculty roles. The terms "quality" and "excellence," used in the first edition of the university standards document, were changed to "basic quality performance" and "high-level performance" in the second edition. Several department heads objected to the change in terminology, preferring the terms used in the first edition. They felt that *excellence* meant something radically different from *high-level performance.* While the new terms were a better fit with annual PSEs, this is just one evaluation measure used at SDSU. There have been problems linking the language of the university standards document to the BOR-COHE language for promotion and tenure, a second measure; and to the assessment of performance relative to merit pay, a third measure. SDSU's standards task force has incorporated tables into the university standards document to reduce ambiguity and confusion over performance levels. Campuses should ensure that the "theory" of the expanded view of scholarship be translated into "practice," by providing information to department chairs on how to use the agreed-upon criteria in decision making and to faculty on how they are being evaluated.

Equity in Department Standards Across the University Are Important

The freedom allowed each department was based on the belief that each could be trusted to be true to its national disciplinary standards. This meant risking that some departments would not put forth a good faith effort to establish criteria that were equivalent to peer institutions with comparable disciplines and comparable faculty roles.

Campuses should allow standards to evolve from the grass roots of an institution, but they should also ensure that the process discourages departments from aiming for the lowest levels of performance. There is always the possibility that allowing individual departments to determine standards of performance may lead to inequity across disciplines in terms of rewards. Indeed, some survey respondents felt that some departments set their standards so low that it gave them an unfair advantage compared to other departments.

Some faculty members said that their departmental document was too qualitative in its indicators, while others felt that it was too quantitative or constricting of creativity. Others said that it was difficult to seriously consider the standards document without a discussion or resolution of what they perceived as a very unfair workload.

Most departmental documents establish relatively high standards of performance. Even so, respondents recommended that a next step would be to require each department to identify two departmental standards statements from other universities that could be used to establish the validity of its disciplinary standards. Furthermore, respondents recommended some effort to assess the impact of workload issues on faculty attitudes about, and use of, the standards documents.

So What? And What Now?

In the end, some concrete result related to the existence of the departmental documents has to make the investment of time and effort worthwhile for the faculty and the university as a whole. Every university that hopes to change faculty standards of performance and rewards must demonstrate the practical relevance of these changes at the local institutional level, in terms of evaluation and rewarding faculty; at the state level, in terms of accountability and higher education budgets; and at the national level, in terms of adherence to disciplinary standards.

We found that these efforts did have a beneficial effect on promotion and tenure decisions and merit pay decisions. However, change of this type requires continual attention. At SDSU, there is ongoing education of all concerned, evaluation of process, and evaluation of impact. Much work remains. Campus leaders hope to have departments compare their standards statements or documents with standards used in comparable departments at other universities. This will provide external validity to the criteria used by departments at SDSU. Both department heads and faculty need additional training, through workshops, on the meaning and measures of scholarship. "Best practice" models from specific departments must be made available to serve as guides to departments wanting to improve their documents. Campus leaders plan to expand the documentation section of the departmental documents, which is currently at the preliminary stage for most departments. Finally, the campus will continue to monitor the process and its impact on the reward system.

The campus study has enabled SDSU to develop a succinct historical account of the steps involved in creating the standards documents, and enabled campus leaders to obtain feedback on the effectiveness of the development process. The account of SDSU's journey, it is hoped, will be useful to other campuses considering similar change.

References

Boyer, E. L. (1990). *Scholarship reconsidered: Priorities of the professoriate.* Princeton, NJ: Carnegie Foundation for the Advancement of Teaching.

Elman, S. E., & Marx Smock, S. (1985). *Professional service and faculty rewards.* Washington, DC: National Association for State Universities and Land-Grant Colleges.

South Dakota Board of Regents and Council on Higher Education. (1992, December 11). *Statement concerning faculty activities.* Interim terms and conditions between South Dakota Board of Regents and Council on Higher Education, an affiliate of the South Dakota Education Association and the National Educational Association of Higher Education. Unpublished document.

South Dakota Board of Regents and Council on Higher Education. (2000). *Agreement between the South Dakota Board of Regents and the Council of Higher Education.* Unpublished document.

South Dakota State University. (1995, October). *Achieving excellence in faculty roles* (1st ed.). Unpublished report.

South Dakota State University. (2002, May). *Achieving excellence in faculty roles* (2nd ed.). Unpublished report.

CHAPTER NINE

OPTIMISM WITH OUR EYES WIDE OPEN

Reconsidering Scholarship at Kansas State University

Victoria L. Clegg and Gretchen R. Esping

> *Who are scholars? Some people think of scholars as the inhabitants of ivory towers or dark corners of great libraries, engaged in esoteric activities. Well, at K-State this is hardly the case.*
> —THE MEANING OF SCHOLARSHIP: A SYNOPSIS, 1999

Kansas State University (KSU), the oldest of the country's land-grant institutions, has a long and valued history of shared governance—a circumstance that is central to its story of reconsidering scholarship. For more than a decade, many faculty and administrators have focused on ways to optimize the two assets—time and talent—upon which all of the university's work depends, leading them to make the case for evaluation and reward systems that truly account for *all* faculty responsibilities and strengths. One major concern was that although KSU had long acknowledged the value of teaching, faculty members who excelled in teaching were not as clearly rewarded as their colleagues who excelled in research.

The faculty and head of each department have, for several decades, jointly developed criteria and procedures for the annual evaluation of faculty members. In 1990, a newly revised university policy emphasized the expectation that each faculty member would meet annually with the department head to jointly establish an individualized agreement (IA) reflecting the faculty member's strengths and interests, while also assuring that the mission of the department is met. The flexible allocation of time and talent, intended to encourage scholarship in all areas of academic work, has been challenging but is slowly being incorporated across campus. Several themes that emerged from analysis of the campus study findings are presented following to help illuminate possible implications for other campuses contemplating similar reform. The story concludes with the lessons learned from this ongoing cultural change and projections about probable next steps.

The Meaning of Scholarship: A Synopsis—a special edition of KSU's Provost Roundtable Series—appeared on local cable television in April 1999. The production drew from contributions by administrators, faculty members, and guest lecturers during the 1997–1998 academic year, when the campus community engaged in discussion about the meaning of scholarship. During that year, the provost invited each of the nine academic deans to present a lecture on the meaning of scholarship, providing their own college's perspective and comparing that perspective to Ernest Boyer's writings in *Scholarship Reconsidered* (1990). Each lecture was followed by a roundtable discussion, where the dean and four or five faculty members from that college discussed the topic of scholarship with the provost. These lectures and roundtable discussions were broadcast over local cable television and KSU's low-power TV channel. Faculty, staff, and administrators could ask questions and offer comments on a threaded message board and through voicemail.

The yearlong discussion, although more focused than informal conversations on the subject, was not really a groundbreaking event. Since 1989, the provost and the academic deans have repeatedly encouraged faculty to examine the nature of scholarship: to discuss what scholarship means at KSU and how the institution's policies and procedures might best be adapted to reflect continuing change in the nature of scholarship. These efforts evolved into an ongoing process of developing and implementing strategies designed to encourage scholarly work in all areas of faculty endeavor. In this chapter, we describe the sparks of change that ignited the flames of serious discussion on our campus, the steps leading to a broader definition of scholarship, and the outcomes from actions taken to date.

HISTORY AND CONTEXT

In September 1863, Kansas State Agricultural College opened with 52 students: 26 men and 26 women. Today, KSU thrives as the state's land-grant institution in the Carnegie classification of Doctoral/ Research Universities–Extensive. More than 19,000 undergraduate students and 3,000 graduate students are enrolled. Approximately 1,200 full-time faculty members are employed on two campuses; nearly 730 are tenured. Degrees are offered in nine colleges: Agriculture; Architecture, Planning and Design; Arts and Sciences; Business Administration; Education; Engineering; Human Ecology; Technology and Aviation; and Veterinary Medicine. The diversity in faculty specialization and versatility in professional responsibility are evidenced within and among the various colleges.

Faculty members have always had a substantial and essential role in the formation of policies and procedures for their departments and colleges, and for the university. Most department administrators are heads; fewer than 10 percent are chairs. Heads serve at the pleasure of the dean with input from the faculty, rather than by election of the faculty. They tend to serve longer as department administrators than do most chairs, and their longer tenure may lead to a more consistent interpretation and application of policy and procedure. They also gain expertise through an extensive professional development program supported by the Office of the Provost.

As late as 1988, the university's written policy concerning annual evaluation, promotion, and tenure indicated that faculty members must "demonstrate superior professional accomplishment and excellence in the performance of their assigned duties which normally include, in varying proportions, teaching, research (or other creative endeavor) and, for a portion of the faculty, Extension activities" (Kansas State University, 1988). Although the words may imply a diversity of assignment and performance expectations, as a practical matter the main focus in the evaluation of faculty effectiveness fell on research and creative endeavor.

Students often ask, "Will I be tested on that?" to judge what is important to learn. Faculty members ask, "Will I be tenured for that?" to judge what is important to perform. The university's policy in 1988 reflected practical reality in the statement that a candidate for tenure "*must* display a productive and creative mind through published research or artistic and creative projects, to be judged for quality as well as for quantity and consistency" (emphasis added). No such definite statements were made for other areas of faculty responsibility.

One of James R. Coffman's first experiences as Kansas State's new provost was a series of conversations, in 1988, with several women faculty who wanted more explicit standards for judging performance, to avoid either the potential or the reality of being judged against a different set of standards than their male colleagues. As a result of those conversations, Coffman asked each dean to closely review the evaluation processes in the departments.

It soon became evident that in most departments, everyone had similar assignments, performance usually was judged against a single, set standard, and the evaluation of faculty was tied to the explicit ranking of members within a department. However, the process in many departments was not a matter of written policy. As Coffman said, "We needed to establish a policy framework for each unit and build to practice" (J. Coffman, personal communication, 1988). Thus KSU's academic community began to explore the nature of faculty scholarship, its meaning and value, and to consider effective ways to evaluate that scholarship.

FORCES FOR CHANGE: FLEXIBLE ALLOCATION OF TIME AND TALENT

In concert with discussions about scholarship, many faculty members and administrators began to make the case for evaluation and reward systems that truly account for *all* faculty responsibilities and strengths.

POLICY FOUNDATIONS FOR FLEXIBLE ALLOCATION

In 1989, Provost Coffman commissioned a task force to develop procedures and guidelines for the annual evaluation of faculty and all unclassified personnel. In 1990, the provost commissioned a second task force to examine the impact of tenure and promotion practices upon institutional excellence and to recommend changes.

Recommendations of the two groups were combined to propose changes in policy and procedure, and, in 1992, by a close margin, the Faculty Senate approved the recommended revisions. Many faculty and administrators vigorously supported the initiative throughout three years of changes to evaluation policies. Most had read *Scholarship Reconsidered*, believed that the university's current view of scholarship was too narrow, and tried to persuade others to think about these issues and to make decisions for change.

An introductory paragraph in the university's *Handbook* (Kansas State University, n.d.) referring to the 1992 policy, states, "Faculty members . . . are those . . . who have the professional expertise and the responsibility for the major university endeavors of teaching, research and other creative endeavor, extension, directed service, and non-directed service. Institutional excellence is enhanced by both faculty specialization and versatility in the kind of work done within and across departments and units. Faculty members will have individual responsibility profiles" (Sec. C). It highlights the diversity of faculty responsibilities with the statement that "the emphasis given to these responsibilities varies among the colleges and departments of the university and may well vary from individual to individual within department" (Sec. C). Thus it laid the foundation for consideration of the flexible allocation of time and talent.

Establishing Departmental Criteria, Standards, and Guidelines

In the early 1990s, the Kansas Board of Regents, charged by the legislature to govern the six state universities, provided a mandate by formalizing expectations for enhanced teaching at the six institutions and promoting systems of faculty evaluation that would compare outcomes against expectations. Provost Coffman and the deans in 1992 charged all departments to develop their own criteria, standards, and guidelines for the evaluation of faculty members in line with the revised policies.

A 45-page resource booklet for faculty and administrators, *Effective Faculty Evaluation: Annual Salary Adjustments, Tenure and Promotion* (Committee Report, 1992), was distributed in the fall of 1992 as an aid to departments and units. Members of the team that devised the booklet recommended that department faculty consider the ideas proposed by Boyer in *Scholarship Reconsidered* (1990) as a way to categorize scholarly activities.

According to university policy, the department faculty and head share primary responsibility for developing and revising the evaluation systems, which must be approved by the college dean and the provost. These evaluation systems are dynamic, with departmental review occurring at least every five years. The availability of all department evaluation documents online enables faculty and administrators to examine the evaluation systems and procedures used across the campus. The department mission statements are also online.

The resource booklet makes the point that "where the responsibilities and goals of the department dictate specialization of effort among faculty members, the weighting of various areas of endeavor must be sufficiently flexible to accommodate the individual assignments" (Committee Report, 1992). However, it also clearly states that the significant variety of responsibilities and assignments among faculty members must be effectively balanced with the department's mission.

In a September 1995 memo to the deans, Provost Coffman reminded the campus of the regents' recommendation to move toward a system comparing evaluation outcomes with expectations. Noting that the recommendation was already reflected in KSU's policy, he emphasized that "a fundamental element of rethinking how to most effectively deploy faculty time and talent is going to be *flexibility* of assignment, in contrast to a departmental norm approach" (J. Coffman, personal communication, 1995).

Later, in May 1998, the Faculty Senate deleted a policy requiring those working toward tenure to exhibit versatility by the ability to function well across major areas of work (for example, teaching, research and other creative endeavors, service, and extension). This decision was made because departmental criteria, standards, and guidelines were to form the basis for judgments about versatility and expertise. This was a significant change because it acknowledged that pretenure faculty assignments could be heavily weighted in one area, as determined by the department, and that university policy would no longer hold faculty accountable to demonstrate versatility across all major areas as originally described.

AN EMPHASIS ON TEACHING

In February 1995, Provost Coffman and the deans charged all departments to review the descriptions of their evaluation systems, with particular attention to the evaluation of teaching. Departments were to establish multiple criteria for judging teaching effectiveness and were to include the scholarship of teaching in faculty evaluations.

That same year, to symbolize the institution's commitment to excellence in undergraduate teaching and learning, the provost established the University Chair for Distinguished Teaching Scholars. Recipients of the honor are selected through a competitive process and appointed to the half-time position for one academic year. They become leaders to the university community in the scholarship of teaching, and hold the title University Distinguished Teaching Scholar for the rest of their career at KSU.

THE CALL TO IMPLEMENT FLEXIBLE ALLOCATION

For several decades, the head and the faculty of each department have jointly developed criteria and procedures for the annual evaluation of faculty members. In 1990, the revised university policy added the expectation that each faculty member would meet annually with the department head to establish personal goals for the upcoming year, within the context of the department mission. The previous year's goals would also be considered during the annual evaluation.

In January 1996, Provost Coffman (personal communication, January 8, 1996) sent a letter directing that departments begin to implement this fundamentally different approach to faculty evaluation. According to his instructions, a department head had to meet with each faculty member, individually, at the beginning of the evaluation period, to set broad terms for allocating the faculty member's time and effort in teaching, research, service, and other activities during the ensuring year, and also to agree on reasonable expectations about performance standards. "The written results of this discussion should be *specific and unique for the individual,*" Coffman wrote, "and consistent with more general criteria and standards for evaluation, promotion, and tenure. Any problem areas which exist from the previous year(s) should also be clarified, along with a plan for addressing them."

In workshops held for department heads and deans through-out early 1996, the provost emphasized five points that remain at the center of today's considerations of faculty scholarship and eval-uation at KSU: (1) time and talent constitute 90 percent of the uni-versity's resources, (2) each department must clearly understand its mission, (3) faculty members must collectively decide how to achieve the mission, (4) the reward system must appropriately rec-ognize the various categories of achievement, and (5) the univer-sity's success depends heavily on maximizing the skills and talents of faculty members according to the department's mission.

THE CAMPUS STUDY

During the past five years of discussion and implementation, a growing sense of progress has emerged as the campus community accepted the challenge of using strategies of individualized or flex-ible faculty assignments to encourage scholarship in all areas of academic work. Provost Coffman, who admits to having "the most or one of the most positive attitudes" about the university's ac-complishments, was eager to conduct a self-study to learn what could be done to further progress. Specifically, the authors set out to assess the full impact of new policies and procedures to encour-age scholarship in all areas of academic work; how these policies and procedures have been accepted and incorporated into the academic culture; and success in elevating the importance of teach-ing—in particular to determine the impact of the University Chair for Distinguished Teaching Scholars.

The campus study applied several perspectives. We began by reviewing the department mission statements and the department evaluation documents that describe policies and procedures for the allocation of faculty time and talent. This provided a sense of what had been accomplished "on paper."

To determine implementation and impact, we went directly to the people—those involved in designing the policies and procedures and those affected by their implementation. Selected department heads from each college, all college deans, and the provost were in-dividually interviewed. We taped the interview sessions, averaging about 40 minutes each, and reviewed transcriptions and interview notes to identify common concerns and patterns.

Faculty members in all academic departments were asked to complete an online survey that combined standardized and open-comment questions. Responses were anonymous, and each faculty member could respond only once. The demographics of the respondents (30 percent of the faculty) are very representative of the university's faculty in age, gender, rank, tenure status, and college affiliation; reasonable conclusions can be drawn from the sample.

WHAT WE LEARNED: EMERGING THEMES

Introducing academic cultural change is never easy, nor is it accomplished without some distress. We examined cultural change with the help of Schein's (1992) and Kuh and Whitt's (1988) work on analyzing institutional culture, which is captured so well by Eckel, Green, Hill, and Mallon (1999), *On Change III: Taking Charge of Change*. As Kuh and Whitt observe, "Understanding institutional culture is analogous to peeling away the many layers of an onion" (p. 41). When changing the culture, the goal is to alter the underlying assumptions and beliefs through a variety of strategies. To make the change permanent, all three layers—artifacts, espoused values, and underlying assumptions or beliefs—must align and agree. If, on the other hand, there is a conflict along the way, for instance, between an institution's espoused values and "how business gets done," then the core assumptions probably remain as they were before, and there is only an illusion of change (Eckel et al., 1999).

The strategy of individualized or flexible faculty assignments, intended to encourage scholarship in all areas of academic work, has been challenging. Nevertheless, the flexible allocation of time and talent is slowly being incorporated across campus, although progress is still scattered. The following five theme statements, based on analysis of our campus study findings, illuminate possible implications for other campuses contemplating similar reform.

THEME 1: The acceptance and implementation of flexible allocation is largely a function of the academic department's culture and traditions.

Each department has a distinctive culture, sense of tradition, and collective experience that sets the stage for accepting or resisting flexible allocation. The influence of shared governance is very strong at KSU, where faculty members expect to play a central role in the formation of policies and procedures for departments, colleges, and the university. In theory and in practice, faculty members have a great amount of freedom and a commensurate responsibility to influence their current situation and to shape their own future.

The department is responsible for devising its own criteria for governance, hiring, and evaluation. While these are crafted within the context of overarching university policy, there is clearly room for diversity and distinctiveness among the departments. Not surprisingly, flexible allocation, a very new concept for most on our campus, is accepted and implemented to varying degrees and with varying levels of satisfaction.

Nearly 90 percent of the department evaluation documents now mention flexibility in the allocation of time and talent, one way or another. Sometimes the *fact* of flexible allocation is stated directly: "Assignments will be based on faculty strengths, departmental and college needs and opportunities, and/or promotion/ tenure status." Other departments quietly allude to the possibility of flexible allocation: the faculty member "is invited to negotiate the distribution of percentages if so desired." Several departments set out customary allocations that will be expected of all faculty members in the department. Others offer ranges deemed appropriate for the allocation of time and talent but note that deviation from the customary expectation is possible. A few offer considerable opportunity for flexibility: "Tenths time assignments are totally negotiable; there are no upper or lower limits as long as the mission and goals of the department are met."

In some departments, the concept of flexible assignment is emerging within the more traditional approach of standard assignments. Annual reviews of faculty evaluation packets reveal that some faculty members are doing their scholarship as research in teaching in their own disciplines. Their colleagues are crediting them for that effort, and department heads are evaluating them on that effort.

A few interdisciplinary departments—by nature a combination of several loosely related programs—have found the flexibility of individualized faculty assignment to be ideal for their situations. The faculty and administrators of these departments contend that the diversity of faculty responsibilities almost requires the more flexible system for the department to be an effective unit. Departments that traditionally have split appointments with the Experiment Stations and the Cooperative Extension Service are a good fit for the more flexible approach, and maintain they have been using a similar system for decades.

Other departments with more focused missions—whether research or teaching—are more resistant to a flexible system of allocation of time and talent. They maintain that such a system simply does not fit their situation, and that expectations must be the same for each faculty member in order to meet goals and mission of the department.

THEME 2: Faculty members are generally optimistic about the theory of flexible allocation of time and talent and its potential benefits for individuals and institutions.

They are more skeptical about implementation. Departmental criteria, standards, and guidelines rest on two important expectations: (1) both the faculty members and the department head will participate in development and review of the department's policies and procedures, and (2) the policies and procedures will be followed in practice. A few written comments from the faculty survey imply that the latter is not universally realized, particularly when it comes to procedures for flexible allocation.

Respondents suggested that not all faculty members were actually evaluated according to the expectations established for their individualized assignments. Comparing the individual's evaluation outcomes with the expectations is critical when flexibility or individualization across faculty assignments, and thus across expectations for performance, exists. When that does not happen in practice, faculty members have reason to be wary of the strategy of flexible allocation.

Some faculty members expressed appreciation for flexible allocation:

- "If you are doing what you enjoy and feel strongly about, you're likely to be functioning at a higher level."
- "Flexible assignment does not attempt to shove everyone into the same mold; [it] forces recruitment of faculty that best meet the needs of the department."
- "We are a department of related but distinctly different goals. It is vital that assignments be individualized in order to meet our students' needs and to meet research goals."
- "We all have our comparative advantages and can each uniquely contribute most to the program and university with individual assignments matching our comparative advantages with program needs."

Others were far more cautious, skeptical, or antagonistic, largely because of experienced or anticipated problems in the implementation of the strategy:

- "It is fair only if all activities are equally rewarded, which they are not."
- "I do worry that this method could be abused to hide incompetence."
- "IAs are used as a punishment for not publishing. It creates a lot of resentment."
- "Putting an undue teaching load on one faculty member because someone else wants more 'free' research time is not fair."
- "The process is fair in theory but unworkable in an academic environment. Department heads are too vulnerable and wisely try to maximize faculty satisfaction and will not be adequately tough negotiators."
- "The minefield is how to equate expectations in different areas so that each person has an appointment that is of similar overall value and load."
- "IAs assure that our most nonproductive tenured faculty can coast along, at their own pace, for as long as they can drag themselves to work and collect a paycheck."

Respondents were split on this issue. Approximately 78 percent indicated that their departments do implement some form of individualized assignments. As Table 9.1 shows, a substantial majority

Table 9.1 Responses of Faculty Members
Implementing Individualized Assignments (IAs)

Survey Items	Yes (%)	No (%)
IAs in my department are determined annually.	83	17
IAs are negotiated between faculty member and department head.	89	11
All faculty assignments in my department are individualized.	68	29
Only tenured faculty members negotiate IAs.	14	81
Faculty members are evaluated in comparison to their goals and expectations as established at the beginning of the evaluation period.	79	20

Survey Items	Agree Strongly (%)	Agree Somewhat (%)
What is best for the department's mission is considered when IAs are determined.	44	42
The strategy of individualized assignments is best for my department.	66	29
I think it's fair to allocate each faculty member's time differently.	64	30
I believe the strategy of IAs might put some faculty careers at risk.	16	28
The process of individualized assignments contributes to more positive faculty morale in my department.	45	39

characterized flexible allocation or individualized assignments as beneficial: individualized assignments are fair, boost morale, and are best for the department.

However, a significant number of respondents believed that the strategy of flexible allocation—also identified as individualized assignments—had the potential to put some careers at risk. As expected, several comments evidence concern that tenure-track faculty could end up with agreements that would not permit them to show the range of achievement expected by their departments. The comments also reveal apprehension that the careers of tenured faculty could be at risk. Respondents noted that an emphasis on research productivity and publication is still a reality in many departments. Research is by no means disparaged in these comments, but it is recognized that those who emphasize teaching or service are likely to be accorded less reward and prestige and may find promotion to full professor very difficult:

- "Teaching is always indicated as being very important, but research funding and national research reputation is usually what gets the largest merit pay increase."
- "The only reality in my profession is 'publish or perish.' Any other arrangement of time jeopardizes a career."

Also, there is the fear that this new strategy may not prevail. If, for example, a new administration—department, college, or university—were not as supportive of flexible allocation of time and talent, the person who forged a career different from those of recent tradition could be in trouble. A few respondents noted that faculty might need to be protected from themselves—that they might negotiate assignments based on doing what they want to do and not what they need to do.

Theme 3: Language describing scholarship in department documents and our academic community has begun to reflect the campus discussions of the past several years.

The collective result can be described as exploratory, thoughtful reconsideration of scholarship realized in varying degrees. Many department evaluation documents now explicitly expand the meaning of scholarship to include multiple facets of faculty work. A few departments include all areas of faculty responsibility—teaching, research, and service—and specifically refer to Boyer's (1990) categories of scholarship. Others use phrases such as "creative work contributing to pedagogy" and work that "promotes excellence in instruction." Some documents use the phrase "scholarship of teaching." While almost half of the documents still refer explicitly to research or research publication when using the term "scholarship," the fact that more than half now reflect an expanded understanding of scholarship is noteworthy.

Personal language offers more telling evidence of an expanding view of scholarship. The word *scholarship* is nearly absent from 25 pages of additional comments from the faculty survey. Instead, respondents describe their faculty responsibilities or use specific designations such as *teaching, research, creative endeavor, community service,* or *advising.* A decade ago the word *scholarship* was far more prominent in faculty comments about faculty work and was used to refer explicitly to research.

When interviewed for this study, deans and department heads did use the word *scholarship* as they explained their views of the flexible allocation of time and talent and the impact of the strategy at KSU. Some described how they and others in their colleges or departments were rethinking the nature of scholarship; others clarified an expanded definition that went beyond research. Even those who continued to apply the word *scholarship* to research and creative endeavor occasionally spoke of the "scholarship of teaching" and the "scholarship of service."

While deans talked very positively about a broader meaning of scholarship, they also expressed reservations about the academic community's readiness to accept these new ideas:

- "Scholarship has three basic requirements, and this goes across the board, whether it is teaching, service or in research. Scholarship (1) must include creative thought; (2) it must result in something tangible; and (3) it must be communicated to your peers."
- "There are different criteria that must be used for different types of scholarship. A different set of expectations. And just because they are different doesn't mean they are deficient."

- "One effect [of the changes] in tenure and promotion decision is greater flexibility in the decisions about what counts. It is still important that a faculty member have some publications, but their prominence in the decision-making process, I think, have kind of been diminished, in part due to this flexibility."
- "The culture doesn't accept different forms of scholarship that readily. This is going to take time."

Department heads usually discussed their department's perspective on the subject, gleaned from communication and collaboration with faculty. Some expressed the more traditional view of scholarship as research; others alluded to an expanded view of scholarship:

- "As we began to work on these interdisciplinary teams, we began to realize that there are different forms of scholarship and different ways we allocate our time to scholarship."
- "Scholarship is understood to be not just research and publishing articles. Scholarship can involve applying what you learn in your research, or I would argue even in your teaching, to your service activities so you can do things as a volunteer or as someone who has expertise in certain areas that really provides service to others."
- "Anything novel in teaching, research or service . . . or administration . . . is considered to be scholarship."
- "It's also important that we have research as well as teaching because that's what a major institution of scholarship is all about. I think it's about right when one assigns approximately equal weightings to those two."

THEME 4: A significantly greater appreciation of teaching as scholarship has developed during the past 10 years but is not universal in all departments.

As noted earlier, KSU administrators and faculty have long respected KSU's educational mission. Both department mission statements and evaluation documents acknowledge, almost universally, the value and importance of "education," "student learning," "instruction," and "teaching." The established departmental criteria, standards, and guidelines for evaluation do show a steadily increasing positive consideration for this critical faculty role.

Unfortunately, a disconcerting number of survey comments indicate that an existing *policy* of valuing teaching and the scholarship of teaching is not always reflected in *practice*. Faculty respondents claimed this occurred in the evaluation practices at the department level, but they were perhaps even more concerned about its occurrence as the evaluation process moved to the college and university levels:

- "I strongly support differing duties as long as the reward systems recognize the contributions as being equally important. Research is still valued much more highly than teaching or service."
- "I understand that a faculty person will most likely not get promoted to full professor if s/he has a primarily teaching and service assignment. So, if a person aspires to be a full professor, that person better maintain a research and writing agenda."
- "Within our department I think individualized assignments have worked well. But when I hear the dean of my college say that he would prefer a senior faculty member wait to apply for promotion to full professor because he does not have enough research publications and this will reflect poorly on the college, I know that the system is not working."

Several faculty members and many department heads offered strong statements favoring a commitment to excellence in both teaching and research. Still, the preceding comments are among many that mirror the continuing debate about the relative merits of research and teaching. Some believed that colleagues who emphasized teaching were simply not as capable. The attitude that teaching is easier than research pervades these comments, and the language often portrays teaching as a "burden" or a "necessary load." Similar comments are made about service but not about research.

The University Chair for Distinguished Teaching Scholars serves as another window onto KSU's appreciation for the scholarship of teaching. Here the message is also mixed. On the one hand, the eight years of this program document a grand success. The eight faculty members selected to serve, to date, have effectively promoted enhanced undergraduate education in a variety of ways; their public presentations and programs have been well attended by faculty and administrators. One chairholder's workshops on improving teaching were so well received that the sessions have continued for nearly five years. The Faculty Exchange for Teaching Excellence also was created to plan and run the programs.

On the other hand, one might assume that each year every college on campus would forward nominees for appointment to this prestigious position. That has not happened. Approximately 70 percent of the nominations have come from two colleges; three colleges have never submitted nominations. One might also assume that the academic community would be well informed about the University Chair for Distinguished Teaching Scholars and the activities of the chairholders. The faculty survey indicates that is not the case. Clearly, there is work to be done. Still, a critical mass of faculty members from across campus, colleges, and disciplines is meeting to listen and to talk about teaching. That represents a significant change from a decade ago.

THEME 5: The changes are spreading and evolving but are not yet anchored in the culture of the institution as a whole.

As Provost Coffman has suggested, and our review of documents and interviews has revealed, we are about one-third of the way to successfully implementing individual assignments at KSU. Kotter (1996) makes the point that the final stage of anchoring change into the overall culture of an organization occurs only at the end of the process, once the changes prove to be better than the old way.

Campuswide and departmental discussions about scholarship have led to broader perceptions of what is valued as scholarship. Successful steps have been taken to create more prestige for teaching, without diminishing research. Some departments use the concept of flexible allocation of time and talent substantively, while others are just beginning to seriously explore its merits and prospects. A few have considered the idea and decided they have neither the elasticity nor the inclination to implement the strategy.

Clearly, some individuals and departments already believe that the case for the change has been made. Their policies, procedures, actions, and words say so. Many believe that in theory it should work but are not yet convinced that the new ways will prevail and have decided to wait and see. Still others have weighed the alternatives and decided to remain with tradition.

LESSONS LEARNED

After more than 10 years of discussion and transition, we can report slow but steady cultural change. No one snapshot can depict this change, not even with a panoramic lens, since the picture in one sector of our campus is not the same as in another. Only a dynamic "video collage" could truly portray the constant movement and modification. Would that be just a little confusing? Sure. But it would depict reality. What have we learned?

One size does not fit all. Provost Coffman, when noting the advantages of broadening the definition of scholarship and offering flexible allocation of faculty time and talent, said, "Everybody is different to begin with. Different strengths. Different interests. During the course of a career, these strengths and interests are very likely to change. To allocate everyone's time [in the same way] is to condemn some individuals to some time—maybe a long time—of dissatisfaction and probably ineffective production" (J. Coffman, personal communication, 2001). We conclude that a similar case can be made for departments. They all are different: different missions, visions, strengths. And over time, these missions, visions, and strengths often change.

"One size fits all" is a myth. Should we be surprised that diverse groups of faculty define scholarship—even broadened views of scholarship—differently? No. The academic community must acknowledge that the differences are real and valid, that being different is not being deficient. Faculty and administrators who assess the worth of scholarly endeavor must judge it in the context of the department's characterization of scholarship.

And KSU *is* striding forward. In 2001, in decisions about annual merit salary increases and promotion and tenure, the department documents were used as the basis for judgments up through the decision-making hierarchy: department committees, department heads, deans, and provost. Not everyone will agree that the system works perfectly, but it is now clear that the processes for these decisions are supposed to include the departmental definitions and expectations of scholarship.

Similarly, a system of flexible allocation has to be flexible; it has to accommodate the varied implementation modes that departmental cultures find effective and comfortable. In the words of one department head, "A flexible system ought to allow little pockets where the system doesn't apply." At the same time, even in those departments that neither formally accepted nor implemented the concept of flexible allocation, the heads always indicated some opportunity for "wiggle room," some way to accommodate the exceptional circumstance that a faculty member might face for a given year.

Department heads play a pivotal role. Faculty members indicated a widespread inclination to appreciate and to accept flexible allocation in theory. It is also true that some voiced discomfort and even grave concern about the way the system is practiced or could be abused. Many connected their reactions—positive and negative—to assumptions and assertions about the pivotal role of the department head in the process of flexible allocation.

The members of a department share responsibility for fulfilling its mission and goals, but the department head often must balance the mission with the goals and desires of the many individual faculty members. As one department head noted, the heads have the "general responsibility to watch out for the needs of the department," even in departments where the faculty appear to make most governance decisions as a collective whole and the head "only" facilitates and consults. Many faculty comments concurred.

Trust is crucial. Several faculty members, while acknowledging the department head's major role in the negotiation of flexible allocations, attributed their satisfaction or dissatisfaction with the process to the attitude and conduct of their head. If the head seemed to lack either the perspective or the discretion to "manage" flexible allocation, or made decisions without discussion and mutual agreement, the faculty member was unhappy with the process. Other faculty members believed that their satisfaction with the process probably related strongly to the department head's win-win mentality—a willingness to listen and to accommodate for the good of the whole department.

Communication and collaborative decision making are vital. Lynton (1998) makes the point that "the effective integration of individual faculty work into collective purposes requires systematic, collaborative decision-making processes" (p. 9) involving both faculty and administrators. As noted earlier, shared governance is an important reality and expectation at KSU. Our conversations with department heads often revealed community decision making in those departments that use flexible allocation to a greater degree. There seems to be a convincing correlation. We do not assume that other departments do not make decisions collaboratively, although we heard about it much less from department heads who reported using flexible allocation only rarely or *not at all.*

Effective communication lies at the heart of effective collaboration. Many people—deans, department heads, and faculty—attributed better communications between department heads and faculty members to a system that emphasizes establishing expectations for faculty performance at the beginning of the evaluation period and encourages flexible allocation of time and talent. Such a system certainly demands *more* communication. Experience suggests that a beneficial outcome has been *improved* communication.

WHAT'S NEXT?

Watching slow progress does not have to be discouraging. Provost Coffman offered his analysis: "I focus on the progress, not the speed of the progress. We aren't 'there' yet, but we're headed in the right direction" (J. Coffman, personal communication, 2002). It will probably be necessary for administrators and faculty to promote even more the use of multiple criteria in the evaluation of faculty work, especially since everyone in the department must clearly understand the range of criteria and standards for evaluation used within an approach of flexible faculty assignments.

Many would support enhancing the value of service as the next big push. "But first," according to Coffman, "we have to extend the notion of individualized assignment or flexible allocation as a positive approach to more—most, if not all—sectors of the university.

Appropriate language in the policies of the department documents is a great beginning. Implementation in ongoing practice is the ultimate sign of success" (J. Coffman, personal communication, 2002).

Implementation in ongoing practice is never accomplished without focused effort and attention. Several deans and a few department heads alluded to university-sponsored opportunities for professional development. They wanted to empower both faculty and administrators—to inform a critical mass of decision makers about ways to evaluate diverse types of scholarship, provide opportunities for people from across the university to come together and share their diverse views, and challenge the academic community to reach beyond their traditions. Such professional development opportunities would extend activities already in place but focus them more sharply and coordinate them at several levels to achieve the desired outcomes.

Discussions about the broader nature of scholarship and the use of flexible allocation of time and talent have also uncovered a growing sense that the university is not necessarily *for* the faculty. One dean flatly stated, "The institution exists to educate students, to develop and disseminate new knowledge, and to provide leadership in service to our various professions and publics. Those missions, however you want to talk about them or think about them, are why the institution is here. We're not here for faculty members . . . or for administrators. This place doesn't exist for any of us. We're the instruments of those three missions." For some faculty and administrators, this is a fairly new idea; others have held it as a given from the beginning. Nevertheless, it is probably at the crux of the discussion.

In his 1998 article about the larger context of faculty work, Lynton advised, "If universities are to have the resilience and adaptability they will need in the decades to come, they must find better ways to make individual faculty members' work contribute to common organizational needs, priorities, and goals" (p. 8). We believe that the system of flexible allocation of time and talent will help KSU meet those challenges. As one dean on our campus noted, "I think faculty understand that we're all in this together and that their departments should act as communities; and for communities to be successful, people need to work toward their own strengths while they share diverse responsibilities." Acknowledging the value of all types of scholarship, allowing each faculty member to realize individual strengths for the good of the institution, making it clear that each has a stake in the achievement of others—all are vital for continued success as an institution of higher education.

References

Boyer, E. L. (1990). *Scholarship reconsidered: Priorities of the professoriate.* Princeton, NJ: Carnegie Foundation for the Advancement of Teaching.

Committee Report. (1992). *Effective faculty evaluation: Annual salary adjustments, tenure, and promotion.* Manhattan: Kansas State University.

Eckel, P., Green, M., Hill, B., & Mallon, W. (1999). *On Change III: Taking charge of change: A primer for colleges and universities.* Washington, DC: American Council on Education.

Kansas State University. (1988). *Faculty handbook.* Manhattan: Author.

Kansas State University. (n.d.). *University handbook.* Manhattan: Author. Retrieved May 15, 2002 from http://www.ksu.edu/academicservices/fhbook

Kotter, J. P. (1996). *Leading change.* Boston: Harvard Business School Press.

Kuh, G. D., & Whitt, E. J. (1988). *The invisible tapestry: Culture in American colleges and universities.* ASHE-ERIC Higher Education Report Vol. 17, No. 1. Washington, DC: George Washington University.

Lynton, E. A. (1998). Reversing the telescope: Fitting individual tasks to common organizational ends. *AAHE Bulletin, 50*(7): 8–10.

The meaning of scholarship: A synopsis. (1999). Provost Roundtable Series, Special Edition, Kansas State University. Videotape.

Schein, E. H. (1992). *Organizational culture and leadership.* San Francisco: Jossey-Bass.

CHAPTER TEN

IDENTIFYING AND MANAGING UNIVERSITY ASSETS

A Campus Study of Portland State University

John Rueter and Talya Bauer

INSTITUTIONAL HISTORY AND CONTEXT

Between 1994 and 1996, Portland State University (PSU) expanded the definition of scholarship used to assess and reward faculty. Three conditions facilitated this change. The first related to PSU's urban history, culture, and values. This context allowed faculty to approach their teaching, learning, and community engagement in scholarly ways. The second condition involved external forces, which challenged faculty to identify and use their intangible assets in the scholarship of teaching, integration, and application. The third condition was, and continues to be, university leadership. Leadership at PSU encourages the faculty to engage in institutional reflection and strategic planning from a scholarly perspective. In the mid-1990s, the synergy among these three conditions prompted PSU to broaden notions of scholarship to include, more centrally, an emphasis on teaching.

The authors acknowledge project support from AAHE and personal support and encouragement from Devorah Lieberman.

This chapter examines the current status of this broadened definition of scholarship within PSU's academic culture. We interviewed 28 faculty members, staff members, and administrators and analyzed documents, such as the university's promotion and tenure guidelines, to understand the process and structures that promote a broader view of scholarship across campus. The analysis suggests that PSU has made progress in using expanded forms of scholarship to both identify and manage the intellectual assets of the institution. It also suggests that PSU is still in the process of implementation and now faces a second generation of challenges.

A SNAPSHOT OF PORTLAND STATE UNIVERSITY

When academic leaders cite examples of institutions at the forefront of implementing Ernest Boyer's (1990) framework for expanded scholarship, they often point to PSU. With a motto of "Let Knowledge Serve the City" and more than five years' experience implementing a broadened definition of scholarship, PSU serves as a model for many urban universities—particularly in encouraging and assessing teaching and engagement under a scholarship rubric. The current study is an opportunity to reflect critically on the university's experience with regard to scholarship, past and present.

Portland State straddles a tree-filled mall in downtown Portland, Oregon, only six blocks from city hall. The Carnegie Foundation classifies PSU as a Doctoral-Granting University II. In 1946, legislative action formed the university to provide educational access to the growing metropolitan population. In fall 2000, the university's headcount showed 12,246 full-time and 4,995 part-time students; however, because of student turnover between terms, it is estimated that more than 36,000 individuals take classes at PSU during a calendar year. Only 11 percent of students live in campus housing. PSU receives state funding through the Oregon University System (OUS), which includes four regional universities and two larger, higher profile universities (Oregon State University and the University of Oregon). There has been recent growth in the student population at PSU, and a major shift toward hiring fixed-term (one- or two-year contracts) and part-time faculty, with such appointments increasing by 136 percent between 1995 and 2001.

These changes indicate a movement away from using tenured and tenure-track faculty to meet student credit-hour demand.

A BRIEF HISTORY TO 1990

In 1990, PSU defined itself with the new descriptor of "urban university." Many current faculty members remember this move to define PSU's urban mission and the fanfare over launching the motto, "Let Knowledge Serve the City." However, PSU set its urban course much earlier, between 1949 and 1955, when it came into being after the flooded-out Vanport Extension Center moved from below the dikes on the Columbia River to downtown Portland and became the College (Dodds, 2000). In this historical account, there is no record of the extension center or the nascent university having a mission statement, except for a commitment to teaching and access. Political support for this mission led to state legislation that created Portland State College.

Two periods prior to 1990 are critical to the development of faculty roles and rewards at PSU: the activist 1960s and the financially and administratively challenged late 1980s. Events during these two periods created a culture that would later be responsive to changes in faculty roles and rewards.

During the 1960s, PSU faculty participated in the growing citizen and political activism of the era. There was a general cultural transition from materialist to postmaterialist values (Inglehart, 1990, 1997) and a shift in priorities from economic development to quality of life. These tradeoffs transformed "basic norms governing politics, work, religion, family, and sexual behavior" (Inglehart, 1997, p. 8). The shift began in the cities and continues as a cultural divide between urban and rural communities (Inglehart, 1997, p. 111). Faculty recruited to PSU in the 1960s elected to work in an environment that aligned with their values of service and access. Many chose to work at PSU, which had a balance of teaching, research, and service, rather than institutions (for example, traditional land-grant universities in "college towns") that focused more rigidly and narrowly on the traditional model of discipline-based research. Faculty members hired during this period eventually became campus leaders and helped shape PSU's culture through what has been described as "elite-directed participation" (Ingle-hart, 1990, p. 336). This type of leadership originated among the general faculty who had no formal, upper-level administrative appointments. Instead, they created ad hoc mechanisms to apply their particular skills and values to resolve specific problems and effect change on campus.

PSU experienced internal politics and financial and student enrollment constraints during the 1980s that also influenced the large-scale changes of the 1990s. In the early 1980s, several budget restrictions forced the administration to focus on cutbacks rather than enrollment growth. Retrenchment was a very real threat; there was a several-month period when each issue of *PSU Currently* (a weekly internal newsletter) had a budget update. Concurrent with this internal campus distress, there was tension between PSU and the Oregon University System (OUS). In 1986, the OUS appointed a PSU president whom the faculty did not support. Budget irregularities compounded the lack of support, and eventually a no-confidence vote by the faculty led to the president's resignation. This episode inspired the faculty to support a process of shared governance centered in the Faculty Senate and in the faculty union, the American Association of University Professors (AAUP). The departure of the president demonstrated the power of organized faculty governance and illustrated the much less predictable, but important, process of emergent faculty leadership. During the period of this dispute, PSU continued to hire faculty with excellent intellectual resources and a strong sense of shared governance. However, during the late 1980s, PSU was essentially leaderless and lacking a common vision and direction.

These two periods significantly influenced current faculty roles and rewards. The same stress factors of budget and competition persist to varying degrees, and the culture of innovation that developed to handle these stresses remains. The faculty and administration learned that they would need to be innovative, take risks, and exercise self-reliance and independence. This has been evident in times when PSU was buffeted by the state budget or the state university system. The external disturbances required innovation, not simply adaptation. Within the institution, faculty have accepted some of this risk while trying to solve problems and find ways to work with limited resources. Distributed risk is part of a classical entrepreneurial approach to management and change. The faculty was, and continues to be, involved in change-oriented activity without the potential for financial reward or, in many cases, even recognition.

REVISION OF THE PROMOTION AND TENURE GUIDELINES

In 1990, the College of Liberal Arts and Sciences (CLAS) released a report on expanded forms of scholarship, based on Ernest Boyer's *Scholarship Reconsidered: Priorities of the Professoriate* (1990). Faculty across the campus became aware of the CLAS report, and interest spread about faculty roles and rewards as framed by Boyer. In fall 1994, the university formed a committee to rewrite the promotion and tenure guidelines. The committee included members appointed by the provost (as recommended by deans and chairs), as well as two representatives from the local AAUP. The committee worked for two academic years on their proposal, which was brought before the University Senate in June 1996. There was easy agreement on most items, which described the processes by which departmental and college promotion and tenure committees would revise their guidelines to include an expanded definition of scholarship. In a discussion that presaged PSU's current situation, some senators worried that promotion and tenure committees would lack specific language to describe what the university termed "scholarship of community outreach." The most contentious issue recorded in the discussion was debate about the "scholarly agenda"—specifically, whether it should be a required, rather than an optional, part of a faculty member's file and whether the faculty could modify it unilaterally. After extensive debate, including a special session, the senate adopted new guidelines in 1996. After this, departments and programs were required to modify their governance guidelines and processes for promotion and tenure review and evaluation, and they were required to explicitly state how they would review different forms of scholarship.

THE CAMPUS STUDY

More than seven years later, all faculty hires and promotions adhere to the promotion and tenure standards found within these guidelines. The current study provided an opportunity to reflect on the processes that led to the adoption of these guidelines and take the lessons forward. PSU received a grant from the American Association for Higher Education to study how multiple forms of scholarship are rewarded in policy and practice. The proposal and subsequent campus study focused on the gradual cultural shift as PSU integrated the expanded definition of scholarship into the many layers of academic culture, including different disciplines, formal and informal reward systems, and strategic planning processes. We identified four major questions:

1. Did PSU experience a culture shift as it redefined scholarship?
2. If so, what were some of the concrete outcomes of this culture shift?
3. What internal forces and conditions led to this culture shift?
4. What external forces and conditions led to this culture shift?

In order to better understand these questions and their answers, we examined historical documents and conducted interviews with faculty, staff, and administrators. We obtained much of the historical information for this project from published sources, the campus newsletter, and other internal documents. These sources enabled us to determine the critical factors that led PSU to broaden the definition of scholarship for assessing and rewarding faculty. After the Human Subjects Research Review Committee waived review of the interview protocol, we did 28 interviews, each scheduled for 30 minutes. We did eight interviews of upper administrators, including the president, provost, two vice provosts, and six deans; and four interviews of middle administrators, including two associate deans directly involved in the promotion and tenure process at the college level. We interviewed 14 faculty members from five of the seven colleges, including four from CLAS, the largest college; five of the faculty members interviewed had been involved in revising the general education program or teaching in it. Finally, we did two interviews with staff who had been involved in the process of creating the new guidelines. The interview questions elicited views about (1) scholarship, (2) PSU's change process, (3) the promotion and tenure guidelines and their implementation, (4) how expanded definitions of scholarship have impacted academic culture, (5) the documentation used to assess scholarship, (6) the university's external reputation, and (7) community partnerships.

FINDINGS

The findings support the hypothesis that internal and external conditions led to a cultural shift as well as a changed perspective on what scholarship is and how it must be supported. One key condition for this shift was an external call for academic accountability, and the other was an internal demand for general education reform. University leaders used these situations to shape a discussion on general education that focused on scholarship rather than governance and to garner support for structures that encouraged multiple forms of scholarly work. Outcomes from the cultural shift include the perception among interviewees that PSU has had a positive change in its promotion and tenure guidelines, an increase in the range of acceptable products that can be used as evidence of scholarship, and external recognition of campus efforts and progress.

INTERNAL AND EXTERNAL FORCES AND OPPORTUNITIES

During the early 1990s, faculty and administration initiated a change process that resulted in broadening the definition of acceptable scholarship for evaluating faculty work. This project was undertaken in the context of two other important calls for reform that ultimately shaped the direction of scholarship at PSU. First, in the early 1990s, there was external pressure from politicians to be accountable to stakeholders for faculty workload and activities and university expenditures. Second, there was dissatisfaction with the general education program among the faculty and a feeling that it needed to be revised.

CALLS FOR ACCOUNTABILITY

In 1989, Oregon's governor formed a commission to address the improvement of doctoral education in Portland and called for increased faculty workload accountability (Dodds, 2000). Leaders at PSU translated this call into an internal dialogue about whether faculty priorities were congruent with institutional priorities. This discussion allowed the faculty and administration to preemptively reformulate questions about accountability into questions about how expanded notions of scholarship could align faculty work and institutional responsibility.

GENERAL EDUCATION REFORM

In the early 1990s, PSU faced a significant problem of student attrition between the freshman and sophomore years. The president and provost initiated campuswide discussions in order to address this problem, inviting interested faculty to join in the discussion and study national trends in general education reform. A volunteer faculty cohort began reading higher education retention literature, conducting site visits to other institutions, and attending higher education conferences. The General Education Working Group, as it became known, grounded its reform process in PSU's scholarly approach to organizational change and general education reform (White, 1994). At the same time as this group was meeting, PSU's president determined that the new general education model should have a strong service-learning (community-based learning) component. The president believed that PSU's location was ideal for seamlessly connecting the city to the university. The emphasis on teaching, curricular reform, retention, service-learning pedagogy, and the scholarly approach to change shaped the conversations that resulted in PSU's redefinition of scholarship.

PORTLAND STATE UNIVERSITY LEADERS

Administrative leadership was crucial for setting new direction, vision, and institutional focus. Campus leaders supported a scholarly approach for engaging faculty in addressing their roles and responsibilities. Whereas previous administrations had thought of PSU faculty as "dusty eggheads that needed to be led into the twenty-first century" (Dodds, 2000, p. 453), the administration of the early 1990s actually fostered a discussion about vision, goals, scholarship, and faculty support. A common theme among those interviewed for this project (and discussed in more detail in the next section of the chapter) was that this kind of inclusive leadership was crucial to the change process.

A key part of the strategy was a deliberate formation of structures that used and transferred knowledge within the institution. Such knowledge transfer is much more than the sharing of information. Sveiby (1997) refers to Polanyi's definition of knowledge as being public but also highly personal. Individuals construct knowledge for themselves, and increasing one's knowledge leads to the "capacity to act" (Sveiby, 1997). By employing a scholarly approach to developing the general education program, PSU demonstrated the capacity for this kind of transfer of knowledge. Current PSU leaders employ similar strategies to address specific initiatives as well as broader strategic planning and institutional vision.

The leaders of the early 1990s engaged faculty members across campus in scholarly discussions about faculty worth and what scholarship had meant and would mean at PSU. Administrators encouraged and financially supported those faculty members interested in higher education trends to attend national higher education conferences, in the hope that they would bring national conversations back to PSU. They did, and new directions within PSU emerged from many of these national and local discussions. From the larger faculty, several individuals became campus leaders, helping the move to greater clarity and sophistication in relation to curricular design, general education, faculty governance, scholarship, faculty support, community-based learning, assessment, and the redesign of promotion and tenure. This collection of faculty and administrative talent propelled PSU forward during its culture shift.

UNIQUE CULTURAL CHARACTERISTICS OF PORTLAND STATE UNIVERSITY

Our analysis of the campus interviews revealed two commonly held beliefs about the culture of PSU in the 1990s. The first was a dedication to student learning, scholarship, and innovation, and the second was a readiness for change. The personal commitment to scholarship described by all the interviewees was profound, to the point where it can be considered a core value of the institution. Many interviewees described PSU as an innovative or entrepreneurial institution where people could try new approaches to issues. Interviewees describing the situation leading up to the reform of the 1990s characterized the campus community as "fed up," with people starting to "wake up" or "grow up." Other interviewees described the reform efforts as an attempt to legitimize or validate the type of work they were already doing.

The culture at PSU is one of the key conditions that supports the adoption and acceptance of expanded forms of scholarship. Other authors describe this culture in different ways. Shulock and Ketcheson (2000) describe PSU as "action oriented," a cultural attribute that explains why PSU undertakes many high-risk projects. Ramaley (2000) notes that innovative academic projects often must meet a double standard that requires a higher burden of proof for new projects than those representing the status quo. Tetreault and Ketcheson (2002) claim that PSU has an "urban" culture, where "*urban* is an idea, a philosophy, an approach, rather than a strictly geographic or sociological term" (p. 42). They also describe how the administration previously positioned institutional transformation as scholarly work, and they refer to this approach as an "epistemology of practice." These recent definitions are likely to be useful in building on the urban history and culture of PSU without limiting the future vision to a geographical region.

SUPPORT STRUCTURES FOR MULTIPLE FORMS OF SCHOLARSHIP

Concurrent with significant campus changes, in 1995, the president and provost created the Center for Academic Excellence (CAE) to support faculty members engaged in teaching, learning, and scholarship. Its mission is to "promote and support academic excellence in teaching, assessment, and community-university partnerships by enhancing faculty scholarship, improving student learning outcomes, and contributing to the Portland metropolitan community"(www.psu.edu). Such coordination of a wide range of activities that support teaching and learning aims to simultaneously improve learning outcomes and enhance scholarship. The following list outlines some of the support available to faculty and graduate students since 1995:

- Community-based learning activities designed to support faculty in developing ongoing and reciprocal relationships with community organizations, businesses, and corporations, and to enhance faculty scholarship in community-based learning and capstone courses.
- Campus Carnegie Conversations, two-hour discussions held monthly, offering faculty members a venue in which to publicly address issues of teaching and learning. The series is part of the Carnegie Foundation's National Series on Teaching and Learning.
- The Scholarship of Teaching Resource Team, a group of faculty members and graduate students who meet monthly to support one another in the scholarship of teaching and the scholarship of engagement. This culminates in campuswide publication of their scholarly work and reflection.
- Scholarly Work in Progress (SWIP) sessions, which encourage faculty members and graduate students to share their "work in progress," get feedback from others, and hear about research support from experts on campus.
- The Engaged Department, an effort to increase community activities and scholarship of community engagement. CAE provided financial assistance to departments selected to participate.

CONCRETE OUTCOMES

Trying to find concrete outcomes from something as intangible as a cultural shift is difficult. An institution and its faculty can espouse values that serve as part of a vision more than as any concrete indicators of change. To address the degree of change in the culture, we interviewed individuals about how their personal opinions had changed and how they believed institutional procedures had changed.

CULTURE SHIFT: TURNING INTELLECTUAL CHANGES INTO COMMUNITY VALUES

The historical research on PSU and the interview data help address whether or not there was a cultural shift toward a new set of commonly held values regarding expanded forms of scholarship, and whether the new values had been woven into the institutional fabric. Interviewees offered a wide variety of responses to the question of whether a shift had occurred, ranging from "The adoption of the new guidelines required a shift in the administration [and] would require continued care in recruiting new administrators to fit into that culture," to "There had been no cultural shift because faculty are essentially being evaluated in the same way as before." Of the 28 interviewees, 12 (43 percent) provided statements indicating a shift toward values that support a broader definition of scholarship; 3 (11 percent) provided statements indicating no shift; 4 (14 percent) provided statements indicating a negative shift; and 9 (32 percent) did not indicate a direction. Several of those who did not indicate a direction were recent employees and therefore had no sense of culture change.

There were more interviewees who thought that there had been a positive cultural shift versus none at all; they were using new definitions of scholarship in hiring and faculty development activities. Their perception that there had been a cultural shift, whether or not they could prove it, allowed them to feel comfortable using the ideas associated with a wider definition of scholarship. Interviewees who believed there had been a culture shift said traditional researchers and scholars had bought into the new guidelines, more people were now willing to listen and consider areas outside their expertise, and the institution had matured as the shift allowed faculty to convert university resources into community resources.

With regard to respondents who indicated no shift in culture, it is possible they held pessimistic views about the likelihood of cultural shift, were generally resistant to change, or had not been on campus long enough to be able to ascertain a shift if any had occurred. Interviewees who believed there had not been a shift said it was really too soon to tell, or that any shift had not significantly changed the way faculty members are evaluated.

Respondents who indicated a negative direction held high expectations about the redefinition of scholarship that had not yet been met, but they were generally positive about the redefinition itself. They interpreted recent activities as a move backward from what they saw as the full potential of a redefinition of scholarship, and said they were afraid the culture was "swinging back toward the traditional model," with deans falling back on traditional criteria and new faculty members focusing more on tenure in their disciplines.

SHIFTS IN ACCEPTABLE PRODUCTS OF SCHOLARSHIP

Evidence from document analysis and interviews suggests that an expansion in the accepted products of scholarship is complementing the expansion in the definition of scholarship (to include teaching and community activities). However, the breadth of what is accepted as evidence of scholarship continues to vary by school or college. Scholarship products in some schools include different types of intellectual properties, and some faculty members and administrators question traditional definitions of "peer review." For example, one school considers the identification of the impact of scholarship on users as potentially more valuable than the evaluation of products by peers in traditional discipline-based journals.

The following emerged in the interviews as examples of "traditional" products and newly recognized scholarship products that are used today to evaluate scholarship at PSU: (1) traditional or disciplinary products, including peer-reviewed publications, peer-reviewed presentations, or projects that are grant funded; (2) documentation demonstrating that a scholar has used expertise to develop interdisciplinary curriculum plans or help shape department curriculum; (3) newly recognized products, including patents or software design, where the scholarly value may be measured by the impact on end users rather than traditional peer review; and (4) new types of measures for the quality and significance of faculty work that are independent of the form (these might include the value of the process of collaboration, significant community activities, or making a university resource into a community resource; the scholarly value of these activities may have to be judged by the promotion and tenure committee directly, rather than relying on external peer review).

Every PSU school and college has made the transition to the more inclusive and broader definition of scholarship. However, the products that are acceptable as evidence for scholarship vary. Traditional forms of scholarship are products that would be recognized within the discipline and have been widely accepted as indicators of intellectual contribution. The traditional forms in one discipline may not be recognized or understood by other disciplines. Although the schools have embraced the broader definition of scholarship, some seem to be more interested than others in looking for different types of evidence to use in evaluation. For example, there is interest in the College of Engineering and Computer Sciences to look for new products of scholarship that build in the evaluation of the impact on the user. A faculty-written software product might have built-in mechanisms for user evaluation that would be considered evidence of the value and quality of the faculty member's contribution to the field. This type of evidence could be used in addition to peer review.

Some interviewees suggested ways in which the schools and colleges could help promote new definitions of what contributes to scholarship. For example, the Graduate School of Education includes faculty contributions to curriculum development as scholarship; the contribution can be evaluated through built-in assessment. Interviews also suggested that some schools have not fully attended to the "burden of proof" issue for new forms and products of scholarship. Many interviewees stated that candidates need to justify and document new products, that is, that the burden of proof lies with them.

Several schools have tried to ease the potential risk of pursuing expanded forms of scholarship. The Graduate School of Education pays attention to the entire promotion and tenure process, from recruitment through promotion, and also engages the candidate's promotion and tenure committee in faculty development. Senior faculty in the Graduate College of Engineering and Computer Science are developing sample products as prototypes for nontenured faculty to use in their own promotion and tenure portfolios. The School of Fine and Performing Arts challenges the promotion and tenure committee to judge the future creative potential of candidates. While most of the schools do not espouse these novel interpretations of scholarly products or the new processes for implementing the guidelines, these examples represent development in the direction of expanding the definition of scholarship.

Variations in the Definition of Scholarship

The most striking outcome is that different and highly personal definitions of scholarship exist. When asked for a definition, each interviewee constructed a definition on the spot. Not one of the

28 interviewees relied on a stock definition. The most common components of a definition included "creating new knowledge," "dissemination to peers through publication or other product," and "contributing to a body of knowledge."

The responses are organized along a continuum divided into four levels (see Table 10.1). Level 1 represents people with a traditional focus on the discipline. Level 2 includes people who hold an expanded view of scholarship but would probably look for traditional, peer-reviewed products. Level 3 people are open to new products, but probably ones that are peer reviewed. Level 4 people feel that scholarship is a process that should be judged on quality; rather than being judged for their own value, products serve as a means to help evaluators understand the underlying value of the process. A few individuals gave responses that did not fit any level.

The interviewees were not asked to respond by these categories. Rather, the categories emerged from the interviews. The difference between Level 3 and Level 4 is that Level 3 still deals with products, whereas a Level 4 definition would open up the possibility of looking at the impact of an activity. The more restrictive end of this range would be more widely accepted, easier to judge fairly, and transportable to other institutions. The less restrictive definitions are more difficult to evaluate and less transportable outside of the institution.

These data indicate that the definition of scholarship that is used by 12 out of the 28 interviewees (43 percent) is consistent with developing new products for scholarship (even though only two schools were using this definition of scholarship at the time of the study). This suggests that there are obstacles to a broader acceptance of new products of scholarship. Among the interviewees, those with the highest-ranking appointments identified most often with Level 3. The two Level 1 definitions, which might be considered the most conservative, were provided by faculty members, not administrators. This is particularly interesting because many other faculty members interviewed thought the administration held more conservative views. In the context of progressing beyond scholarship to valuing and managing all the intangible assets of a university, the Level 4 definition is the most permissive and would attribute scholarship value to the most activities. Level 4 looks at the attributes of a scholar in action—or the process rather than the product. As Sveiby (1998) posited, "If we measure

TABLE 10.1 LEVELS AND DEFINITIONS OF SCHOLARSHIP

Level and Definition of Scholarship	Respondents (Number/Percentage of Total)	Example Statements
Level 1: Traditional definition	2/7%	Discovery of new knowledge and extension of existing knowledge in one's professional or academic domain (that is, traditional research with traditional peer-reviewed products)
Level 2: Expanded definition	8/29%	Discovery, application, transmission, and integration of knowledge with traditional, peer-reviewed products
Level 3: Expanded definition that includes new products	12/43%	Discovery, application, transmission, and integration of knowledge that is disseminated, uses appropriate methods, and is situated in a community of discourse
		Discovery, application, transmission, and integration of knowledge that directly impacts the discipline, practitioners, or members of the community who can use it (documented action and process as important as publications)
Level 4: Expanded definition that includes process and impact as well as products	2/7%	Contributions to the development of knowledge for the benefit of the discipline or a body of people who can use it
		Characteristics of a practitioner who reflects on the process of teaching, discovering, or applying knowledge, done as a public act
Respondents who did not fit into this scheme	4/14%	

the new with the tools of the old, we will not 'see' the new" (p. 220). PSU needs to consider creating and testing methods for understanding creative faculty work that focus on examining the work directly rather than relying on peer review, which by definition relies on an established community of scholars. Some valuable assets are created outside of these established communities and thus would not be measurable.

The interviews also revealed the need for a common definition for the term "scholarship of teaching." As one high-level administrator said, "There is still confusion over being a good teacher versus a reflective teacher." In the context of evaluation, this person would recognize the high value of good teaching but would only consider it scholarship if it were reflective and published. Several comments from faculty and staff members suggested that scholarship of teaching and learning may be evaluated using a fundamentally different process than traditional research. Whereas traditional research is evaluated mostly on the products, such as publications, the evaluation of the scholarship of teaching may rely on evaluation of processes.

EXTERNAL VALIDATION OF AN EXPANDED DEFINITION OF SCHOLARSHIP

The national, external community recognizes the significant changes undertaken at PSU. In 1994, the *Journal of General Education* devoted an entire issue to PSU's general education reform, with a lead article by Charles White (1994). Several years later, in 1997, the university received the National Pew Leadership for Education Reform Award. Representatives from hundreds of campuses have made site visits, and many campuses have adopted forms of PSU's general education program. The W. K. Kellogg Foundation invited PSU to become part of a 26-campus consortium, the Urban University of the 21st Century; in 2002, PSU received one of the Hesburgh certificates of merit from TIAA-CREF; and in 2003, *U.S. News and World Report* ranked PSU as one of the top 10 schools for student learning communities, service-learning, and senior capstones (*U.S. News and World Report,* 2003). These awards and recognition confirm what PSU has to offer to the national discussion.

Lessons Learned: Looking Back Before Leaping Forward

This chapter has four main conclusions. First, PSU went through a transition that led to growth through scholarship, not governance. The university applied a scholarly approach to its own internal change process and created a new vision and implementation of scholarship, general education, and community partnership. This can be seen as an act of institutional *cognition*. Varela, Thompson, and Rosh (1999) define *cognition* as "embodied action" (p. 172) or an enactment that results in a new version "from a background of understanding" (p. 149). Maturana and Varela's (1992) definition states that cognition is "an ongoing bringing forth of a world through the process of living itself" (p. 11). Interpreting the activities that led to the expanded definition of scholarship as examples of institutional cognition is important, because cognition requires more than thought; it requires action. At the same time that the faculty was involved in discussing its roles, it was also creating and implementing general education reform. This sparked new conversations about involvement in teaching and service, which in turn influenced concurrent conversations about the definition of scholarship.

Second, the expanded forms of scholarship helped the faculty and administration identify intangible assets. In applying the rigorous approaches associated with scholarship to projects at PSU, the university was able to leverage valuable assets and make them more effective in meeting institutional goals. With the broadened locus of scholarship, more value was placed on activities already undertaken by the faculty—PSU simply found a way to acknowledge its intangible assets. Though faculty members lacked a common name for it, many were already involved in the scholarship of teaching, classroom research, and the scholarship of engagement. For example, many faculty members, departments, and schools had built networks of professional collaborations in the Portland metropolitan area, but had not identified these efforts as related to scholarship. Making these intangible assets visible also allowed them to be better managed. PSU is continuing efforts to more effectively assess the impact of these assets on all stakeholders.

Third, PSU is still undergoing the transformative process of expanding the definition of scholarship. There is a range of acceptance across the institution regarding the expanded forms of scholarship. Some schools are committed to using traditional products and processes in their faculty evaluation, whereas others are developing new products of scholarship and even new definitions of the impact of scholarship.

Finally, departments, colleges, and the university itself are all involved in projects that may improve understanding about scholarly impacts. This, in turn, should lead to deeper and broader understanding of traditional scholarship, the scholarship of teaching, and the scholarship of engagement.

IMPLICATIONS FOR OTHER CAMPUSES

Four characteristics of PSU's change process may be useful for other campuses as they attempt to broaden the definition of scholarship used in institutional policy and practice.

1. *Increase open dialogue.* Throughout our deliberations, PSU faculty and administrators joined in national conversations about scholarship sponsored by AAHE, the Carnegie Foundation, and others. This exposed campus constituents to new ideas. In addition, campus leaders worked to ensure that all faculty members, deans, and administrators had opportunities to discuss and consider promotion and tenure changes. Thus, there was almost universal buy-in. Cultural shifts can occur when there are enough people in responsible positions to affect change. In Inglehart's (1990) mobilization model, the general public participates in change even though it holds no formal leadership roles. According to Inglehart, an elite group will increase in an institution owing to generational shifts and the normal promotion of people into positions with more responsibility. Within PSU, many senior faculty participated in the promotion and tenure policy changes even though they weren't administrators. These senior faculty, many of whom had been hired during the activist 1960s, understood the importance of this shift in the definition of scholarship. They had

the skills to cause change because of their experiences at PSU. Ramaley (2000) claims that if only one-third of the faculty agrees that an idea is legitimate, there can be "substantive changes in the intellectual environment and values of an institution" (p. 9). PSU benefited twice from this change: first, from the actual change in the guidelines, and, second, from developing an institutionally embedded process for change. The second benefit is an asset that has led to a more adaptable institution.

2. *Support new learning.* During our change process, the campus created the Center for Academic Excellence, which supports scholarly activities as well as offering a venue for producing scholarship. Having a campus "home" that supports these conversations and their ultimate implementation is key to success.

3. *Take risks.* Another crucial aspect in the process that redefined scholarship at PSU is that the transition contained an element of risk. Obviously, the nature of the risks will vary by institution, but risk taking as a process is crucial to innovation in faculty roles and rewards.

4. *Reward innovation.* One of the main reasons the campus expanded its definition of scholarship was to be able to confer faculty rewards in different areas. During the process of moving toward these new definitions, the president and provost demonstrated the institution's commitment to rewarding innovation by supporting faculty activities that generated new ideas, such as teaching with technology or creating new general education curricula and courses. It was important that the administration found ways to support activities that were new or on the cutting edge of a discipline. This support helped innovative faculty members to thrive and encouraged their more hesitant colleagues to develop and adopt innovations as well. It was a tangible means of spreading the reform.

All of the characteristics are portable. Any institution that wants to engage in a discussion about broadening the promotion and tenure guidelines to include a broader definition of scholarship would likely be able to bring in the national discussion, engage participation from all levels, and support innovation from the highest levels.

CURRENT STATUS AND FUTURE QUESTIONS

PSU is now asking hard questions as it enters the second generation of reform. Should faculty in departments that have not embraced the broader definition be encouraged to take part in teaching and engagement scholarship? Will this effort to broaden the forms of scholarship still be relevant if universities rely more heavily on fixed-term and adjunct faculty? Are the standards rigorous enough for evaluating newer forms of scholarship? Have the reforms cost PSU anything in faculty turnover, prestige, or national ranking? These questions and their answers are both testing and invigorating our academic culture and its ability to sustain multiple forms of scholarly work.

References

Boyer, E. L. (1990). *Scholarship reconsidered: Priorities of the professoriate.* Princeton, NJ: Carnegie Foundation for the Advancement of Teaching.

Dodds, G. B. (2000). *The college that would not die: The first fifty years of Portland State University, 1946–1996.* Portland: Oregon Historical Society Press.

Inglehart, R. (1990). *Culture shift in advanced industrial society.* Princeton, NJ: Princeton University Press.

Inglehart, R. (1997). *Modernization and postmodernization: Culture, economic, and political change in 43 societies.* Princeton, NJ: Princeton University Press.

Maturana, H. R., & Varela, F. (1992). *The tree of knowledge: The biological roots of human understanding.* Boston: Shambhala.

Ramaley, J. A. (2000). Embracing civic responsibility. *AAHE Bulletin, 52*(7): 9.

Shulock, N. B., & Ketcheson, K. (2000). Two approaches to assessing the metropolitan university mission. *Metropolitan Universities, 10*(4): 63–72.

Sveiby, K. (1997). *The new organizational wealth: Managing and measuring knowledge-based assets.* San Francisco: Berrett-Koehler.

Sveiby, K. (1998). *Measuring intangibles and intellectual capital—An emerging first standard.* Retrieved August 18, 2003, from http://www.sveiby.com/articles/EmergingStandard.html

Tetreault, M., & Ketcheson, K. (2002). Creating a shared understanding of institutional knowledge through an electronic institutional portfolio. *Metropolitan Universities, 13*(3): 40–49.

U.S. News and World Report. (2003). *America's best colleges, 2003 edition.* Washington, DC: Author.

Varela, F. J., Thompson, E., & Rosh, E. (1999). *The embodied mind: Cognitive science and human experience.* Cambridge: MIT Press.

White, C. R. (1994). A model for comprehensive reform in general education: Portland State University. *Journal of General Education, 43*(3): 168–229.

CHAPTER ELEVEN

SIGNS OF CHANGE AT A RESEARCH-EXTENSIVE UNIVERSITY

Promoting the Scholarship
of Teaching and Learning at
Arizona State University

Don Evans, Judy Grace, and Duane Roen

INSTITUTIONAL CONTEXT

Arizona State University (ASU) consists of three campuses dispersed within metropolitan Phoenix: Main Campus in Tempe; West Campus in northwest Phoenix, near Glendale; and East Campus in southeast Mesa. In addition, the Extended Campus, which is administered from ASU's Downtown Center and involves faculty from all three campuses, is situated in downtown Phoenix. In fall 2002, the total enrollment for the three campuses was 55,491 students (Auffret, 2002, p. 1). In 1994, ASU achieved Research I status, and it holds Research Extensive status in the current (2000) Carnegie classification system. The university was among 12 campuses selected for the *Newsweek* magazine list of "America's Hot Schools" for 2002–2003 (www.asu.edu). Today, ASU is recruiting the very best students and most renowned scholars—not only because of the Arizona weather, but also because of the reputation of its academic programs and research centers.

CHANGING THE CULTURE
AROUND TEACHING

Many scholars have used the concept of paradigm shift, since Thomas Kuhn introduced it in 1962, to explain change in scores of fields, including many beyond the realm of the physical and life sciences (Kuhn, 1970). Although there must be caution in using Kuhn's framework to explain change in the academic reward system at ASU, certain features seem readily applicable. Among them is Kuhn's concept of normal science, defined as "research firmly based upon one or more past scientific achievements, achievements that some particular scientific community acknowledges for a time as supplying the foundation for its further practice" (p. 10). Paralleling Kuhn's normal science is philosopher Richard Rorty's (1979) concept of normal discourse, defined as "that which is conducted within an agreed-upon set of conventions about what counts as a relevant contribution, what counts as answering a question, what counts as having a good argument for that answer or a good criticism of it." He goes on to note that "abnormal discourse is what happens when someone joins in the discourse who is ignorant of these conventions or who sets them aside" (p. 320).

The normal discourse about promotion and tenure at ASU for the last two decades of the 20th century valorized the features of Research I universities as the old Carnegie classification system defined them—a heavy emphasis on traditional research and discovery, and the external funding supporting such a mission. That emphasis led to ASU's achieving Research I status in 1994. In 1999, ASU's then president, Lattie F. Coor, noted, "Our focal point for strengthening this campus and our design for the future is to continue building our overall profile as a leading, growing, competitive research university" (Billingsley, 1999). An increase in the number of research awards during the 1990s reflected the institution's commitment to external funding. In 1992, ASU was awarded $54.5 million in external funding, and that number increased to $122.8 million by 2001 (Vice President for Research and Economic Affairs, 2001). The strong focus on achieving and maintaining Research I status sometimes overshadowed conversations about other aspects of its mission—most important, teaching.

This chapter examines the forces that contributed to a change in the normal discourse around scholarship at ASU. Specifically, it explores how a large research university began to focus more attention on effective teaching, scholarly teaching, and the scholarship of teaching. At ASU, internal forces for change arose at the grassroots level and were driven and supported by the administration. Highly visible efforts, able to draw funding and sustain dialogue over a significant period of time, show the evolution in a change process that actually occurred as a dynamic interchange between many segments of the institution. We explore how an interdisciplinary collaborative, ASU's Center for Research on Education in Science, Mathematics, Engineering, and Technology (CRESMET), acted as a catalyst in changing the larger institutional discourse on teaching scholarship. Further, we reflect on ASU's process for changing its promotion and tenure guidelines as a result of the broader cultural changes happening around the subject of scholarship.

External Forces for Change

Although ASU remains strongly committed to its research mission, both external and internal factors have encouraged it to generate more discourse about its teaching mission during the past half-decade. At the national level, changes in the Carnegie classification system in 2000 expanded the descriptors for research universities. Under the new Carnegie system, ASU falls into the category of Doctoral/Research Universities-Extensive. The change in designation is important because it subtly modifies the role of research. For institutions such as ASU, the new designation helps focus more attention on the effects and benefits of research and slightly less on the quantity of external funding. The shift is evident in the opening paragraph of the 2001 "Annual Sponsored Projects Report" from the vice provost for research. It emphasizes the direct influence of research on students: "As a major public institution of higher education it is imperative that Arizona State University seek ways to enhance the educational experience of students. Research and other sponsored project activity serves as a major contributor to this endeavor by providing new ideas to faculty and state-of-the-art equipment to the classrooms and laboratories. These grants and contracts also provided 2,550 ASU graduate and undergraduate students with student employment opportunities with wage/salary payments" (Vice President for Research and Economic Affairs, 2001).

Many researchers, policymakers, and organizations have championed the scholarship of teaching and learning during the last two decades of the 20th century, including the Carnegie Foundation for the Advancement of Teaching, the U.S. Department of Education, the Pew Charitable Trusts, the American Association for Higher Education (AAHE), the National Center for Higher Education Management Systems (NCHEMS), and more recently and locally, the Arizona Board of Regents. While Lee Shulman, president of the Carnegie Foundation for the Advancement of Teaching, contends that the paradigm shift of focusing on the scholarship of teaching and learning is difficult, because "those who engage in innovative acts of teaching rarely build upon the work of others" (Shulman, n.d.), the efforts of the individuals and groups noted have been responsible for making teaching more visible both inside and outside the academy.

McLean and Callarman (2002) described the process by which the Arizona Board of Regents prescribed post-tenure review for faculty at all three state universities in 1996. Because post-tenure review at ASU focused more attention on teaching and especially on undergraduate education, it also prompted some interest in rewarding faculty who teach effectively.

External forces, such as national and state conversations about faculty responsibilities, have broadly affected ASU's practices and policies and fostered notable pockets of public discussion on effective teaching. Additionally, efforts in discipline-specific societies have encouraged institutions in the past decade to develop better models for assessing and rewarding teaching as scholarship.

INTERNAL FORCES FOR CHANGE: CRESMET AND ACEPT

During the past 10 years, forces within ASU also fostered change in how the campus community thinks about and rewards teaching. For example, CRESMET is an alliance of ASU's colleges of Education, Engineering and Applied Sciences, and Liberal Arts and Sciences. Its establishment as a university-wide center in 1995 was an outgrowth of a National Science Foundation (NSF)–funded program to improve the delivery of the science and mathematics courses that education majors take to fulfill their degrees and Arizona's teacher certification requirements. The Arizona Collaborative for Excellence in the Preparation of Teachers (ACEPT), one of several NSF-sponsored state teacher collaboratives, was a joint effort of several institutions of higher education and a large number of K–12 schools in the state to implement science and mathematics education reforms to produce better K–12 teachers. Reform of K–12 science and mathematics education and teacher preparation programs has become a national pursuit, for many reasons.

The ACEPT program and the Arizona teacher collaborative recognized that the courses in which ASU's education majors were learning science and mathematics were traditional in their delivery: 50-minute, "talking-head" lectures, with instructor-modeled problem solving in recitation sections and "canned" experiments in laboratories. These elements seemed antithetical to national model teaching and learning standards for K–12. If new teachers were to implement inquiry-based instruction in K–12 classrooms, as suggested by national leaders (National Council of Teachers of Mathematics, 2000; National Research Council, 1995), they had to see inquiry-based science and mathematics instruction modeled in their courses. The paradigm for university teaching in these courses began to change.

The way in which the ACEPT program prompted a change in the traditional teaching paradigm offered one possible model for other ASU programs to use. CRESMET's goals included continuing to expand an inquiry-based model in teacher education courses in science, technology, engineering, and mathematics (STEM) programs at ASU, promoting the model in courses for majors in STEM disciplines at ASU, and promoting the model in STEM disciplines at other institutions. CRESMET's staff believed that this inquiry-based teaching could be a catalyst for enhancing the scholarship of teaching across all colleges at ASU.

Although CRESMET is intended to be more research- than outreach-oriented, it has sustained faculty development efforts begun in ACEPT. Thus, CRESMET shares faculty development responsibilities with the Center for Learning and Teaching Excellence, a university-level outreach organization. The two centers have held workshops and retreats on topics such as active and cooperative learning, visualization in the digital age, and distance learning.

BUILDING A LEARNING COMMUNITY OF EDUCATION SCHOLARS

After being involved with several systemic reform efforts, including the ACEPT program, one of the CRESMET associate directors and his coauthors reached the profoundly simple conclusion that "partnerships build reform" (Middleton, Sawada, Judson, Bloom, & Turley, 2002). This principle underlies the concept of a learning community—learning experiences that are linked or clustered around a theme or topic for a cohort of individuals. Vast numbers of research studies have shown that learning communities are highly effective in supporting pursuits ranging from treating substance abuse to mustering citizen-based referendums, to teaching cohort classes in education.

One of CRESMET's prime goals is to maintain a learning community of scholars. Because its initiatives and activities are highly interdisciplinary, CRESMET's director has forged lasting partnerships with other support units on campus. In one such relationship, CRESMET and ASU's Center for Learning and Teaching Excellence have initiated campus discussions about the scholarship of teaching and learning, including numerous faculty workshops. In addition, CRESMET plans and sponsors activities aimed at bringing together education scholars in STEM fields for discussions and renewal. Activities have included a semester-long, weekly seminar attended by approximately 30 faculty members, most of whom came from STEM disciplines. CRESMET faculty members also met in a daylong poster symposium to share their ongoing research on teaching and learning. Another semester, CRESMET faculty members met weekly on the topic of partnering with K–12 schools. Throughout the year, CRESMET faculty members attend periodic brownbag lunches featuring national and international specialists in STEM education.

Developing Better Assessment Techniques

During the first two years of the five-year funded program, ACEPT participants realized that although they believed their "reformed" classroom methods were effective, they were not using assessments that would allow their beliefs to be verified in any consistent manner. The program hired a full-time assessment expert to address this omission. The resulting assessment technique became one of the program's greatest legacies. In what is called the "Reformed Teacher Observation Protocol" (RTOP), trained observers relate what a teacher does in the classroom to facilitate student learning. Details on the RTOP can be found in Sawada et al. (2002).

Applying the ACEPT-CRESMET Model of ASU to Faculty Development

The experience gained in the ACEPT program and several other funded, multiyear projects that ultimately grew into CRESMET provides evidence that it takes three to five years for a faculty member to transit from a traditional, teacher-centered paradigm to a learner-centered paradigm where the faculty member's primary role is to facilitate student learning. This transition is the key factor in moving from effective teaching to the scholarship of teaching.

Furthermore, enacting the scholarship of teaching can take more than five years. The faculty member needs appropriately staged faculty development, support from peers pursuing similar goals, encouragement and reassurance from the department administration, and perhaps a waiver on having student evaluations used in the annual review process. The last is often necessary to lower the risk for instructors who incorporate learner-centered instructional techniques in their classrooms. Students subjected to these new learning environments have often had 12 or more years of teacher-centered instruction as their only model for good instruction. Many of them expect "good" instructors to provide all the reasoning, all the data, and all the answers—in short, to do all the work involved in learning. They often resent having to take initiative and responsibility for their own learning—as is expected in inquiry-based environments—and they often voice this resentment in anonymous student evaluations of the instructor.

The idea of appropriately staged intervention (in this case, faculty development) is a change management technique that academe shares with the business world. E. M. Rogers (1995), writing about the business world, identifies five stages of innovation: knowledge, persuasion, decision, implementation, confirmation. How rapidly a person moves through these stages depends on a number of factors. Typically, approximately 15 percent of people—the adventuresome and early adopters—easily and quickly transition through the stages. Another 35 percent move more slowly and deliberately through the stages, while the final 50 percent—which includes skeptics—are more resistant.

A one-size-fits-all faculty development model will not move people through all five stages of the innovation-decision process. Those in Stage 2 will require different types of faculty development than those in Stage 4, for example. That is why workshops have a poor record of driving change, unless a good program supports attendees as they continue to move through the process. Without this support, a large fraction of attendees will regress.

The Campus Study

In spring 2002, ASU applied to AAHE for a grant to examine the degree to which CRESMET's and similar teaching-centered efforts at ASU had moved the predominantly research culture closer to one that discusses, supports, and rewards the scholarship of teaching. Specifically, the authors wanted to know:

1. Are there signs of change in our institutional initiatives and commitments?
2. Are there signs of change in our formal reward structure?
3. Are there signs of change in our discourse and culture (for example, in how participants are talking about teaching and experiencing the culture around teaching or scholarship)?

In order to better understand these issues, we looked for evidence of change in several places. The ACEPT evaluator examined the effectiveness of ACEPT programs and activities. We examined:

(1) major teaching initiatives that have developed since 1995, (2) evidence of more visible conversations about teaching and the scholarship of teaching and learning on campus, and (3) promotion and tenure policy changes related to teaching. Finally, we interviewed constituents across ASU's campuses.

SIGNS OF CHANGE: INSTITUTIONAL INITIATIVES AND COMMITMENTS

ACEPT-Sponsored Activities

At the conclusion of the five-year ACEPT project, the campus commissioned Michael Lang of the Maricopa County Community College District to investigate the overall project and its outcomes (Lang, 1999). His draft report includes summaries of interviews and surveys conducted to ascertain the perceptions of the success of the ACEPT team and its leadership abilities. Among other things, he noted that regular communication among project participants had developed a cohesive vision of ACEPT's goals, as well as a sense of inclusion among stakeholders.

ACEPT faculty members had a long history of working together, which helped establish a clear vision of how to approach curriculum reforms and contributed to their ability to quickly initiate and implement their goals to better prepare science and mathematics teachers. As a result, ACEPT team members were seen by other faculty as having high credibility, by "walking the talk" of reform practices and modeling collaboration through their own curriculum activities. The team's justification for change was based upon research on instructional practices, and members modeled a new attitude of experimentation and risk taking in their own instructional practices. They capitalized on the diversity of faculty from all partnering institutions, and with their commitment achieved sustainable reformed curricula. In addition, ACEPT Summer Faculty Workshops established learning communities among participants as well as with the ACEPT team members.

External evaluators reported that ACEPT reforms had affected more than 80 percent of the participating faculty by 1999; that the learning curve for participants for a transition to the scholarship of teaching ranged from three to seven years; and that community acceptance for such changes required a "synergism of intellectual, social and political skills" (ACEPT, 2002, p. 15). Evaluators also observed that there was more work to do in aligning the reward system with scholarly teaching practices.

Summer and Winter Institutes

In addition to evaluating ACEPT-sponsored programs, the authors looked for signs of a positive environment for the scholarship of teaching in university-wide initiatives and programs. Each May and June since 2000, several of the teaching and learning support offices have collaborated to offer ASU's Summer Institute on College Teaching, which includes approximately 12 one-week courses. Each December and January, the same groups offer the ASU Winter Institute on College Teaching, which includes two or three one-week courses during the intersession period between fall and spring semesters. Although learner-centered education is not the most prominent feature of every course in the institutes, reviews of course syllabi, lessons, and evaluations suggest that the learner-centered education theme has a substantial influence on the majority of the courses.

In these courses, faculty from ASU and the Maricopa County Community College District focus on using learning goals as the foundations for teaching and assessment. Between summer 2000 and summer 2002, the institute registration numbers grew from 63 to 145 participants.

ENCOURAGEMENT FROM THE ARIZONA BOARD OF REGENTS

The Arizona Board of Regents has emphasized learner-centered education for the past few years, as exemplified by a Web site devoted to principles and examples of learner-centered education. The regents' vision stresses active learning, assessment, access, and workforce development. ASU's Center for Learning and Teaching Excellence, with a good deal of influence from CRESMET, has contributed to that Web site (Arizona Board of Regents, 2003).

In April 2002, the regents awarded ASU, Northern Arizona University, and the University of Arizona a $100,000 grant to engage the faculty in learner-centered practices, especially the use of goals to design active learning and assessment in their courses.

Forty-five faculty members and six teaching assistants from all three universities revised their courses. The enthusiasm for the project was so great that the participants initiated conversations in their home departments, encouraging their colleagues to engage in similar reform. Some have even worked on group grant proposals to expand the project to include more faculty. Further, in December 2003, the Arizona Board of Regents awarded the three universities another $100,000 to continue the work.

UNIVERSITY-WIDE CONVERSATIONS AND LEVELS OF PARTICIPATION

With assistance from AAHE and the Carnegie Foundation for the Advancement of Teaching, as well as financial support from the Office of the Provost, ASU held university-wide conversations about the scholarship of teaching and learning in January 2002. Among those joining the discussion that day were Mary Taylor Huber, a senior scholar at the Carnegie Foundation; Patricia Hutchings, codirector of the Higher Education Program of the Carnegie Academy for the Scholarship of Teaching and Learning; and two Carnegie Foundation scholars. At a luncheon meeting for academic chairs and assistant and associate deans at all three campuses, the guests discussed strategies for using the scholarship of teaching and learning in promotion and tenure policies and procedures. Later that day, they engaged the same group of administrators, as well as faculty, in conversations about the topic.

As an indication of interest in teaching and learning, in the 2001–2002 fiscal year, more than 1,200 faculty members and teaching assistants participated in activities sponsored by ASU's Center for Learning and Teaching Excellence and CRESMET. One of the most salient signs that the culture is changing is that, in spring 2002, the university finished designing the ASU Distinguished Teaching Academy. Among other things, the academy honors and supports faculty engaged in effective teaching, scholarly teaching, and particularly the scholarship of teaching. For years, ASU has awarded Regents Professorships, which strongly favor faculty with stellar national or international records in research or creative activity. The establishment of the ASU Distinguished Teaching Academy is evidence of an equally strong commitment to teaching. The academy received a jumpstart in October 2002, when the ASU Parents Association offered a $10,000 gift to support its activities.

As part of the current study, we asked academic deans and chairs about teaching awards for faculty in their colleges and departments. Of the 21 departments and colleges responding, most indicated they had added teaching awards in the past five years. As a result of this survey of administrators (and with encouragement from ASU's new president), we began compiling a complete list of teaching awards and will maintain a Web site to house it.

Finally, another indication of the growing interest in the scholarship of teaching is the frequency with which the phrase "scholarship of teaching" appears on ASU Web sites. It has appeared more frequently with each passing month during the past three years: for example, in December 2002, it appeared on 2,580 ASU sites, up from 2,170 only four months earlier.

Criteria for Promotion and Tenure and University Culture

In fall 1999, the vice provost for academic personnel established the Tenure and Promotion Policy Review Task Force to draft new guidelines for promotion and tenure. Milton Glick , executive vice president and provost, identified the key reasons for seeking a change in policies. He noted that while there was much rhetoric about the importance and the beneficial interaction of teaching, research, and service, "policy and practice seldom keep up with the rhetoric, especially with regard to promotion and tenure" (personal communication, July 2, 2002). It was therefore vital to bring policy and rhetoric into alignment, a task made difficult by several factors. To begin with, the measurement of research quality and impact was better understood than the measurement of teaching and service. Then there was the question of whether faculty members prepared to critique a colleague's research might not find it hard to critique teaching or service. "We also have a far greater differentiation in both quality and quantity between our best and worst researchers than between our best and worst teachers," Glick wrote, "which reduces our ability to make distinctions." At ASU, he argued, the goal was to raise the bar, certainly, but also to broaden it to encompass additional methods for gaining promotion while setting a higher level of expectation: "We also recognize that a workload distribution of 40 percent research, 40 percent teaching, 20 percent service is a fiction and that we need to recognize different profiles of faculty but within the context that we must not grant tenure to any faculty who are not outstanding teachers and researchers."

During fall 2000, the task force engaged the campus community in face-to-face and online discussions about the draft guidelines, discussions in which CRESMET faculty members actively participated. The conversations evoked a range of issues and concerns, among them whether the institution was ready to focus on teaching to the desired extent; how to evaluate teaching in the best and fairest way; how to place greater emphasis on teaching while continuing a strong research focus; and the extent to which the scholarship of teaching and learning could constitute legitimate research and be valued by all departments and faculty.

The Academic Senate, consisting of faculty members from across the institution, discussed revisions to the draft during the 2000–2001 and 2002–2003 academic years, and the institution began implementation. The senate's recommendations contained concrete and specific language showing wide support for the culture shift (Academic Senate, 2002; Promotion and Tenure Task Force, 2001). The changes included a statement that efforts to establish a national reputation should not be limited to research and creative activity. The senate balanced this statement with another to the effect that expecting excellence in teaching should not be understood as diminishing excellence in research and creative activity. It declared, also, that the pursuit of excellence and full engagement were required in all activities and assignments "so that all contributions toward achieving the university mission are appropriately considered," and it noted the desirability of establishing "common evidentiary elements" for evaluating faculty work. Faculty should be evaluated according to several measures of teaching effectiveness, the senate advised, and it was important to have peer review of teaching materials and the development of "learning environments." It stressed the need for "high quality evidence and documentation" in each area and stated that "the scholarship of teaching and learning will be valued."

PARTICIPATING IN THE
AAHE SUMMER ACADEMY

A seven-member team from all three campuses participated in an AAHE Summer Academy in July 2002. The team focused on strategies for evaluating teaching within ASU's revised promotion and tenure guidelines—guidelines that are flexible enough to meet the needs of departments and colleges with different missions and emphases. First, the team developed strategies for the peer review of teaching as well as the self-critique of teaching. While the campus will probably continue to use some form of student evaluation of teaching, leaders plan to augment that with other kinds of evaluation to achieve triangulation. Effective peer evaluation and self-critique can also do much to encourage conversations about teaching within and among departments.

Second, the team has developed strategies that offer greater flexibility in promotion to full professor. For example, a faculty member could be promoted based on a strong record of effective teaching (leading to substantial learning), scholarly teaching (grounded in the sources and resources of the discipline), and the scholarship of teaching, where, as Lee Shulman (2000) notes, "our work as teachers becomes public, peer-reviewed and critiqued, and exchanged with other members of our professional communities so they, in turn, can build on our work" (p. 49). Although full implementation of the guidelines will take several years, all departments have developed plans for including the peer review of teaching.

SIGNS OF CHANGE IN DISCOURSE AND
CULTURE: NARRATIVES FROM THE GROUND

Participant narratives can yield a good deal of information about cultural change. We asked a cross-section of ASU's administration and faculty to share experiences with institutional change, and we offer the following excerpts to capture the essence of their responses.

A REGENTS' PROFESSOR'S VIEW

Regents' Professor Jane Maienschein has a dual appointment in the departments of philosophy and biology. Noting some of the changes that had occurred since she arrived at ASU in 1981, she observed that upon receiving the College of Liberal Arts and Sciences Teaching Award (in a "quite lame" ceremony) after the first full year of her appointment, she was treated to remarks from peers such as "Too bad, now you won't get tenure." The winners of teaching awards, and indeed anyone who paid serious attention to teaching undergraduates, never got tenure, or so she was told informally by colleagues. Yet today, two decades later, she and another winner that year were still on the faculty, suggesting that the common wisdom had been wrong. Indeed, since those days there had been a major change in "climate and values," and junior faculty who won teaching awards were enthusiastically supported by their colleagues and gained the sense of being recognized for something important: "The message today is that it is possible to care and even care passionately about teaching and still be a serious researcher and professional." In both departments where she has an appointment, recent decisions about retention, tenure, and promotion to full professor "have looked seriously at teaching as part of the profile of excellence."

A Perspective From Biology

Allison Whitmer, manager of the Undergraduate Biology Enrichment Program, offers the following perspective on a culture of support regarding the scholarship of teaching at ASU, over the past five years: "I had the good fortune of becoming a member of the Department of Biology in 1999. . . . The positive attitude about educating students does much more than provide a comfortable environment for its faculty. The focus on teaching and student learning at ASU has been instrumental in our ability to procure extramural funding for our projects . . . which has allowed us to continue our scholarship in science education."

A Dean's Perspective

Anne Schneider, Dean of the College of Public Programs, observes that change is occurring in practices: "Some of the colleges (certainly ours) have already insisted on quality teaching and have done so by stressing this during the second- and fourth-year reviews—well before a tenure decision is made. We tell faculty that student evaluations are a solid indication of whether the students are receptive to their teaching style and material. We stress that peer review of their syllabi and materials indicates whether the course is current, scholarly, and relevant to the curriculum."

THE VIEW OF THE PRESIDENT OF THE ACADEMIC SENATE

Many senior faculty leaders have said that the new emphasis will encourage a renewed focus on the scholarship of teaching. The 2002–2003 president of ASU's Academic Senate, George Watson, is optimistic:

> I have high hopes that the new promotion and tenure guidelines will effectively address a considerable number of issues extant under the old system. Previous guidelines did not provide adequate recognition for teaching and service. The new guidelines elevate the teaching enterprise and expand the realm of recognized service work. The consequence is not intended to provide less emphasis on research, but a greater recognition of the importance of effective teaching from all of our tenured and tenure-track faculty. . . . I see considerable progress over the past decade regarding teaching here at ASU along a number of dimensions. Renaming the faculty development office as the Center for Learning and Teaching Excellence symbolizes the increased attention given to the teaching and learning process on campus. Moreover, an increase in the resources of the center and a concomitant increase in its service to the academic community also represent progress. There is much more that could be detailed, but certainly these highlights stand as beacons that have been shining more of our light on the teaching and learning enterprise.

A VIEW FROM EAST CAMPUS

The culture at ASU-East, the institution's newest campus in the metropolitan Phoenix area, fosters a strong commitment to teaching and learning—especially in applied sciences and engineering. Barry Maid, who joined the faculty several years ago, offers these comments:

> My experience in more than 20 years as a tenure-track or tenured faculty member is that institutions of higher education all talk much about teaching but don't always show that teaching is really

valued on campus. I think we can tell much about how a campus really values teaching by examining who does it and how it is rewarded. Since coming to ASU-East in January 2000, I have observed that almost everyone teaches. It is simply what we do. It's part of the campus culture. Administrators teach. So, listening to our new president, Michael Crow, say "Teaching is our prime directive" indicates that the highest levels of administration are asserting what is already occurring at Arizona State University.

THE VIEW FROM THE PRESIDENT

Michael Crow became ASU's president on July 1, 2002. He offers another strong indication—perhaps the strongest yet—that the culture is changing. In an address to the academic chairs and associate and assistant deans at their annual retreat in August 2002, he offered a vision for ASU that he has reiterated often since then, in settings ranging from the university-wide meeting of the Academic Assembly to the weekly newspaper for faculty and staff. Among other things, he stated, "We are teachers first and foremost" (September 5, 2002). He also articulated four principles for the university, which further emphasize the importance of teaching, scholarly teaching, and the scholarship of teaching (September 16, 2002, p. 6):

1. Teaching is our prime directive. We are teachers. I am a teacher; you are teachers; the institution is a teacher. I can't think of anything more important than that. That is the prime directive.
2. Scholarship is our pathway to better teaching. Scholarship, in whatever form each of us takes it, is essential to the quality of our teaching. There's a whole range of things that scholarship means, but all of us must be creatively engaged in pushing back the edges of whatever it is we do if we hope to be great teachers.
3. If teaching is our prime directive, creative expression in all forms is our highest goal. We have a responsibility to be creative.
4. We must be an institution built around openness and access to our learning environment for all. Whatever we're doing, the energy we create, the creativity that we stimulate, the teaching we do, if we sequester it, hold it inside, or wall it off, it's greatly diminished.

PROSPECTS FOR THE FUTURE

In an era of rapid institutional growth but shrinking state resources and support for higher education, ASU must be strategic in fulfilling its mission of teaching, research, and service. It must seize the opportunity to enhance the teaching portion of its mission and integrate teaching and research (the scholarship of teaching and discovery) in synergistic and symbiotic ways. Campus constituents are optimistic that the work done thus far can result in such synergy and symbiosis.

Although it will take some time to know whether the project has succeeded, the university will realize the extent of success when language about teaching and learning appears in department and college promotion and tenure procedures in the next few years. Of course, campus leaders will understand the degree of success even more fully when specific promotion and tenure cases come up for review. While some departments and colleges may change their procedures relatively quickly, some units may take longer. Still, there are already indications of changes in how departments evaluate teaching. For instance, a growing number of department Web sites include new procedures for the peer review of teaching—something that was relatively rare a year or two ago.

In the short run, campus leaders plan to offer workshops, conversations, Web resources, and print resources for departments and colleges as they prepare for change. Participation will provide some indication of success in stimulating the scholarship of teaching and learning. In the long run, plans are to collect further data to document change in the initiatives, promotion and tenure decisions, and campus discourse and culture.

LESSONS LEARNED

We began this chapter by examining the forces that contributed to cultural change within one institution. We explored how a large research university began to focus more attention on effective teaching, scholarly teaching, and the scholarship of teaching. We explored how an interdisciplinary collaborative, CRESMET, acted as a catalyst in changing the larger institutional picture around faculty involvement in, understanding of, and rewards for teaching scholarship. Finally, we reflected on the process for changing promotion and tenure guidelines—the primary means for systematically addressing faculty roles and rewards.

There are many lessons to be learned from ASU's experience. As any basic management textbook would note, leadership plays a most important role. While leadership by ASU's president and provost was essential, faculty leaders, such as members of the Academic Assembly and heads of large research centers, also had important roles. Funding associated with the centers helped to sustain the efforts long enough to establish broad faculty participation and gather and document information about enhanced student learning outcomes. Additionally, the centers were able to combine the scholarship of teaching and the scholarship of discovery. Collaborative efforts made the discussion highly visible and moved the process along rapidly relative to the institution's large size and complexity. Finally, a complex institution such as a research university was able to offer discussion forums and avenues of inquiry from many units. Efforts were driven by the grass roots, encouraged by the upper administration, and carried out in many venues, some more successfully than others. In the end, the campus found a good mix of soil and nutrients to transplant seedlings of the scholarship of teaching to the institutional field. The seedlings have taken root. The campus looks forward to reaping the harvest, season after season.

References

Academic Senate. (2002, February 18). *Academic Senate minutes.* Retrieved December 22, 2003, from ASU Academic Senate Web site: http://www.asu.edu/provost/asenate/minutes/Summ021802.htm

ACEPT. (2002). *ACEPT final report.* Tempe: Arizona State University. Retrieved December 22, 2003, from ACEPT Web site: http://acept.la.asu.edu/final_report/

Arizona Board of Regents. (2003). *Learner-centered education in the Arizona university system.* Retrieved December 22, 2003, from Arizona Board of Regents Learner-Centered Education Web site: http://www.abor.asu.edu/4_special_programs/lce/index_lce.html

Auffret, S. (2002, September 27). University enrollment more diverse, academically prepared. *ASU Insight, 1:* 6.

Billingsley, C. (1999, Fall). *ASU vision*. Retrieved August 18, 2003, from Arizona State University, President's Office Web site: http://www.asu.edu/president/graduate.html

Crow, M. (2002, September 5). *Address to Academic Assembly*. Retrieved August 18, 2003, from Web site of ASU President's Office: http://www.asu.edu/president/speeches/speech_acadassembly.html

Crow, M. (2002, September 16). Four guiding principles drive Crow's vision for ASU. *ASU Insight, 1:* 6. Retrieved December 22, 2003, from ASU News & Information Web site: http://www.asu.edu/asunews/university/acadassembly_speech_091602.htm

Kuhn, T. (1970). *The structure of scientific revolutions* (2nd ed., expanded). Chicago: University of Chicago Press.

Lang, M. (1999). *Review of ACEPT program*. Unpublished report.

McLean, S. V., & Callarman, T. (2002). Tracking evolving meanings: Five years of post-tenure review in Arizona. In C. M. Licata & J. C. Morreale (Eds.), *Post-tenure faculty review and renewal: Experienced voices* (pp. 50–65). Washington, DC: American Association for Higher Education.

Middleton, J. A., Sawada, D., Judson, E., Bloom, I., & Turley, J. (2002). Relationships build reform: Developing partnerships for research in teacher education. In L. D. English (Ed.), *Handbook of international research in mathematics education* (pp. 409–431). Mahwah, NJ: Lawrence Erlbaum.

National Council of Teachers of Mathematics. (2000). *Principles and standards for school mathematics*. Reston, VA: National Council of Teachers of Mathematics.

National Research Council. (1995). *National science education standards*. Washington, DC: National Academy Press.

Promotion and Tenure Task Force. (2001, February). *Review of faculty evaluation processes and criteria*. Retrieved December 22, 2003, from ASU provost's Web site: http://www.asu.edu/provost/reports/final_tenure_promo.doc

Rogers, E. M. (1995). *Diffusion of innovations* (4th ed.). New York: Free Press.

Rorty, R. (1979). *Philosophy and the mirror of nature*. Princeton, NJ: Princeton University Press.

Sawada, D., Piburn, M., Judson, E., Turley, J., Falconer, K., Benford, R., et al. (2002). Measuring reform practices in science and mathematics classrooms: The Reformed Teaching Observation Protocol. *School Science and Mathematics, 102*(6): 245–253.

Shulman, L. (2000). From Minsk to Pinsk: Why a scholarship of teaching and learning. *Journal of Scholarship of Teaching and Learning, 1*(1):

49–53. Retrieved August 18, 2003, from Indiana University Web site: http://www.iusb.edu/~josotl/Vol1No1/shulman.pdf

Shulman, L. (n.d.). Carnegie Academy for the Scholarship of Teaching and Learning (CASTL). Retrieved December 22, 2003, from Carnegie Foundation for the Advancement of Teaching Web site: http://www.carnegiefoundation.org/CASTL/

Vice President for Research and Economic Affairs. (2001). *Sponsored projects annual report 2001*. Tempe: Arizona State University. Retrieved December 22, 2003, from ASU Web site: http://researchnet.asu.edu/pi/Annual_Report_2001/

Chapter Twelve

Broadening the Definition of Scholarship

A Strategy to Recognize and Reward Clinician-Teachers at the University of Colorado School of Medicine

Steven R. Lowenstein and Robin A. Harvan

Background: Faculty Roles in Medical Schools

Medical schools, like most universities, have three core missions: teaching, research, and service, which form the traditional "three-legged stool" (Levinson & Rubenstein, 2000). Teaching has long been a priority in medical schools, as faculty are entrusted with the responsibility of educating the next generation of physicians and physician-scientists (Skeff & Mutha, 1998). Research is also a visible and highly regarded responsibility of medical school faculty. During the past century, medical school faculty have made discoveries that have elucidated the physiologic, environmental, behavioral, molecular, and genetic foundations of disease, and they have developed the means to treat and prevent hundreds of illnesses and disabilities. Excellence in research is routinely rewarded in medical schools, as productive medical scientists win research funding, space, institutional support, and national and international prestige. It is also no secret that research achievements have always been weighted most heavily in promotion and tenure decisions (Levinson & Rubenstein, 1999).

Regarding service—the third leg of the academic stool—medical schools are very different from other universities. In most non-medical universities, "service" consists mainly of donated time, leadership posts, committee and task force membership, and other activities that benefit the university or the community. In contrast, medical schools have a more conspicuous service mission—namely, providing direct medical care to patients. Indeed, the majority of medical school faculty are physicians, and for many, providing patient care is a dominant part of their job assignments.

This chapter presents a strategy to reform policies and procedures for promotion and tenure to recognize and reward clinician-teachers. The University of Colorado School of Medicine (SOM) conducted a campus study to determine whether revised rules for promotion and tenure, which emphasize alternative forms of scholarship and acknowledge the relationship among teaching, research, and clinical service, have had an impact. This chapter also presents the results of the campus study.

The Importance of Clinical Practice

At the University of Colorado SOM, the importance of clinical service is clearly articulated. The *School of Medicine Rules* (University of Colorado, 1997), which govern promotion and tenure, state, "Experience has repeatedly demonstrated that meaningful teaching . . . is impossible unless the teacher also has ongoing involvement in patient care, so that his/her teaching is relevant to actual practice and so that he/she may keep abreast of the latest developments in patient care and communicate these to . . . students. In addition, clinical research loses its focus when it is not ultimately related to actual clinical work" (p. 15). Also important, the *Rules* add, "The funding of all activities of the School of Medicine is [also] heavily dependent upon its clinical activities, and increasingly so, as federal support of research and teaching declines" (p. 15).

Increasingly, U.S. medical schools depend upon the work performed by clinicians for large shares of their operating revenue. Medical schools have evolved into large academic health centers, or academic health "corporations," which consist of the medical school, affiliated public and private hospitals, outpatient clinics, community-based medical practices, faculty practice plans, and other entities. Modern academic health centers rely extensively on contracts with managed care organizations and ever-expanding networks of primary practice sites. Not surprisingly, large cadres of clinicians are required to meet the increasing demand for medical care. Between 1986 and 1995, the number of full-time clinician-faculty increased 52 percent at public medical schools, with almost no change in the number of basic science faculty or medical students. Between 1965 and 1990, there was a 200-fold increase in clinical income in medical schools (Ludmerer, 1999). In the early 1960s, medical schools derived only 3–6 percent of their total revenues from patient care (with the rest from sponsored research, contracts, state funds, or private philanthropy); today, medical schools derive 40–50 percent of their revenues from direct medical care (Levinson & Rubenstein, 2000; Ludmerer, 1999).

In the competitive managed care environment, reimbursements to hospitals and physicians for medical services have decreased, and it is no longer possible to charge higher rates to offset the extra costs of teaching (Commonwealth Fund, 1997). Academic health centers have had to increase their patient volumes and assign more patient care duties to individual faculty (Kuttner, 1999; Viggiano, Shub & Giere, 2000). A business climate, with an emphasis on revenue and the "bottom line," prevails at many medical schools and competes for the time and attention of the faculty (Barchi & Lowery, 2000). Medical schools are increasingly concerned with "organizational structure, business discipline, resource management and accountability" (Cohen & Goodell, 2000). Clinically oriented medical school faculty members lead ever more frenetic lives, with little "protected" time for research or other creative scholarly work. One recent study found a strongly negative correlation between the penetration of managed care in a community and the academic productivity of medical school faculty (Campbell, Weissman, & Blumenthal, 1998).

Who Are the Clinician-Teachers?

Clinician-teachers today have unique job assignments. As defined by Branch, Kroenke, and Levinson (1997), they are full-time faculty who spend 75–90 percent of their time in clinical practice and teaching and who are serious about both tasks. Research is usually a minor component of their work (Beasley et al., 1997). Clinician-teachers have large teaching loads in a variety of clinical settings, such as offices and outpatient clinics, hospital wards, intensive care units, and operating rooms. Usually, they are available evenings, nights, and weekends, both to supervise residents and students and to attend to urgent patient care needs (Levinson & Rubenstein, 1999).

There are other unique and distinctly nonacademic demands on clinician-teachers. In the era of managed care and practice oversight, clinician-teachers spend increasing amounts of time communicating with insurance companies, coordinating specialty referrals for their patients, adhering to regulations and clinical care guidelines, managing drug formularies, and complying with paperwork requirements for quality improvement and utilization management reviews (Levinson, Branch, & Kroenke, 1998).

Clinician-teachers also have heavy teaching loads. Like Sir William Osler (1849–1919), who believed that students learn best by doing, they teach by example (Wright, Kern, & Kolodner, 1998), with their practices serving as model teaching units for medical students and residents (Branch, Kroenke, & Levinson, 1997; Levinson, Branch, & Kroenke, 1998; Levinson & Rubenstein, 1999, 2000; Wright, Kern, & Kolodner, 1998). Often, clinician-teachers are asked to design new curricula for medical students, interns, and residents. Because of their expertise in patient care, they often are asked to teach courses in history-taking and physical examination, clinical decision making, "keeping up" with the literature, doctor-patient communication, medical ethics, and other topics known variously as medical humanism, the art of medicine, the foundations of doctoring, or simply "getting to know your patient" (Branch, Kroenke, & Levinson, 1997; Levinson, Branch, & Kroenke, 1998; Levinson & Rubenstein, 1999, 2000; Wright, Kern, & Kolodner, 1998).

RECOGNIZING AND REWARDING CLINICIAN-TEACHERS IN ACADEMIC MEDICAL CENTERS

A remarkable disconnect has developed in many medical schools between the job assignments of clinician-teachers and the traditional requirements for career advancement. Busy clinicians are often judged by their hospitals and departments based on the number of patients seen per month (or per hour), patient satisfaction, waiting times, practice income, and other measures of "the bottom line." Salaries for clinician-teachers are often boosted by large incentives, based on patient "through-put" and clinical revenue. In contrast, promotion committees value teaching performance, scholarly achievement, and national reputation (Levinson, Branch, & Kroenke, 1998; Levinson & Rubenstein, 1999, 2000). It is often observed that the number of patients seen per month, practice income, and other measures of "clinical productivity" are inversely proportional to academic productivity (Beasley et al., 1997); promotions committees seldom consider them with regard to promotion and tenure.

Given that medical schools are increasingly dependent on clinician-teachers, several questions arise. What can be done to help clinician-teachers manage the extraordinary demands on their time? What support will they need to enable them to succeed as scholars in their university communities? Is it reasonable to expect clinician-educators to conduct traditional, hypothesis-driven research, compete for funding, or establish national reputations— long considered key credentials for advancement and tenure in American universities (Levinson & Rubenstein, 1999, 2000)? In a practical sense, the question is how to recognize, promote, and retain valuable clinician-educators who have talents and skills that are widely sought in the private medical sector.

Within this context, the University of Colorado SOM decided to review and revise its policies and procedures for faculty promotion and tenure. Emphasis was given to broadening the definition of scholarship, particularly for recognizing and rewarding clinician-teachers.

RECOGNIZING ALTERNATIVE FORMS OF SCHOLARSHIP AND REWARDING CLINICIAN-TEACHERS

The University of Colorado SOM is a public medical school within the University of Colorado System. The medical school was established in 1883, "since the Regents believed that the lives and health of the people of Colorado are not second in importance to any other interest that can be subserved by the State University." In

1883, the SOM consisted of two rooms, along with "two professors, two instructors, and two hastily recruited students" (Claman & Shikes, 2000, p. 12). Today, the SOM enrolls 126 new medical students each year and includes 22 affiliated hospitals and centers, 90 specialty clinics, more than 1,200 full-time faculty, and more than 2,500 volunteer and part-time faculty. In 2000–2001, its budget was more than $508 million, including revenues from patient care, research grants, gifts and endowments, tuition, and state support.

RECENT CHANGES TO THE PROMOTION POLICIES

In 1986, with the regents' approval, the SOM adopted three separate tracks for faculty promotion. The main promotion track was the tenure track, in which faculty were expected to demonstrate "excellence in teaching or scholarly work" to advance to associate professor. Within this track, "quantity of clinical effort [was] not considered sufficient grounds" for promotion, although outstanding clinical contributions could "enhance a candidate's status for promotion in the tenure track," if performance was judged to be excellent in scholarly work and teaching (University of Colorado, 1997, p. 59).

To accommodate faculty members with more highly focused careers, two specialty tracks were devised. These were considered parallel to the faculty ranks of associate professor and professor, although not eligible for tenure. The SOM defined a Specialty Track/Research for basic scientists. To qualify for promotion to associate professor in this track, faculty members had to demonstrate "excellence in research and scholarly activity, with original publications in peer-reviewed journals and national recognition in their field, as evidenced by . . . invitations to address national scientific meetings and research funding from peer-reviewed sources" (University of Colorado, 1997). Only minimal teaching was required.

In the Specialty Track/Clinical, which was designed for clinician-teachers, associate professors were expected to devote a majority of effort to clinical care and teaching and to demonstrate excellence in both. They were expected to present evidence of "continuing scholarly activity," and although this requirement was not well defined, it was noted that "this need not principally be original research published in peer-reviewed journals nor represent the clinician-educator's major academic activity" (University of Colorado, 1997).

In 1997, the SOM again reformed its promotion and tenure policies, this time creating a single, tenure-eligible track system. Citing Ernest Boyer's *Scholarship Reconsidered* (1990), the SOM expanded the definition of scholarship to include the scholarships of discovery, integration, teaching, and application of knowledge. The new *School of Medicine Rules* (University of Colorado, 1997), state, "All faculty will be required to participate in scholarship, as broadly defined. The products of all scholarship must be in a format that can be evaluated, which would normally mean a written format. . . . The School will recognize the four types of scholarship as adapted and modified from concepts developed by Ernest Boyer" (p. 18). The revised *Rules* define each of the four types of scholarship and provide more than 60 examples that are pertinent to academic physicians, scientists, and teachers.

The *Rules* emphasize a broad definition of scholarship, but with the requisite that all scholarship must reflect creative, interpretive, or innovative work and that, to be meaningful, it must be able to be shared, read, understood, and critiqued by others. For awards of tenure, the revised *Rules* also embraced a broad (but still rigorous) definition of scholarship:

> The first requisite for an award of tenure is excellence in scholarship, which has led to a national or international reputation. Scholarship is defined, in the context of an award of tenure, as the long, continued, systematic study of phenomena or events which leads to a competent mastery of one or more of the medical, allied health or related basic sciences disciplines. More narrowly, scholarship refers to advanced study that leads to the acquisition of knowledge in a particular field, along with accuracy and skill in investigation and the demonstration of powers of critical analysis in interpretation of such knowledge. *While the foregoing primarily refers to the scholarship of discovery, it may also include exceptional examples of the scholarship of application, integration and teaching.* (University of Colorado, 1997, p. 19)

The revised *Rules* maintain the "up-or-out" probationary system for all assistant professors. Review for promotion to associate professor must occur by the beginning of the seventh year of service as assistant professor, and faculty members who are not promoted according to this schedule are given one year's notice of non-renewal. Extensions to the seven-year probationary period may be granted by the dean for various career interruptions, including illness, family obligations, or significant changes in career focus or responsibilities.

Balance Between Scholarship and Teaching

The revised *Rules* reinforce, unambiguously, that both scholarship and teaching excellence are primary institutional goals. For example, faculty in every discipline and at every rank must demonstrate at least meritorious performance in scholarship and teaching before promotion may be considered. A higher standard, "excellence," is required before awarding tenure. Indeed, according to the revised *Rules,* tenure is reserved for individuals who are "recognized as outstanding and influential teachers." And while "the balance between accomplishments in scholarship and teaching may vary considerably from one candidate to another, both scholarship and teaching excellence must be present before tenure is granted" (University of Colorado, 1997, p. 19).

Implementation of the New Rules for Promotion and Tenure

In addition to redefining scholarship, the revised *Rules* led to other key changes: (1) the standards for evaluation of faculty were rewritten with greater clarity; (2) candidates for promotion were encouraged to outline areas of *meritorious* performance and areas of *excellence,* reflecting their job assignments and their principal areas of focus and achievement; (3) faculty were encouraged to present multiple products of scholarship, using clinical, teaching, and service portfolios; (4) teaching was given greater weight and parity, and candidates for promotion and tenure were required to develop teacher's statements and portfolios; and (5) promotion and tenure awards were made into separate processes. Having expanded the definitions of scholarship and having added rigor to the evaluation of teaching, it was possible for the SOM to effect one final change: the school eliminated the three-track system for faculty, and all faculty, from basic scientists to clinician-educators, were reunited into a single, equal, tenure-eligible track.

Support for Clinician-Teachers

One important objective of revising the *Rules* in 1997 was to assist the growing number of clinician-educators by aligning the promotion policies of the SOM and the job assignments of the clinically oriented faculty. In fact, the revised *Rules* highlight a unique aspect of medical scholarship—namely, that teaching students and engaging in research are usually more relevant and focused if the faculty member is also engaged in clinical work. According to the revised *Rules*, "Excellence in clinical work for physicians cannot be completely separated from excellence in research and teaching and should not be separated from these performance criteria in overall consideration of a faculty member for promotion and tenure" (University of Colorado, 1997, p. 15).

Assessing Scholarship for Clinician-Teachers

Rather than keeping the separate pathway for clinician-teachers, the SOM incorporated Boyer's broad definition of scholarship into its rules for promotion and tenure. One objective was to recognize forms of scholarship that were alternatives to hypothesis-driven research, including translational, interpretive, and interdisciplinary scholarly work. Another purpose was to raise teaching and clinical practice to their proper stature. The changes were, in a sense, an admission that the SOM is not solely a research institution, and that faculty members must be encouraged and rewarded not only for activities that produce knowledge, but also for activities that integrate and synthesize knowledge, apply knowledge, and impart knowledge to others. Indeed, alternative forms of scholarship, as defined by Boyer, might prove to be highly relevant to the practice and teaching of medicine.

More practically, the SOM recognized that faculty contributions varied and a more pluralistic measuring system was needed. Faculty could not be evaluated solely on the basis of research funding, peer-reviewed publications, and national and international reputations. Original research publications, while still highly valued, could no longer remain the sole criterion for promotion. Presentations about innovative curricula, development of novel teaching methods, and receipt of training grants (the scholarship of teaching) would now take their rightful place along with review articles, case reports and book chapters (the scholarship of integration), and leadership roles in patient-care quality improvement, investigational drug studies, patient guidelines, and public health policy (the scholarship of application).

Faculty members were encouraged to document their work in nontraditional areas of scholarship, communicate how it qualifies as scholarship, and be reflective about their achievements. The *Rules* clearly state that "all products of scholarship must be in a format that can be evaluated, which would normally mean a written format" (p. 15). They place a strong emphasis on tangible and visible products of scholarship that can be presented to the schoolwide faculty promotions committee, which is charged with evaluating the faculty member and recommending for or against promotion.

Evaluation of teaching effectiveness is also a critical component of the promotion process for clinician-teachers. The *Rules* include a detailed matrix that outlines the criteria for evaluating teaching performance. Ratings by learners (students, residents, and other trainees) receive the most weight, but peer ratings, course administration, mentoring, innovative curricula, and other examples of teaching scholarship are also considered. In addition, faculty members are asked to develop teaching portfolios and are encouraged to identify their teaching strengths and weaknesses and to use the university's Health Sciences Center Office of Education and other resources to improve their teaching skills.

Progress in Encouraging, Assessing, and Rewarding Multiple Forms of Scholarship

The campus self-study sought to determine whether the revised rules for promotion and tenure, which emphasize alternative forms of scholarship and acknowledge the relationships among teaching, research, and clinical practice, have had an impact on promotion practices. We wanted to determine whether the decisions of the

SOM Faculty Promotions Committee had demonstrated a commitment to rewarding multiple forms of scholarship.

REVIEW OF PROMOTION DECISIONS

We analyzed promotion decisions that occurred during a two-year period (academic years 2000–2001 and 2001–2002). As noted earlier, promotion and tenure are separate decisions, although they may occur concurrently. This study examined only assistant professors seeking promotion to associate professor without tenure, and specifically, only clinician-teachers—those faculty members whose job responsibilities lay exclusively or primarily in teaching and clinical practice. We gathered information about promotion decisions by reviewing a set of documents for each faculty candidate: (1) minutes of the schoolwide Faculty Promotions Committee; (2) votes for or against promotion; (3) the curriculum vitae submitted by the candidate; (4) letters of support written by the candidate's department chair and by the departmental faculty promotions committee; and (5) all evidence of scholarship, published and unpublished, submitted by the candidate as part of the promotion dossier.

RESULTS: PROMOTION DECISIONS
FOR CLINICIAN-TEACHERS

During the two-year period of this review, the Faculty Promotions Committee considered 198 dossiers, including 69 assistant professors seeking promotion whose roles in the SOM were exclusively or primarily clinical work and teaching. We reviewed the dossiers and supporting materials for these 69 clinician-teachers, with particular attention to publication records and other examples of scholarship. Of the 69 clinician-teachers who sought promotion to associate professor, 66 (96 percent) were approved and 3 were rejected.

Table 12.1 summarizes the publication records of the 66 candidates. The number of first- or senior-author peer-reviewed publications ranged from 0 to 29; the mean number of peer-reviewed first- or senior-author publications was 7.6, while the median and 25th percentiles were 5 and 3, respectively. The table also lists the means, medians, 25th percentiles, and ranges for coauthored, peer-reviewed publications and for "other" publications (which typ-

TABLE 12.1 PUBLICATIONS BY CLINICIAN-TEACHERS
PROMOTED TO ASSOCIATE PROFESSOR (N = 66)

	Peer-Reviewed Publications				
	First or Senior Author	Contributing Author	Total Peer-Reviewed Publications	Book Chapters & Other Publications	Total: All Publications
Minimum	0	0	0	1	1
Maximum	29	63	85	36	88
Mean	7.6	8.2	15.5	7.7	22.7
Median	5	6	11	6	19.5
25th percentile	3	3	5.5	3	11

ically included invited editorials, book chapters, case reports, or solicited articles in lower-tier journals).

These data reveal that faculty members varied considerably in their publication records. If first- or senior-authored peer-reviewed publications are the traditional yardstick for judging scholarly productivity, half of the faculty members were promoted despite having published five or fewer papers; one-fourth were promoted with three or fewer publications; and at least one faculty member had no written publications of any kind. However, a detailed examination of the records indicates that these faculty members had brought other, "alternative" products of scholarship to the table.

Recognizing Alternative Forms of Scholarship

The 69 dossiers that we reviewed for this study contained numerous examples of clinical, teaching, and applied scholarship. Most would have been discarded prior to adoption of the new *Rules*. The most common products were works of integration—"creative syntheses [or] original interpretations, demonstrating connections across disciplines or bringing new insights to bear on original research" (University of Colorado, 1997, p. 18). For example, several clinician-teachers had edited review textbooks or CD-ROMs; others had submitted compendia of practice guidelines, some in electronic or PalmPilot® format, covering such topics as diabetes management, disease prevention in indigent care settings, smoking cessation, end-of-life care, congestive heart failure, and health problems during pregnancy. These works were rated based on several criteria, including originality, grounding in scientific evidence, and use and acceptance by peers.

The scholarship of application includes efforts to "build bridges between theory and practice and apply knowledge to practical problems" (University of Colorado, 1997, p. 18). Some faculty members had written comprehensive, disease-specific patient care guidelines, which the Faculty Promotions Committee regarded as examples of the scholarship of application. Given the most weight were guidelines adopted by peers and tested in patients, and those that included quality and outcomes measures indicating improvements in patient care.

Faculty members were also awarded credit for publishing case reports. In medicine, case reports highlight unusual manifestations of common diseases, describe odd conditions, or highlight the benefits (or harms) of medical treatments or procedures. Case reports have long been considered "inferior" to original research, since they place less emphasis on scientific method or the collection of quantitative data. Yet case reports are, by their very nature, original, bedside observations that are communicated in written form to other clinicians. They represent an appropriate type of scholarship for academic physicians who are engaged fully in the practice of clinical medicine.

PROMOTION AND TENURE ILLUSTRATIONS

The following samples illustrate different clinician-teacher faculty profiles considered for promotion to the associate professor rank. Examples of alternative forms of scholarship in teaching, integration, and application are provided.

SCHOLARSHIP OF TEACHING

One assistant professor had committed more than 90 percent of her work week to clinical practice and teaching. She worked in an outpatient clinic, caring primarily for homeless, impoverished, and uninsured patients. In seven years as an assistant professor, she had published only three papers, and these were coauthored reviews. However, she had written an educational manual focusing on principles of caring for uninsured and underserved patients, and this had been distributed to, and used by, medical students and residents rotating at several homeless and indigent care clinics. Upon review, this manual was judged to be an excellent example of teaching scholarship. It was also an example of the scholarship of application, since it described innovative techniques to improve health care delivery in a particularly challenging setting.

A family physician had been an assistant professor for six years. This very creative faculty member was a specialist in end-of-life care and the spiritual aspects of healing and caring. In addition to his busy clinical practice, he served as medical director of several hospices and hospice alliances. He developed competency-based curricula for medical students and family medicine residents, covering the care of dying patients, pain palliation, and spirituality, that were adopted by family medicine residencies throughout the state. In addition, his work in curriculum development had been recognized nationally, as evidenced by a large number of invited presentations and by receipt of a large training grant.

SCHOLARSHIP OF INTEGRATION

A specialist in the psychology of healing after severe burn injuries was promoted to associate professor despite a dossier that included no peer-reviewed publications. However, she offered tangible evidence of scholarship and proof of a well-defined area of focus and expertise. At the time of her review, she had presented seven scientific papers at national meetings and delivered 20 additional invited lectures at other medical schools. She had written two patient education booklets that described the stages of recovery after burns, the need for supportive services, and the benefits of burn camps for children. She had also helped write and produce five peer-reviewed videotapes about the emotional experiences of children with burn injuries, aimed at audiences of parents, providers, and community leaders.

A faculty radiologist was promoted to associate professor with a record of just five publications, none in peer-reviewed journals. She had focused on computer-assisted learning in radiology, both in her department and nationally, and had developed a computerized radiology teaching curriculum for medical students and a Web-based radiology teaching file for residents and students. These learning tools included evaluation worksheets that enabled medical students to provide feedback to the department in order to improve the teaching files. She published a summary of this work in a journal (an invited, non-peer-reviewed contribution). She also wrote an extensive self-assessment program for community-based radiologists that contains 150 thoroughly referenced, researched, and tested questions about key topics in chest radiology. The questions were adopted by the American College of Radiology's Continuous Professional Improvement project and are now available to practice-based radiologists around the country. Her contributions were judged as outstanding examples of the scholarship of teaching and integration.

SCHOLARSHIP OF APPLICATION

An assistant professor served as medical director of several busy ambulatory clinics that were described by external referees as among the best-known and most imaginative in the nation. He had just two publications, but he had received several large practice management grants that enabled him to develop, test, and implement innovative health care delivery techniques. Among the most novel were systems to integrate the care delivered by students, physicians, physicians' assistants, and other health professionals, in psychology, pharmacy, occupational medicine, sports medicine, and other disciplines. He had also developed state-of-the-art practice management curricula for learners in these settings, which outlined novel approaches to integrate clinical care and teaching and conserve resources. There was evidence that his practice management curricula and programs had improved health care delivery and reduced overhead and other costs. After careful review, the Faculty Promotions Committee accepted these achievements as products of the scholarship of application.

A general internist with a heavy, ongoing clinical load had become one of the school's experts on electronic medical record systems. At first, this was primarily an administrative assignment, for which the hospital provided modest salary support. Later, however, he published four papers and two abstracts describing how electronic medical records could be harnessed to improve documentation and efficiency, help disseminate up-to-date clinical guidelines, enhance the teaching of residents and students rotating through the clinical practice site, and support outpatient-based clinical research.

A busy assistant professor, who specialized in infectious diseases, devoted approximately 80 percent of his work week to patient care duties and teaching. He served as director of a busy clinic for patients with AIDS and HIV-related diseases. As practice director, he developed several innovative strategies to coordinate medical and pharmacy services, and he demonstrated that these strategies reduced the need for hospital admission for patients with AIDS. He submitted carefully analyzed data demonstrating dramatic reductions in mortality and costs, and each of these improvements in outcomes exceeded national benchmarks and the improvements that might be expected only from the use of newer drugs to treat AIDS and AIDS-related infections. Although the Faculty Promotions Committee encouraged him to publish his results more widely in peer-reviewed journals, the committee accepted his written practice descriptions, interventions, and outcomes summaries as meritorious examples of the scholarship of application.

A member of the geriatrics faculty spent several years developing methods to improve the medical care of older patients, based on early recognition of common geriatric syndromes combined with estimates of functional decline, mortality risk, and adaptive capacities. His written scholarship included five white papers invited by health maintenance organizations, professional societies, a national foundation, and two government agencies (Medicare and the Congressional Budget Office). These papers outlined health services research priorities for geriatric care and formed the basis of a subsequent funding initiative by a large national foundation. While not published in traditional medical journals, his work had been accepted by a broad and respected community of scholars and policymakers and led to new insights regarding the delivery of health services to senior citizens. This body of work was rated as an exceptional example of the scholarship of application—addressing consequential public health problems, proposing solutions, and helping shape public policy.

THREE CANDIDATES WHO WERE NOT PROMOTED

Three clinician-teachers were not promoted during the campus study period, though they had been busy in their practices, were energetic and effective teachers, received consistently high ratings by students, and participated in quality improvement activities. One of them had served as director of a fellowship training program. They received no credit for scholarship, because they had no tangible products of scholarship to "communicate to peers and other scholars" or to the Faculty Promotions Committee. The fellowship training program director had been personally responsible for the hands-on education of numerous physicians-in-training and had been responsible for recruiting residents and fellows, organizing the curriculum, establishing competency standards, and evaluating trainees. However, he could not provide evidence of creative or innovative scholarship that could be read, understood, or critiqued by others. Two other faculty members also sought promotion as clinician-teachers. Their dossiers included numerous documents submitted as evidence of teaching scholarship, but the promotions committee determined that they consisted of course materials, such as lecture notes, handouts, or PowerPoint slides, that drew from the work of others and did not reflect creative or innovative syntheses or explorations of student learning that had been shared outside the classroom. The Faculty Promotions Committee concurred with Beattie (2000), who argued that "[teaching] scholarship is incomplete unless communication to peers and other scholars occurs in addition to presentation to the usual audience of students" (p. 874).

SUMMARY AND DISCUSSION

The campus study suggests that, at the University of Colorado School of Medicine, clinician-teachers are being evaluated for promotion using Boyer's (1990) expanded definition of scholarship. Although publications and other traditional measures of the scholarship of discovery are still sought and valued by the SOM's promotions committee, scholarship in the other domains (integration, application, and teaching) is also recognized. Some faculty members were promoted to associate professor with no peer-reviewed publications, indicating that the concept of a "minimum number of publications" has been eliminated.

Each new faculty member at the SOM receives a copy of the *Rules* (University of Colorado, 1997). Boyer (1990) is cited in the *Rules,* which also include definitions and examples of achievements in the four domains of scholarship that are pertinent to physicians and medical scientists. The *Rules* emphasize that all scholarship must reflect creative, interpretive, or innovative work and that "the products of scholarship must be in a format that can be evaluated" (p. 18). Documentation of the products of scholarship is the cornerstone of the evaluation process at the SOM. According to Glassick, Huber, and Maeroff (1997), "The quality of a faculty member's performance in any of the four areas of scholarship can be best assessed on the basis of evidence that speaks directly to the standards for judging the work. Such documentation requires rich and varied material that the scholar and others assemble over time to make the case on the scholar's behalf" (p. 37).

During the two-year period of the campus study, 66 clinician-teachers were promoted from assistant to associate professor, each having demonstrated "excellence" (the SOM's highest standard) in either teaching or clinical service. Each was also required to demonstrate at least "meritorious" accomplishments in scholarship. Many met this requirement by submitting published case reports, videotapes, CD-ROMs, innovative curricula, computer-assisted learning tools, public policy white papers, descriptions of important quality improvement projects, or clinical guidelines that led to improvements in patient care. Grants were often recognized as evidence of scholarship, although frequently these were from nontraditional sources, such as foundations, the state government, or hospitals. The faculty promotions committee informally rated each product of scholarship, based on criteria such as originality, suitability for peer review, impact, and use and acceptance by respected clinicians and scholars.

The SOM took steps to redefine scholarship and recognize the contributions of clinician-teachers, for a simple but compelling reason: clinician-teachers are vital to the school's success. Whatever the future structure or priorities, the SOM will need energetic, caring, and well-trained clinicians who devote their careers to improving the culture of teaching and the quality of patient care.

The campus study also demonstrates that it may not always be necessary to have separate tracks or promotion pathways for clinician-educators. Separate tracks or promotion standards have been established at more than half of all U.S. medical schools (Beasley et al., 1997). In contrast, the University of Colorado SOM sought to acknowledge clinician-teachers by recognizing a broad array of scholarly achievements within a single, unified faculty track in which all have equal access to promotion and tenure. As Beasley pointed out, it may be more "important to ensure that appropriate methods are in place to evaluate clinician-educators than to worry about whether a school has a separate track" in which to promote them (Beasley et al., 1997, p. 728).

Of course, it will not be enough just to expand the definition of scholarship. Clinician-teachers will also need concrete support to be successful. They may require workshops to enhance their instructional skills, training in data analysis or outcomes research, protected time for scholarship, salary or other support for teaching, skilled mentors, and a supportive structure that enables them to remain "connected" to the academic missions of the university (Williams et al., 1998). They must be informed about opportunities to participate in innovative forms of scholarship that are relevant to their work as teachers and physicians. In addition, clinician-teachers will have to learn the best ways to document their scholarly achievements—how to transform teaching and clinical service into products of scholarship that are creative, original, reflective, and suitable for peer review (Fincher et al., 2000). Most important, unless the new scholarship policies are publicized widely, "junior faculty members [may] wrongly perceive that traditional research is their only opportunity for scholarly work in the college" (Nora et al., 2000, p. 915).

Medical schools will need to develop better methods of measuring clinical and teaching excellence. There still are no accepted standards across medical schools for assessing alternative products of scholarship without relying on old yardsticks such as research data, published papers, and grants. The University of Colorado SOM decided to recognize and reward exceptional examples of the scholarship of teaching, integration, and application, but it has not developed or tested any tools with which to do so. The SOM *Rules* emphasize documentation and sharing of the products of scholarship, but evaluation is more difficult. Formal peer review, resulting in publication, is the traditional form of evaluation. But what are the "publication equivalents" (Marks, 2000) of scholarship for clinician-teachers? Valid and reliable methods of peer review, acceptable to academic clinician-teachers, still need to be explored. Schools will have to develop fair, reproducible standards with which to assess the creativity, dissemination, and impact of nontraditional forms of scholarship. Stated differently, we need an acceptable means to determine where high-quality teaching and clinical service end and the scholarship of teaching, integration, and application begins (Fincher et al., 2000; Glassick, 2000).

CONCLUSION

At the University of Colorado SOM, and in many other American medical universities, clinician-teachers are growing in number and importance. They can no longer be evaluated using the same methods and standards that are applied to research-intensive faculty. When it comes to evaluating performance or recommending promotion, the emphasis must shift from winning grants, conducting hypothesis-driven research, and publishing, toward an appreciation of scholarship that is more closely tied to what clinician-teachers actually do. Expanding the definition of teaching is appropriate and necessary if clinician-educators are to be recognized as faculty and valued as integral to the academic life and fiscal health of a medical school. Expanding the definition of scholarship is one way to "integrate clinician-teachers into the fabric of [the] contemporary medical school" (Levinson & Rubenstein, 2000, p. 907; see also Branch, Kroenke, & Levinson, 1997; Levinson, Branch, & Kroenke, 1998; Levinson & Rubenstein, 1999), rather than treating them as "hired hands."

At the University of Colorado SOM, the principles articulated in Boyer's (1990) *Scholarship Reconsidered* now play a significant role in shaping faculty roles and rewards. Boyer's expanded definition of scholarship is applicable to the real work that clinician-teachers do. This expanded definition helps recognize faculty members who teach every day and care for patients, alongside those who simply study them. It is also an attempt to realign the reward system at a medical school with a tripartite mission. As Kenneth Ludmerer

observed in his landmark work *Time to Heal* (1999), medical faculty
have two homes (and two sets of masters): "One home is in the
University and the other is in the modern health care delivery system" (p. 336). Scholarship is taking place, and must be recognized,
in both houses.

References
Barchi, R. L., & Lowery, B. J. (2000). Scholarship in the medical faculty
from the university perspective: Retaining academic values. *Academic
Medicine, 75:* 899–905.
Beasley, B. W., Wright, S. M., Cofrancesco, J., Babbott, S. F., Thomas, P. A.,
& Bass, E. B. (1997). Promotion criteria for clinician-educators in
the United States and Canada. *Journal of the American Medical Associ-
ation, 278:* 723–728.
Beattie, D. (2000). Expanding the view of scholarship: Introduction. *Aca-
demic Medicine, 75:* 871–876.
Boyer, E. L. (1990). *Scholarship reconsidered: Priorities of the professoriate.* Prince-
ton, NJ: Carnegie Foundation for the Advancement of Teaching.
Branch, W. T., Kroenke, K., & Levinson, W. (1997). The clinician-educator—
Present and future roles. *Journal of General Internal Medicine, 12*
(Suppl.): S1-S4.
Campbell, E., Weissman, J., & Blumenthal, D. (1998). Relationship be-
tween market competition and the activities and attitudes of med-
ical school faculty. *Obstetric Gynecological Survey, 53:* 36–38.
Claman, H. N., & Shikes, R. H. (2000). *The University of Colorado School of
Medicine: A millennial history.* Denver: A. B. Hirschfeld.
Cohen, H. J., & Goodell, B. (2000). Lessons on repairing distressed aca-
demic medical centers. *Academic Clinical Practice, 13*(1): 1–14.
Commonwealth Fund. (1997). *Leveling the playing field: Financing the mis-
sions of academic health centers* (Findings and recommendations of the
Commonwealth Fund task force on academic health centers). New
York: Author.
Fincher, R. E., Simpson, D. E., Mennin, S. P., Rosenfeld, G. C., Rothman, A.,
McGrew, M. C., Hansen, P. A., Mazmanian, P. E., & Turnbull, J. M.
(2000). Scholarship in teaching: An imperative for the 21st century.
Academic Medicine, 75: 887–894.
Glassick, C. E. (2000). Boyer's expanded definitions of scholarship, the
standards for assessing scholarship and the elusiveness of the schol-
arship of teaching. *Academic Medicine, 75:* 877–880.
Glassick, C. E., Huber, M. T., & Maeroff, G. I. (1997). *Scholarship assessed:
Evaluation of the professoriate.* San Francisco: Jossey-Bass.

Kuttner, R. (1999). Managed care and medical education. *New England Journal of Medicine, 341:* 1092–1096.

Levinson, W., Branch, W. T., & Kroenke, K. (1998). Clinician-educators in academic medical centers: A two-part challenge. *Annual of Internal Medicine, 129:* 59–64.

Levinson, W., & Rubenstein, A. (1999). Mission critical—Integrating clinician-educators into academic medical centers. *New England Journal of Medicine, 341:* 840–843.

Levinson, W., & Rubenstein, A. (2000). Integrating clinician-educators into academic medical centers: Challenges and potential solutions. *Academic Medicine, 75:* 906–912.

Ludmerer, K. M. (1999). *Time to heal: American medical education from the turn of the century to the era of managed care.* New York: Oxford University Press.

Marks, E. S. (2000). Defining scholarship at the Uniformed Services University of the Health Sciences Center School of Medicine: A study in cultures. *Academic Medicine, 75:* 935–939.

Nora, L. M., Pomeroy, C., Curry, T. E., Hill, N. S., Tibbs, P. A., & Wilson, E. A. (2000). Revising appointment, promotion and tenure procedures to incorporate an expanded definition of scholarship: The University of Kentucky experience. *Academic Medicine, 75:* 913–924.

Skeff, K. M., & Mutha, S. (1998). Role models—Guiding the future of medicine. *New England Journal of Medicine, 339:* 2015–2017.

University of Colorado. (1997). *The School of Medicine rules.* Denver: Author.

Viggiano, T. R., Shub, C., & Giere, R. W. (2000). The Mayo Clinic's Clinician-Educator Award: A program to encourage educational innovation and scholarship. *Academic Medicine, 75:* 940–943.

Williams, R. L., Zyzanski, S. J., Flocke, S. A., et al. (1998). Critical success factors for promotion and tenure in family medicine departments. *Academic Medicine, 73:* 333–335.

Wright, S. M., Kern, D. E., Kolodner, K., et al. (1998). Attributes of excellent attending-physician role models. *New England Journal of Medicine, 339:* 1986–1993.

PART THREE

NATIONAL PERSPECTIVES

EFFECTS OF ENCOURAGING MULTIPLE FORMS OF SCHOLARSHIP NATIONWIDE AND ACROSS INSTITUTIONAL TYPES

KerryAnn O'Meara

Ernest Boyer's *Scholarship Reconsidered* (1990) encouraged hundreds of colleges and universities to redefine scholarship and amend their reward systems to better acknowledge, support, and reward faculty involvement in multiple forms of scholarship. Some campuses revised mission and planning documents, others changed promotion and tenure criteria, and still others created flexible workload programs (Diamond, 1999; Rice & Sorcinelli, 2002; Trower, 2000).

Much has changed over the past decade. A small but growing group of scholars and academic leaders is trying to understand the extent of reform in faculty roles and rewards prompted by *Scholarship Reconsidered*. The Carnegie Foundation surveyed chief academic

The author thanks Joseph Berger and Deborah Hirsch for their review of an earlier report from which this chapter was drafted; Larry Braskamp and Mary Huber for their suggestions and comments; R. Eugene Rice for his guidance of this project and feedback on this chapter; and Atlantic Philanthropies and an anonymous donor for their financial support of the research.

officers (CAOs) at four-year colleges and universities in 1994 and found that 80 percent of the institutions had recently reexamined or planned to reexamine their workloads; 62 percent reported that *Scholarship Reconsidered* played a part in discussions of faculty roles and rewards (Glassick, Huber, & Maeroff, 1997). Likewise, the Carnegie Foundation's 1997 national survey of college and university faculty explored the emphasis put on different forms of scholarship during the previous five years and found that nearly half of faculty at research universities said greater emphasis was being placed on teaching (Huber, 2002).

Seldin (1993) found as many as a thousand colleges and universities experimenting with portfolios to document scholarly work in teaching. In 1997, I examined 400 promotion and tenure documents for the New England Resource Center for Higher Education and found that 6.5 percent of the institutions had changed formal policy to encourage and reward service as a form of scholarship in faculty evaluation (O'Meara, 1997). In 2000, the Harvard Project on Faculty Appointments analyzed more than 200 promotion and tenure documents. A small percentage of institutions were found to have written the four domains of scholarship discussed in *Scholarship Reconsidered* (discovery, teaching, integration, application) into their guidelines for promotion and tenure or modified existing language to reflect a broader view (O'Meara, 2000, pp. 156–157). Finally, Braxton, Luckey, and Holland (2002) explored the extent to which faculty members were engaging in each of the four domains of scholarship and which domains were institutionalized into their academic work. They found that all four domains had attained the most basic or structural-level institutionalization; the scholarships of discovery and teaching had attained procedural-level institutionalization (wherein the activity is a regular part of workload); but only the scholarship of discovery achieved incorporation-level institutionalization (wherein faculty values and assumptions support the activity).

The movement to encourage multiple forms of scholarship has affected most institutions, but each type has responded differently, based on the context of faculty roles and rewards within it. Overall, the movement to encourage multiple forms of scholarship arrived at research universities at a time when they were being criticized for neglecting undergraduate education and for being ivory towers with little responsibility to apply knowledge to community problems (Checkoway, 2001; Geiger, 1999). A very narrow view of scholarship as peer-reviewed journal articles and books dominated faculty evaluation in these institutions. At the same time, doctoral and comprehensive universities (especially those located in urban areas) were involved or becoming more involved in regional or community problem solving, linking graduate and undergraduate programs to community concerns, and examining how faculty involvement in economic community development and linkages to schools would fit with established faculty roles and expectations for scholarship (Aldersley, 1995; Braskamp & Wergin, 1998; Cohen, 1998; Crosson, 1983; Finnegan, 1993; Ramaley, 2000).

By the early 1990s, master's-granting colleges and universities were experiencing a mission crisis, with some arguing that their future lay in increasing the productivity of graduate programs and faculty research, while others clung to their distinctive teaching and service missions (Berberet, 2002). Liberal arts colleges, with their established emphasis on teaching, were creating learning communities and engaging students in service-learning. These campuses were struggling with how to integrate interdisciplinary work and classroom assessment into faculty rewards (Eby, 1996; Prince, 2000). Likewise, some baccalaureate institutions were trying to figure out how they could engage faculty in professional development and scholarship of any kind, given heavy faculty course and advising loads and community service requirements (Boyer, 1990; Ruscio, 1987).

One of Boyer's main points in *Scholarship Reconsidered* was that colleges and universities and their faculties should emphasize the forms of scholarship most appropriate to their missions and not try to emulate the faculty roles and rewards at research universities in a quest for prestige. To maintain the diversity of higher education, Boyer prescribed the types of scholarship he thought colleges and universities in each institutional type should emphasize. For example, he recommended an emphasis on discovery for research universities, and teaching for baccalaureate institutions. Braxton et al. (2002) studied the degree to which the different forms of scholarship had been institutionalized into faculty work life in four disciplines. They found that faculty values for involvement in the scholarships of application, integration, and teaching matched

Boyer's domain emphasis (p. 103), but that across institutional types, the scholarship of discovery persisted as the most legitimate and preferred method of faculty scholarship. They suggested that changes in graduate education, the academic reward system, and the methods for assessing scholarship were keys to fully institutionalizing all forms of scholarship across institutional types.

This is where the American Association for Higher Education (AAHE) stepped in. The Forum on Faculty Roles and Rewards decided to examine the impact of policy changes on all types of four-year institutions. From late fall 2001 through early spring 2002, we conducted a national survey of CAOs to gauge the extent of changes to formal reward systems to encourage multiple forms of scholarship, and the impact of those changes over the previous 10 years. I conducted the survey as a research associate with the "Forum on Faculty Roles and Rewards on the Encouraging Multiple Forms of Scholarship" project, directed by R. Eugene Rice.

CAOs play a critical role in ensuring the integrity and fairness of the faculty evaluation process and in promoting growth and morale among members of the faculty (Diamond, 1993). Their pivotal role in setting standards for and assessing faculty work and their ability to describe change in roles and rewards across the campus made them ideal participants for this study. There are, admittedly, a few drawbacks. The larger the institution, the more difficult it is for the CAO to generalize when reporting on changes in academic culture. In addition, CAOs involved in reform efforts may have a professional stake in reporting positive outcomes. We sought to address these limitations by asking questions in different ways and by convening additional, qualitative focus groups to validate survey findings.

The following research questions shaped our survey research:

1. To what extent have campuses made formal changes to their reward systems to encourage multiple forms of scholarship over the last decade?
2. What kinds of formal changes were made?
3. What were the catalysts for making these changes and the barriers to implementing them?
4. Did making formal policy changes have an impact on faculty work life, reward systems, institutional effectiveness, or academic

cultures? If so, what kinds of impact? Were there any noticeable differences between campuses that made formal changes and those that did not, in terms of faculty work life, reward systems, institutional effectiveness, or academic cultures?

To complete our Web-based survey, during late fall 2001 we mailed an invitation to 1,452 CAOs of nonprofit four-year colleges and universities (identified by the 2000 Carnegie classification system) and sent a follow-up written copy to those who did not complete the Web version. Exactly half of the CAOs completed the survey (two-thirds on the Web and the rest on paper). The findings reported in this chapter rest on these 729 responses, which represent half of the CAOs in four-year nonprofit colleges and universities in the United States. When compared to the Carnegie classification system and broken down by institutional type, the AAHE national survey responses mirror the national profile. The next section of this chapter presents the survey findings, followed by a discussion of differences among institutional types.

UNDERSTANDING THE IMPACT OF FORMAL POLICY CHANGE

For more than a decade, advocates for multiple forms of scholarship have argued the need to make formal changes to official university policies, structures, and academic reward systems (Diamond, 1999; Driscoll & Lynton, 1999; Glassick et al., 1997; O'Meara, 1997; Rice, Sorcinelli, & Austin, 2000). The most popular policy reforms suggested in a review of the literature were (1) changing institutional mission and planning documents to acknowledge a broader definition of scholarship, (2) amending promotion and tenure or contract language and criteria, (3) providing opportunities for flexible workload programs, and (4) providing incentive grants. Research shows that hundreds of campuses have made one of these formal reforms over the past decade (Diamond, 1999; Glassick et al., 1997; O'Meara, 1997, 2000; Rice & Sorcinelli, 2002), but little empirical research has been conducted to see if, in fact, initiating what we define as "formal policy reform" results in any greater benefits than "informal" efforts. For this study, we defined formal policy reform as including one of the four changes listed. We call institutions "traditional" if they did not make any of these four changes. However, informal efforts (individual encouragement, unfunded support groups, workshops on portfolio development) may have been made on the traditional campuses over the past decade.

These two categories of reform and traditional are not entirely distinct. A campus might have been working to change promotion and tenure materials while completing the survey, or had a program that did not fit into the first category and had to choose traditional when, in fact, something was in place or was about to take place to encourage multiple forms of scholarship. Nevertheless, this imperfect structure allows us to understand the impact of the most popular formal policy efforts on faculty work life, reward systems, institutional effectiveness, and academic cultures.

We created two survey paths. We asked CAOs to choose a path by identifying with one of the following statements:

1. "Within the last 10 years my institution has made formal changes to our mission, planning documents, and/or faculty evaluation policy to encourage multiple forms of scholarly work."
2. "Within the last 10 years my institution has maintained traditional definitions of scholarly work in our mission, planning documents, and/or faculty evaluation policy. By traditional we refer to scholarship primarily as abstract and analytical research."

We refer to those who identified their campuses using the first statement as "reform-institution CAOs," and those who identified their campuses using the second statement as "traditional-institution CAOs." I have presented our findings in three categories: (1) the extent and kinds of formal policy reform, (2) catalysts and barriers, and (3) the impact of formal policy reform on faculty work life, reward systems, and academic culture.

FORMAL CHANGES

Findings suggest that, over the past decade, most four-year institutions have initiated formal policies and procedures to encourage and reward multiple forms of scholarship. Two of every three

CAOs (68 percent) reported that their institution had changed mission and planning documents, amended faculty evaluation criteria, provided incentive grants, or developed flexible workload programs to encourage and reward a broader definition of scholarship; roughly 1 of every 3 (32 percent) reported that their institution had not. Table 13.1 divides responses by the two survey paths and three major Carnegie institutional-type categories.

We asked CAOs at reform institutions to identify each policy reform during the past 10 years that encouraged multiple forms of scholarship, and to identify one or more of the four reforms we listed. The reforms most frequently identified were expanding the definition of scholarship in faculty evaluation policies (76 percent) and providing incentive grants for multiple forms of scholarship (75 percent). Approximately 45 percent of CAOs noted that they had expanded the definition of scholarship written into institutional mission and planning documents, and 41 percent reported that their institution had used the expanded definition of scholarship to develop flexible workload programs (in the spirit of Boyer's "creativity contracts").

The popularity of creativity contracts, "an arrangement by which faculty members define professional goals for a three to five year period, possibly shifting from one principal scholarly focus to

TABLE 13.1 REFORM AND TRADITIONAL CAMPUSES BY TYPE

Institutional Type	Reform (Number/ Percentage of Total)	Traditional (Number/ Percentage of Total)	Subtotal/ Percentage of Grand Total
Doctoral universities	88/18%	48/21%	136/19%
Master's colleges and universities	230/46%	80/35%	310/43%
Baccalaureate colleges	178/36%	103/44%	281/38%
Did not respond or could not be determined	2/0%	0/0%	2/0%
Total	498/68%	231/32%	729/100%

Note: Due to rounding, percentages may not equal 100.

another" (Boyer, 1990, p. 48), seems to have increased slightly over the past five to 10 years. When Glassick et al. (1997) asked CAOs whether they encouraged faculty "to shift their scholarly focus from time to time (concentrating on teaching or research, for example)" in 1994, 29 percent responded that the idea had been introduced or considered at their institution. While our CAO respondents in 2001–2002 remarked on the implementation of flexible workload programs at a rate lower than the other formal changes (41 percept), nonetheless, this vehicle for change seems to have become slightly more common since 1994.

Catalysts and Barriers

Over the past 10 years, many forces have pushed institutions to establish a closer rewards balance among teaching, research, and service and to support multiple forms of scholarship (Austin, 2002a; Rice & Sorcinelli, 2002). We reviewed the literature on change in faculty roles and rewards and grouped the likely catalysts into three categories: external pressures, cultural elements, and leadership. We then developed a list of factors for each category. At reform institutions, we asked CAOs if, and to what extent, any of these factors influenced their institution's decision to amend reward systems to encourage and reward multiple forms of scholarship. Table A.1 (see Appendix) outlines the responses.

Leadership factors, such as leadership by the provost (57 percent), cultural factors such as the institution's commitment to teaching (73 percent), engagement, and professional service (44 percent), and aligning reward systems with mission to meet institutional goals (49 percent) proved to be major influences (40 percent or more) on the institution's decision to change policy. It is important to acknowledge that CAOs may have shown bias in reporting their own leadership as a major factor. Most reform-institution CAOs did not rate external factors as major influences. However, 32 percent of them identified one factor, ideas generated by the discussion of Boyer's *Scholarship Reconsidered* (1990), as a major influence. When we combined major- and minor-influence responses and compared them with the no-influence categories, we saw a similar pattern. About as many reform-institution CAOs reported that external factors were not an influence as reported that they were (with the influence of *Scholarship Reconsidered* being an exception).

However, when we combined major and minor categories, we found that leadership from the provost, president, and other administrators, and grassroots efforts by faculty (leadership factors) emerged as influences for most reform-institution CAOs, as well as mission alignment, commitment to teaching, and professional service (cultural factors). Overall, the fact that more than half of reform-institution CAOs reported that 10 of the 15 factors were a major or minor influence suggests that, rather than one factor, like the institution's commitment to teaching, it was the interaction of leadership, mission, and the discussions generated by *Scholarship Reconsidered* that worked synergistically to spark reform.

Barriers to change have been identified in studies of academic reward systems (Braxton et al., 2002; Eckel, Green, Hill, & Mallon, 1999; Kezar, 2001; Rice & Sorcinelli, 2002). Many research universities have attempted change to elevate the status of the scholarship of teaching, while many liberal arts colleges have tried to alter a culture focused on teaching and institutional service to one that rewards teaching as a form of scholarship and also encourages discovery and integration. After reviewing the literature on change in faculty roles and rewards, we grouped the likely barriers into the same three categories that we used for catalysts: external pressures, cultural elements, and leadership. We then developed a list of barriers for each category, and asked CAOs if and to what extent any of these barriers influenced their institution's efforts (formal or otherwise).

Reform-institution CAOs and traditional-institution CAOs gave very similar responses to most items, indicating that regardless of the type of reforms, the same obstacles thwart the encouragement and reward of multiple forms of scholarship. Table A.2 (see Appendix) presents a list of 20 potential barriers and the extent to which all CAOs believed those barriers were present on their campuses.

Among 20 potential barriers, the following six were considered most important by all CAOs: (1) faculty concerns about unrealistic expectations that they must excel in all areas at the same time; (2) greater confusion and ambiguity for faculty about what really counts for promotion and tenure; (3) vested interest of some faculty in maintaining the status quo; (4) difficulty in expanding a consistent definition of scholarship across the university; (5) confusion about the definitions of teaching, research, and service as scholarship; and (6) faculty graduate school training and socialization toward traditional definitions of scholarship. Each barrier is embedded in an institution's academic culture and speaks to a need for greater leadership from CAOs, deans, and department chairs in making these cultures more receptive to and trusting of the implementation of a broader definition of scholarship in reward systems. The last barrier, socialization toward traditional definitions of scholarship, points to the importance of efforts like the "Preparing Future Faculty Program" discussed by Jerry Gaff in Chapter 3. Many CAOs report that a lack of socialization and training toward this framework prevents faculty involvement in the scholarships of teaching and engagement (Braxton et al., 2002).

In five areas, subsequent analysis (O'Meara, forthcoming) indicated significant differences between reform and traditional institutions. Reform-institution CAOs were significantly more likely than traditional-institution CAOs to report the following areas as barriers: (1) the political nature of faculty evaluation, (2) excessive paperwork for faculty evaluation, (3) insufficient training for department chairs and deans, (4) faculty concerns about unrealistic expectations that they excel in all areas at the same time, and (5) unevenness in applying new criteria and standards within and across units. These findings suggest that formally implementing a broader definition of scholarship in policy and practice has created additional strain on faculty and their reward systems. Rice and Sorcinelli (2002) observed that the broader conception of scholarship and new ways to document different forms of scholarly work have in many cases multiplied the scholarly responsibilities of early career faculty, sometimes making the tenure process more difficult. Since early career faculty already consider promotion and tenure as "vague, ambiguous, and elusive" (Rice & Sorcinelli, 2002, p. 119), they find that the perceived increase in the number of hoops to jump through makes engaging in alternative forms of scholarship seem prohibitive.

IMPACT OF REFORM ON FACULTY WORK LIFE, REWARD SYSTEMS, INSTITUTIONAL EFFECTIVENESS, AND ACADEMIC CULTURE

The framework of a broader definition of scholarship was developed with the purpose of helping campuses realign their faculty workload, reward system, and mission, and to enhance faculty well-being by ensuring that more of the "mosaic of faculty" was rewarded (Boyer, 1990, p. 27; Walker, 2002). Advocates of expanding the definition of scholarship claim that a number of benefits accrue to their campuses as a result (Diamond, 1999; Hutchings & Shulman, 1999; Seldin, 1993; Wergin, 1994). Recent research and case studies have also found certain institutional benefits associated with changes in academic reward systems of this sort (Braxton et al., 2002; O'Meara, 2002a, 2002b; Zahorski & Cognard, 1999). Thus, we wanted to explore whether CAOs at reform institutions had experienced increases or improvements in faculty work life and reward systems, and whether they attributed these increases or improvements to their formal policy reform.

It is important, for a sense of context, to note the areas where CAOs did and did not observe improvements and increases over the past decade. More than half of all CAOs observed increases in the following kinds of faculty activity: involvement in the scholarship of teaching, service-learning, grant applications, publications, presentations at national conferences, external funding, attention to undergraduate learning, and relationships with the community. More than a third of all CAOs observed increases in the following kinds of activities: scholarship of integration, student contact, and scholarship of engagement and professional service. About half of all CAOs reported increases in areas related to institutional effectiveness, including ability of the institution to meet goals and objectives, congruence between faculty priorities and institutional mission, and faculty recruitment. However, fewer than a third of CAOs reported increases in the following faculty work life areas: applications for promotion from associate to full professor, probability of a successful tenure decision, promotion to full professor, satisfaction with roles and rewards, retention and satisfaction of faculty of color, and evidence of senior faculty vitality. An exception was the area of retention and satisfaction of women faculty, where half of CAOs reported an increase. When we compared responses from CAOs at reform and traditional institutions, we found that the former were much more likely than the latter to report increases and improvements in almost every aspect of faculty work life and institutional effectiveness.[1]

We also asked CAOs if they attributed any of the increases and improvements to their institution's formal (reform) or informal (traditional) efforts to encourage multiple forms of scholarship.

Table A.3 (see Appendix) lists the kinds of improvements and increases that institutions might have experienced over the previous 10 years, followed by the percentage of all CAOs, reform-campus CAOs, and traditional-campus CAOs who believed increases or improvements in these areas were influenced by their institution's efforts to encourage multiple forms of scholarship. As Table A.3 indicates, a much higher percentage of CAOs at reform institutions reported that their institution's efforts had influenced observed increases and improvements.[2]

Reward systems in academic communities are about "what counts." That is the issue that researchers have found baffles junior faculty as they try to judge how their work will be "counted" for tenure and promotion (Boice, 1992). Expectations for quantity and quality of scholarship are often considered moving targets (Rice et al., 2000). Over the past five years, research on faculty productivity has suggested that while standards for faculty work may be a moving target, they have consistently been moving in the same direction—upward—as institutions of all types try to emulate the research productivity of the most selective research universities (Dey, Milem, & Berger, 1997).

Our findings suggest that research expectations have continued to increase, even as more and more campuses formally recognize multiple forms of scholarship. Most CAOs (51 percent) reported that research counted more now than 10 years before on their campus. Rather than thwarting the upward trend in research expectations, our findings suggest that the two events—rising research and writing expectations and a broader definition of scholarship—have occurred simultaneously. These findings are consistent with previous survey research indicating that while teaching and engagement count more at four-year institutions, so too does research (Huber, 2002).

Most CAOs at reform institutions felt that each activity (teaching, service, publication productivity, service to the institution, and service to the discipline) counted more now than it did 10 years ago, while most CAOs at traditional institutions reported each activity counted about the same (Table A.4 in Appendix). Data regarding all CAOs' responses to this question appeared in O'Meara and Braskamp (2005). Publication productivity counted more than previously in institutions that had made formal policy reform, which seems curious, until we consider all the baccalaureate institutions that used Boyer's framework to move from a culture where no scholarship was conducted at all to one where some traditional writing was encouraged and rewarded. This finding is consistent with an increase in writing expectations at institutions that formally encouraged multiple forms of scholarship. While these institutions may have expanded the range of acceptable kinds of writing to include products of engagement and teaching scholarship, nonetheless writing in these areas is still considered a rising expectation.

To assess the influence of formal policy reform on promotion and tenure decisions, we asked several questions concerning different candidate profiles and their probability for success (Table A.5 in Appendix). We found that chances to achieve tenure and promotion, based on excelling in teaching or in engagement, have increased more substantially for reform than for traditional institutions.[3]

Chait (2002) has observed that "the probability of a favorable decision among candidates formally considered for tenure has not varied by institutional type and also has not changed materially" (p. 25), with the probability of tenure last calculated, in 1993, as a little better than 7 in 10 by the National Center for Educational Statistics (NCES) (Chait, 2002, p. 18). While making formal policy changes seems to have improved chances for faculty engaged in teaching and engagement to achieve promotion and tenure, and this is an important finding, it should not obscure the fact that, overall, most CAOs reported that the chances for tenure and promotion had stayed the same. The consistency between these two findings suggests a great stability in the chances for promotion and tenure once a candidate is formally reviewed—a stability that may be immune to policy reform. However, neither the NCES responses nor those by our CAOs reveal whether reforms had increased the number of people retained until tenure-decision year or applying for promotion to full professor. Women and faculty of color are reported to leave the tenure track prior to the tenure-decision year in greater numbers than their peers, and this attrition is attributed, in part, to a lack of recognition of their involvement in teaching and service activities. Likewise, many mid-career faculty never apply for promotion because of the lack of recognition they believe their teaching and engagement activities will receive. Further research should explore the impact of policy reform on faculty retention.

We wanted to understand whether formal efforts to encourage multiple forms of scholarship had influenced the criteria used to assess scholarship. We asked CAOs about the degree to which a list of criteria may have influenced the final decision by faculty committees to recommend or deny tenure and promotion (Table A.6 in Appendix). At traditional institutions, CAOs identified the traditional criteria, such as whether something was published, where it was published, and its impact on the disciplines, as major influences on promotion and tenure. While reform-institution CAOs reported these traditional criteria as major influences, they also identified, as equally or more important influences, criteria often considered critical to the positive and effective evaluation of teaching and service scholarship, such as the impact of the scholarship on the state or local community, the institution, students, the mission of the institution, and the academic unit. Our findings suggest that making formal changes in reward systems does influence the kinds of work that are considered scholarship, who is valued (teaching and service scholars as well as researchers), and how scholarship is evaluated (impact on mission).

How individuals make meaning of change within academic communities will be influenced by their role (faculty member, department chair, dean), discipline, career stage, and institutional type. While research suggests that some subgroups may be more likely to embrace a broader definition of scholarship than others, scholars of organizational change in higher education have found that real change must penetrate the entire institution (Eckel et al., 1999; Kezar, 2001; Kuh & Whitt, 1988; Van Maanen & Schein, 1979). Accordingly, we wanted to identify where CAOs perceived pockets of support or resistance among institutional subcultures defined by academic role, discipline, and career stage.

All CAO perceptions, and CAO perceptions from traditional and reform institutions, are outlined in Table A.7 (in the Appendix). In all three groups, the rankings remained the same: faculty in the social sciences were considered to be most supportive of a broader definition of scholarship, followed by faculty in the humanities, the professional schools, and the natural sciences. All groups viewed junior faculty as most supportive of an expanded definition of scholarship, followed by mid-career faculty and senior faculty. Deans were considered the most supportive of an expanded definition of scholarship, followed by president or chancellor, department chairs, and boards of trustees.[4] Reform-institution CAOs reported much higher levels of support for a broader definition of scholarship, from all constituents, than did traditional-institution CAOs. However, it is not clear from these findings whether policy reform helped to create a supportive environment, or if the supportive environment sparked the policy reform.

Conscious or unconscious values, or "widely held beliefs or sentiments about the importance of certain goals, activities, relations and feelings" (Kuh & Whitt, 1988, p. 23), affect behavior in organizations. Over the past 10 years, advocates of teaching scholarship and engagement scholarship have tried to alter what Rice (1996, p. 8) called the "assumptive world" of the academic professional, which prizes individual over collaborative activity, disciplinary over interdisciplinary work, and basic research over all other forms of scholarship. We wanted to know, from the perspective of CAOs, whether the different activities of teaching, application, and integrative work were commonly valued or believed to be forms of scholarship (Table A.8 in Appendix). Those who embrace a broader definition of scholarship will be pleased to find that of all CAOs surveyed, 71 percent agreed or strongly agreed that their campus faculty had developed a more complex or nuanced view of scholarship, 67 percent that participatory-action research was commonly considered scholarship, 62 percent that aspects of teaching were commonly considered scholarship, 57 percent that engagement was commonly considered scholarship, and 78 percent that integrative work was commonly considered scholarship. When we compared reform and traditional CAO responses to the question of what kinds of activities were commonly considered scholarship, we found great differences. In every area mentioned, most of the reform-institution CAOs reported that they agreed or strongly agreed that these activities were commonly considered forms of scholarship, whereas most traditional-institution CAOs disagreed or strongly disagreed.

In 1987, Clark made us aware of the diversity of faculty work life experiences in different types of colleges and universities. To understand the implications of the survey data in context, it is important to embed them in a discussion of institutional type.

FRAMING BARRIERS AND STRATEGIES BY INSTITUTIONAL TYPE

In this section I analyze the barriers that thwart and the strategies that support faculty involvement in multiple forms of scholarship. Drawing on data from the nine campus studies, the national survey of chief academic officers (CAOs), focus groups conducted with CAOs in New England four-year colleges and universities, and research on organizational change in faculty work life, I note the role that institutional type plays in both the kinds of barriers and the most effective strategies to get beyond them. The discussion proceeds according to the institutional type in which the data suggested they were most prevalent, relevant, or emergent. However, the significance of examples is not restricted to the type being discussed, since the same barrier likely exists in all of the institutional types to some degree, and the same strategy might be used to address it in many institutional types. Consequently, Table 13.2 outlines barriers and strategies. I used the Carnegie classification system (2000) for colleges and universities, a well-known tool for distinguishing between institutional types, to differentiate among four-year institutions.

BACCALAUREATE INSTITUTIONS

Teaching load is perhaps most likely to be a formidable barrier in baccalaureate institutions, where it is often as heavy as five courses per semester. In many baccalaureate institutions, the movement to encourage multiple forms of scholarship has meant trying to encourage any form of scholarship, or even professional development, among faculty whose time is fully devoted to teaching and advising. For example, faculty and administrators at Franklin College cited the heavy teaching load—four courses per semester—as providing inadequate time for faculty to do any substantial reflection and writing. Likewise, Madonna University required a heavy teaching load, and faculty were also engaged in considerable advising, registration, and committee work, as well as expected to attend university events and activities in the community. Fear that encouraging multiple forms of scholarship would result in unrealistic expectations for an already overwhelmed faculty seems to be

TABLE 13.2 BARRIERS TO AND STRATEGIES FOR
ENCOURAGING MULTIPLE FORMS OF SCHOLARSHIP

Institution Type	Barriers	Strategies
Baccalaureate	Heavy teaching and advising load	Reducing course loads, offering incentive grants and sabbaticals
	Faculty training and expertise	Providing training at teaching and learning centers
	Resources	Partnering junior and senior faculty, student affairs, and faculty
		Linking scholarship to the institution's unique mission
	Confusion and ambiguity about what really counts for promotion and tenure	Arranging meetings between candidates and personnel committee
	Desire to maintain the status quo in policies about scholarship	Hosting open forums, opportunities for dialogue, and campuswide discussion
Master's	Mission drift	Offering leadership and raising the profile of teaching and engagement through speeches, awards, press, and so forth
	Bias of new junior faculty in favor of discovery	Offering graduate school programs that prepare whole scholars
		Giving orientations that socialize faculty to a broadened definition of scholarship
		Mentoring and role modeling by senior faculty

TABLE 13.2 BARRIERS TO AND STRATEGIES FOR
ENCOURAGING MULTIPLE FORMS OF SCHOLARSHIP *(continued)*

Institution Type	Barriers	Strategies
Doctoral	Overloaded plate	Offering creativity contracts
		Making departments— not individuals—the focus of evaluation
	Department chairs insufficiently trained to support faculty in newer forms of scholarship	Offering professional development for department chairs and deans
	Inconsistent definition of scholarship across the university	Allowing flexibility and autonomy but requiring accountability
	Test-case fear	Supporting risk takers and innovators, especially through promotion and tenure
Research	Values and beliefs favoring discovery over other forms of scholarship	Focusing on image and increasing the visibility of teaching and engagement in key venues
		Supporting teaching and engagement scholarship through distribution of resources
	Political nature of faculty evaluation	Amending promotion and tenure documents to include a broader definition of scholarship
		Developing trust
	Difficulty in establishing benchmarks for excellence in teaching and engagement	Linking internal reviews to national awards and peer-review procedures
	Lack of standards and encouragement from disciplinary associations	Developing department standards documents for excellence in multiple forms of scholarship

at the root of much resistance at baccalaureate colleges. Resistance also seems to come from senior faculty members, who completed traditional requirements for scholarship despite the heavy workload and expect junior faculty to do the same. Likewise, several CAOs of unionized baccalaureate institutions reported that the *protective nature of faculty unions,* in making sure nothing "extra" is added to a faculty member's official responsibilities, thwarts efforts to redefine scholarship.

Another common barrier is *faculty morale and feelings of competence* in engaging in multiple forms of scholarship. Given that many mid-career and senior faculty in baccalaureate and some master's institutions have spent their careers devoting 80–100 percent of their time to teaching, advising, curriculum reform, and shared governance, they may not feel competent or confident initiating research projects or other forms of scholarship. Some may have lost touch with their disciplines as they became more devoted to institutional concerns.

One approach to alleviating the time problem is to *offer reduced course loads and incentive grants* and to devise sabbaticals aimed at encouraging scholarship. Most CAOs at baccalaureate institutions have used this approach. Findings from the AAHE survey confirmed that baccalaureate institutions were the institutional type most likely to have implemented this strategy over the past 10 years. Kenneth Zahorski (1994) has written eloquently about the potential for stimulating faculty vitality and interest in scholarship through well-planned sabbaticals. One caution about these strategies: they can be expensive, and if incentive grants and reduced course loads are awarded to more junior than senior faculty, senior faculty may become jealous. Care must be taken to provide financial support across both career stages and types of scholarship activity.

One of the best suggestions in this book comes from Madonna University's case, an inexpensive strategy that provides a win-win for everyone. The university developed partnerships between junior and senior faculty and between Academic and Student Affairs to work on newer forms of scholarship such as classroom research, participatory action research, or interdisciplinary curriculum development. In this way, faculty fresh out of research universities could merge their expertise in methods with the senior faculty's knowledge of classrooms, teaching methods, and content. Madonna

University also encouraged partnerships between faculty and staff colleagues in the library or in the offices of service-learning, disability resources, multicultural affairs, and continuing and professional education.

Members of organizations may resist change because they do not understand it or do not feel in control of it (Kanter, 1985). Many of the cases in this book, as well as the CAOs in our New England focus groups, mentioned the importance of *holding open forums* for faculty to express concerns while a redefinition of scholarship is being discussed or changes are being made to promotion and tenure documents or other faculty evaluation procedures. Open forums and increased dialogue across disciplinary lines are all useful, because the more interaction, the more opportunities individuals have to develop new mental models or change the way they think about scholarship and their work (Senge, 1990).

In the AAHE survey of CAOs, 69 percent of those at baccalaureate institutions reported that "greater confusion and ambiguity for faculty about what really counts for promotion and tenure" was a barrier. This highlights the importance of having candidates meet with personnel committees before preparing their portfolios, to review new language or procedures.

Another effective strategy for institutions with heavy teaching and advising commitments is to encourage faculty to link their scholarship to the unique mission of the institution. A good example of this strategy comes from the Albany State University study. This institution was struggling to maintain its historic commitment to minority and underserved students while responding to state requirements to increase faculty scholarly productivity. Its strategy of linking faculty scholarship to student needs was akin to making lemonade when served lemons. The university's president encouraged faculty to study their own students, develop strategies to increase student retention, improve student test-taking skills, and disseminate their findings to similar institutions. In doing so, faculty engaged in the scholarships of teaching and engagement without feeling that they were abandoning their institutional mission. Kezar (2001) notes that connecting the process of change to individual faculty and institutional identity is a proven strategy for moving campuses forward.

When an institution that has traditionally not encouraged or expected faculty involvement in scholarship tries to move toward those expectations, it is indeed attempting a significant culture shift. It is very important that the leadership be intentional about the messages that they send to faculty concerning roles, rewards, and the direction of the institution. Academic leaders must send consistent, even relentless messages that the institution is moving in a given direction, one that will strengthen, not reject, the traditional values and commitments. The CAO of a small baccalaureate college in New England remarked that "the most important thing is that the administration make a commitment to communicating that the culture needs to change regarding scholarship."

MASTER'S INSTITUTIONS

The *orientation and bias* of recently recruited junior faculty toward research constitutes a major barrier, especially for master's institutions. Studies and projects have found that graduate students continue to be socialized to assume traditional research roles to the exclusion of other training, despite the fact that most of the institutions they will be employed in require a greater balance of responsibilities (Austin, 2002b; Burgan, 1998; Rice, 1996; Richlin, 1993). Research by Braxton et al. (2002) found that graduate education was a major barrier to institutionalization of the four domains of scholarship. Not only does most graduate education not prepare students with skills to engage in the application, integration, and teaching forms of scholarship, but it can predispose faculty against engaging in these forms of scholarship (Richlin, 1993). Findings of the AAHE survey indicate that 54 percent of CAOs in master's institutions agreed that "the research orientation of newly recruited faculty is a barrier," and 72 percent agreed that "faculty graduate school training and socialization toward traditional definitions of scholarship" act as a barrier to encouraging multiple forms of scholarship. The CAO from one New England master's institution said, "Doctoral programs acculturate people into research orientations. When we get new faculty from environments where discovery and grants is the gold standard, we have to work against that and reeducate them."

One catalyst for *Scholarship Reconsidered* was a sense by Boyer and others that baccalaureate, master's, and doctoral universities were moving away from their missions and becoming more imitative of research universities in faculty roles and rewards. Efforts to increase the institution's standing in ranking systems act as a major barrier, by causing mission drift, which pushes faculty to emphasize discovery to the exclusion of all other forms of scholarship, even those that directly relate to the institutional mission. Mission drift most directly affects institutions in the middle of the Carnegie classification, which often struggle with their identity and purpose in relation to the institutions directly below and above in the hierarchy. According to the AAHE survey, 45 percent of master's university CAOs found that the "ratcheting up of research expectations to improve institutional or department rankings" was a barrier. CAOs in the New England focus groups said that accrediting associations that review programs without a sensitivity to institutional mission often contributed to mission drift by making recommendations requiring a greater research orientation to the exclusion of other forms of scholarship.

For master's institutions, *preparing graduate students to be "whole scholars"* is a critical recruitment and socialization strategy. Graduate training should foster scholarship in each of the four domains (Braxton et al. 2002; Gaff & Lambert, 1996). Most Preparing Future Faculty programs (see Jerry Gaff's section of Chapter 3) are at research and doctoral universities, but master's institutions have an important role to play in partnering with research universities to develop intern opportunities for graduate students. Master's institutions that develop such partnerships will acquire a new recruiting tool and will benefit from better prepared and more holistic scholars, ready for the kinds of faculty roles that exist in master's institutions.

Another strategy is to provide a new faculty orientation and follow-up programs that socialize faculty to the campus culture and to the broadened definition of scholarship. Programs should explain the broadened definition of scholarship to early career faculty and discuss the kinds of work done by their department colleagues in each of the four domains. Sorcinelli's (2000) research and best practices suggest the importance of communicating performance expectations to early career faculty. Programs that intentionally pair senior and junior faculty in mentoring relationships can orient new faculty to a broadened definition of scholarship through role modeling.

Mission drift cannot be curbed solely by addressing new faculty. Aligning or realigning mission and reward systems requires constant attention to the institutional artifacts, everyday policies, procedures, and workings that influence values and beliefs (Schein, 1992). For example, institutional goals should give the scholarship of teaching and engagement as much weight as discovery research, or even more, accomplishments in these areas should receive the same amount of attention, through on-campus awards, newspaper coverage of accomplishments, and the criteria for giving merit awards and recruiting "star" faculty. In managing the balance between different forms of scholarship, academic leaders and faculty leaders can shape their cultures so as to encourage mission and reward system alignment.

DOCTORAL INSTITUTIONS

Early career faculty are facing an *overloaded plate* (Rice et al., 2000), and in recent years, "scholarly responsibilities of early career faculty have not only broadened but also increased" (p. 16). Numerous studies indicate increasing faculty workloads and expectations (Berberet, 2002).

Most of the CAOs in the AAHE survey reported that research counted more than it did 10 years previously, suggesting that research expectations have continued to increase, at the same time as more campuses formally recognize multiple forms of scholarship. Faculty now feel obliged to excel at all forms of scholarship simultaneously. According to the AAHE survey findings, 79 percent of doctoral university CAOs agreed that "faculty concerns about unrealistic expectations that faculty excel in all areas at the same time" was a barrier to encouraging multiple forms of scholarship. This problem was especially difficult for doctoral universities where a new emphasis on teaching was added to already high research and outreach expectations.

One method for helping faculty cope with an excess of roles is to restructure positions through what Boyer referred as "creativity contracts," discussed in the first section of this chapter. Findings from the AAHE survey indicate that creativity contracts have been most popular at doctoral institutions, where 55 percent of CAOs reported that their campuses had initiated them in the last decade. The authors of Kansas State University's campus study discuss their success with "optimizing time and talent" through the development of individual responsibility profiles.

Another way of unloading the faculty plate is to make departments the focus of evaluation, not individual faculty. Ernest Lynton (1998) discussed this strategy eloquently in "Reversing the Telescope," where he argued for evaluating units, as opposed to individuals, for their overall contributions in terms of research, teaching, and service. According to Lynton, the collegial dialogue and collaboration generated by this approach could foster a greater sense of campus community and decrease unrealistic expectations that faculty excel in everything simultaneously.

"Insufficient training for department chairs and deans" was cited by 73 percent of doctoral university CAOs as a barrier in the AAHE survey. One of the most important strategies for addressing the overloaded-plate problem is providing leadership development for department chairs, to give them the skills for assisting faculty in balancing their roles (Bensimon, Ward, & Sanders, 2000; Wergin & Swingen, 2000). Teaching and learning centers provide another option, being wonderful places for faculty to receive support for multiple forms of scholarship (Sorcinelli, 2002). Portland State University's campus study mentions the crucial role of teaching and learning centers for encouraging faculty in the scholarship of teaching and engagement. Centers can help faculty prepare their dossiers, provide model portfolios, and in general streamline and simplify the documentation process.

Another barrier that many large doctoral and comprehensive universities face is trying to establish a consistent definition of scholarship across the university. The AAHE survey found that 82 percent of CAOs in doctoral universities saw this issue as a barrier. Since departments have considerable autonomy in how they implement university mandates, the revision of a university's faculty handbook and personnel policy does not guarantee that the broader definition of scholarship will be applied the same way, or to the same degree, in physics as in English. As the authors of the Kansas State University and South Dakota State University campus studies point out, the effort to achieve uniformity among units in defining and assessing scholarship should provide flexibility and autonomy but require accountability. Departments need sufficient autonomy to integrate their disciplinary standards into university standards, but each unit should be accountable for showing that it actually followed university procedures for valuing multiple forms of scholarship in faculty evaluation decisions.

Research Institutions

Values that favor discovery over all other forms of scholarship are a major barrier in research universities. In academic communities, deeply held norms and values influence salary increases, tenure, and promotion, and may also influence the involvement of faculty in various forms of scholarship. In a study on the evaluation of service as a form of scholarship for promotion and tenure, I found that certain values inhibited appreciating the importance of multiple forms of scholarly work. These values can be summarized in the following statements:

- "Scholarship is empirical research disseminated to the academic community."
- "Scholarly work is completed apart from practitioners."
- "The best scholarship brings the most prestige to our positions."
- "Traditional research requires more professional knowledge than other forms of scholarship."
- "Writing is scholarly because of where it is as opposed to what it is." (O'Meara, 2002a, p. 67)

These values were most pronounced at research universities.

Another barrier is the use of faculty evaluation criteria that favor discovery above all other forms of scholarship. An institution may commit to a broader definition of scholarship, but if it applies the traditional criteria for evaluating research to the assessment of newer forms of scholarship, then teaching and service scholarship will almost always appear lacking. Braxton et al. (2002) noted that "the process used to assess faculty scholarship is a main barrier to the institutionalization of the four domains" (p. 75).[5]

At research and doctoral universities, disciplinary norms and standards strongly influence faculty. The fact that most disciplinary associations have not encouraged or provided standards for teaching and engagement scholarship has slowed their acceptance in many departments. Either disciplines are lagging behind or faculty are unaware of their efforts, but in the meantime, departments lack disciplinary norms for multiple forms of scholarly work. Research-institution CAOs in the AAHE survey reported in greater numbers than any other institutional type that "the stance of disciplinary associations in some fields (59 percent) and difficulty in documenting alternative forms of scholarship for promotion and tenure (79 percent)" were barriers.

Anyone who studies or works in a college or university knows that faculty evaluation can be highly political. Kezar (2001) observed that the decentralized authority of many universities, coupled with the fact that universities are highly value laden, encourages political activity. Not surprisingly, 65 percent of CAOs in research universities, in the AAHE survey, cited the "political nature of faculty evaluation" as a significant barrier. Within every university are people who have a vested interest in maintaining the status quo. Survey findings indicate that 82 percent of CAOs in research universities experienced vested interests of some faculty in maintaining the status quo. In addition, those who have a vested interest in defining scholarship more broadly must still confront test-case fear, the concern among the first faculty to be reviewed that new promotion and tenure policies will not really be used by those making personnel decisions.

Given the key importance of the promotion and tenure system (Chait, 1995), *amending promotion, tenure, and other evaluation documents* to include a broader definition of scholarship can provide important "cultural armor" for faculty involved in engagement or teaching scholarship (O'Meara, 2002b). Indeed, amending these documents has been one of the most popular strategies used by colleges and universities of all types. Three-fourths of research and doctoral university CAOs reported that their institutions had expanded the definition of scholarship used in faculty evaluation. All of the campus study chapters in this book describe changes made to formal faculty evaluation policy. This strategy is both political and symbolic, for it sends a clear message to faculty that the institution values multiple forms of scholarship, and it serves as a contract between the university and the faculty member, protecting career choices.

However, no matter what the policies, some faculty will feel vulnerable and will doubt that their colleagues will adequately honor the university's commitment to reward activity in teaching or engagement scholarship. Thus, developing trust among the university, the faculty member, the department chair, and the dean is key. Kansas State University's campus study assigned trust a pivotal role in the implementation of a flexible allocation system. Faculty had to trust that, when the time came to make decisions about raises, merit pay, and other rewards, the department chair would value their allocation toward teaching scholarship as highly as someone else's allocation toward discovery. Acceptance and implementation of flexible allocation is, to a great degree, a function of culture and traditions in the academic department. Faculty must believe that the contract will be honored and they will be evaluated based on their new workloads.

In addition to building trust, an institution can do a great deal to influence values and beliefs by raising the profile of reform. A focus on image can be an important change strategy when attempting reform within academic cultures (Kezar, 2001). Methods include, for example, presenting awards for faculty engagement at graduation ceremonies, hosting dinners to celebrate faculty involvement in the scholarship of teaching, and public references to interdisciplinary faculty projects by presidents and CAOs. Finally, internal review processes should be linked, when possible, to national efforts in engagement and teaching. For example, the National Review Board for the Scholarship of Engagement provides external peer review and evaluation (www.scholarshipofengagement.org). The Carnegie Foundation for the Advancement of Teaching annually invites faculty from across the country to become Carnegie Scholars and work with a group of outstanding faculty on innovations in pedagogy and learning (www.carnegiefoundation.org). Finally, the New England Resource Center for Higher Education (www.nerche.org) gives the Ernest Lynton Award to a faculty member who has excelled in professional service. Any of these programs can provide evidence of national recognition and impact and assist faculty in making their case for promotion and tenure.

IMPLICATIONS AND CONCLUSIONS

The findings of this study indicate two kinds of barriers that merit future research. The first set seems to be an unintended consequence of policy reform. Expanding the definition of scholarship used in faculty evaluation and mission statements has caused greater confusion and ambiguity for faculty about what really counts for promotion and tenure. In addition, department chairs, deans, and faculty still lack the skills and knowledge to effectively document or assess the scholarships of teaching, integration, and application. Across the country, leaders in assessing teaching scholarship (Huber, 2002; Seldin, 1993) and the scholarship of application (Driscoll & Lynton, 1999) have worked hard to help hundreds of campuses grapple with these issues. But clearly more work needs to be done. Conducting leadership development for department chairs to support new faculty as they try to document teaching and engagement scholarship will be an important strategy to overcome these barriers (Bensimon et al., 2000). Developing department standards and policies for scholarship in each of the four domains will also be important for reducing ambiguity and uncertainty.

The second set of barriers is more complex and best described as the "overloaded-plate problem" (Rice et al., 2000). Faculty activity in the scholarships of teaching, application, and service-learning was reported to have increased over the previous decade. But faculty activity in external funding, presentations at national conferences, grant applications, and publications also increased. While involvement in the scholarships of teaching, integration, and application does not necessarily exclude faculty from activity in external funding, publications, and presentations, the overlap is likely to be a small proportion of the whole. Furthermore, our findings indicate that research expectations for faculty have increased, even at campuses that reward multiple forms of scholarship. These findings are consistent with other recent studies, which found that, during the past two decades, faculty in every institutional type spent more time on research (Dey et al., 1997) and that expectations for every area of faculty work had increased (Huber, 2002).

Increases in faculty activity have not been accompanied by reports from a majority of all CAOs indicating an increase in faculty satisfaction with roles and rewards, evidence of increased senior faculty vitality, retention of faculty of color, or applications for promotion. According to CAOs at both reform and traditional institutions, faculty identified unrealistic expectations that they excel in all areas at the same time as the primary barrier to encouraging and rewarding multiple forms of scholarship. If activity continues to increase in all areas of faculty work, and expectations for every area continue to rise without a corresponding sense that faculty are being rewarded and sustained in their careers, turnover and burnout may increase.

Making formal policy changes, such as redefining scholarship for faculty evaluation, has improved the alignment of workload, talents, and mission. Findings from the survey suggest that broadening the definition of scholarship used in faculty evaluation and mission statements, developing flexible workload programs, and providing incentive grants improve faculty work life, institutional effectiveness, and academic culture (at least from the CAO perspective), and should be considered important responses to the overloaded-plate problem.

Perhaps most important is the need for institutions to reconsider the relative weight they give to all forms of scholarship vis-à-vis other important faculty activities that maintain and nurture academic communities. While the major thrust of *Scholarship Reconsidered* was to reframe scholarship beyond traditional research, Boyer also encouraged acknowledging all faculty work that serves the mission of an institution. Today we have a more diverse student body, fewer resources, and fewer faculty to meet new needs. These are just a few of the many reasons faculty are being called to greater engagement with their students and within their institutions. Engagement is critical to student success and to the missions of departments, colleges, and institutions, but may not be scholarship as defined by Boyer (1990) and by Glassick et al. (1997). The Associated New American Colleges are recommending that the criteria for assessing scholarship be extended to governance and institutional service (Berberet, 1999). Unless reward systems place more weight on faculty involvement in internal service, advising, effective teaching, and outreach activities, we will continue to see a collapse of shared governance, greater distance between students and faculty, and a faculty whose well-being and commitment are in question.

In the discussion of how institutional type is related to reform efforts, it is clear each institutional type confronts distinct challenges. For example, non-elite baccalaureate institutions face, by far, the biggest structural challenges to involving faculty in multiple forms of scholarship by virtue of the heavy teaching loads and scarcity of resources. Master's institutions, a middle child of the Carnegie system, also face problems with faculty time. Their greatest struggles, however, are probably in recruiting and retaining faculty who will support their primary teaching and service missions, and in the tendency of faculty or leadership to let the reward system drift away from the primary mission in the quest for prestige or higher national rankings. Doctoral universities have always emphasized research, but often in ways compatible with local, regional, and state concerns. Their faculty have felt the weight of increased expectations most heavily, as teaching and integration became greater concerns in the 1990s and were added to already significant research and outreach expectations. Faculty need the freedom to emphasize one area of scholarship over another and not feel that they must excel in all areas of scholarship simultaneously, and they need help in documenting engagement and teaching as forms of scholarship for promotion and tenure. Faculty in research universities who engage in teaching, engagement, or integration as their primary form of scholarship are often working against dominant values and norms and, possibly, even against a mission that suggests that discovery is what they should be doing. What these faculty most need is "cover." They need help in linking their scholarship to national programs and efforts, making it visible on campus, and having it peer reviewed and published.

Across all institutional types each faculty member has the ability to contribute scholarly talent in important ways that benefit the institutions and ultimately the public good. The crux of the matter, amid all the discussion of politics, programs, and policies, is that we are talking about discovering talent, developing talent, and enjoying the benefits of talent. We can reap a great harvest if we seek creative ways to cultivate and nurture faculty scholarship of all kinds.

Notes

1. Each item mentioned is not entirely discrete and may be interrelated with others. For example, faculty involvement in the scholarship of teaching may entail increased attention to undergraduate learning.

Likewise, involvement in service-learning may affect relationships with the community and involve grant-writing to seek support. Future research is needed to explore whether participation in newer forms of scholarship is also increasing faculty involvement in more traditional activities, such as publication, presentations, or external funding, and to elucidate the interrelationships.

2. In interpreting these findings, it is important to consider the possibility of bias on the part of reform-institution CAOs, who, as a result of looking for certain kinds of outcomes, found them (Weick, 1995). Those at traditional institutions may have been less likely to look for data confirming that their informal efforts were having specific outcomes. Regardless, the differences between CAO responses suggests that most reform-institution CAOs found tangible benefits in faculty work life and institutional effectiveness as a result of formal efforts to encourage multiple forms of scholarship—benefits that traditional campuses were less likely to experience.

3. In another set of questions concerning reward systems, reform-institution CAOs reported a higher percentage of promotion and tenure candidates who emphasized teaching or engagement scholarship than traditional-institution CAOs. Asked what proportion of those cases was successful, more than 50 percent of all CAOs reported that it was a majority. Fewer than 6 percent of all CAOs said the cases were unsuccessful in each category; 15–35 percent of all CAOs reported they did not know the answer or did not respond to the question. When we compared the paths, we found that reform-institution CAOs reported slightly more successful teaching and engagement cases than traditional-institution CAOs. For example, engagement scholars were reported to be successful by 58 percent of reform-institution CAOs, compared with 36 percent of traditional-institution CAOs. Traditional-institution CAOs were slightly more likely than reform-institution CAOs to report that they did not know the success rate of candidates, or did not respond to the question.

4. More than 71 percent of all CAOs found junior faculty supportive of an expanded definition of scholarship. This may seem surprising, given recent research showing that early career faculty are the ones most likely to suffer from an "overloaded plate," a situation possibly made worse by attempts to transform every area of faculty work into scholarship. There are at least two possible explanations. Rice et al. (2000) conducted more than 350 interviews as part of their "Heeding New Voices" study, and found that soon-to-be faculty and early career faculty reported "a strong sense of engagement, expressed as strong social commitments and a desire that their academic work be part of a larger life mission to give back to their local communities

and improve society" (p. 6). They found this sentiment especially strong among women and minority faculty. Possibly this "new academic generation" (Finkelstein, Seal, & Schuster, 1998) of junior faculty is more deeply involved than their senior colleagues in work that has not traditionally been rewarded on their campuses, and they want their work to be acknowledged. However, these findings might also reflect the CAOs' impression of junior faculty as generally open to most new reforms, eager to please early in their careers, and more flexible in their views of scholarship or evaluation.

5. However, the problem is not only that the assessment criteria are flawed. There are technical challenges in trying to assess the rigor of this work and establish benchmarks for excellence. Many faculty members involved in newer forms of teaching and engagement scholarship are working on disciplinary frontiers that have not yet gained solid indicators of quality or credible dissemination strategies. In the AAHE survey, research-institution CAOs reported in greater numbers than other institutional types (79 percent) that "difficulty in documenting multiple forms of scholarship for promotion and tenure" was a barrier.

References

Aldersley, S. F. (1995). Upward drift is alive and well: Research/doctoral model still attractive to institutions. *Change, 27*(5): 50–56.

Austin, A. (2002a). Creating a bridge to the future: Preparing new faculty to face changing expectations in a shifting context. *Review of Higher Education,* 26(2): 119–144.

Austin, A. (2002b). Preparing the next generation of faculty: Graduate school as socialization to the academic career. *Journal of Higher Education, 73*(1): 94–122.

Bensimon, E. M., Ward, K., & Sanders, K. (2000). *The department chair's role in developing new faculty into teachers and scholars.* Bolton, MA: Anker.

Berberet, J. (1999). The professoriate and institutional citizenship: Toward a scholarship of service. *Liberal Education,* 85(4): 33–39.

Berberet, J. (2002). The new academic compact. In L. A. McMillin & J. Berberet (Eds.), *The new academic compact: Revisioning the relationship between faculty and their institutions* (pp. 3–28). Bolton, MA: Anker.

Boice, R. (1992). *The new faculty member.* San Francisco: Jossey-Bass.

Boyer, E. (1990). *Scholarship reconsidered: Priorities of the professoriate.* Princeton, NJ: Carnegie Foundation for the Advancement of Teaching.

Braskamp, L. A., & Wergin, J. F. (1998). Forming a new social partnership. In W. G. Tierney (Ed.), *The responsive university: Restructuring for high performance* (pp. 62–91). Baltimore: Johns Hopkins University Press.

Braxton, J., Luckey, W., & Holland, P. (2002). *Institutionalizing a broader view of scholarship through Boyer's four domains.* ASHE-ERIC Higher Education Report Vol. 29, No. 2. San Francisco: Jossey-Bass.

Burgan, M. (1998). Academic citizenship: A fading vision. *Liberal Education, 84*(4): 16–21.

Chait, R. (1995). The future of academic tenure. *Priorities, 3:* 1–11.

Chait, R. (2002). Gleanings. In R. Chait (Ed.), *The questions of tenure* (pp. 309–323). Cambridge, MA: Harvard University Press.

Checkoway, B. (2001). Renewing the civic mission of the American research university. *Journal of Higher Education, 72*(2): 125–147.

Clark, B. (1987). *The academic life: Small worlds, different worlds.* New York: Carnegie Foundation for the Advancement of Teaching.

Cohen, A. (1998). *The shaping of American higher education: Emergence and growth of the contemporary system.* San Francisco: Jossey-Bass.

Crosson, P. (1983). *Public service in higher education: Practices and priorities.* ASHE-ERIC Higher Education Research Report (ED 284 515). Washington, DC: George Washington University.

Dey, E. L., Milem, J. F., & Berger, J. B. (1997). Changing patterns of publication productivity: Accumulative advantage or institutional isomorphism? *Sociology of Education, 70*(4): 308–323.

Diamond, R. M. (1993). Instituting change in faculty reward systems. In R. M. Diamond & B. E. Adam (Eds.), *Recognizing faculty work: Reward systems for the year 2000* (pp. 13–22). New Directions for Higher Education, no. 81. San Francisco: Jossey-Bass.

Diamond, R. M. (1999). *Aligning faculty rewards with institutional mission.* Bolton, MA: Anker.

Driscoll, A., & Lynton, E. A. (1999). *Making outreach visible: A guide to documenting professional service and outreach.* Washington, DC: American Association for Higher Education.

Eby, J. W. (1996). Linking service and scholarship. In R. Sigmon (Ed.), *Journey to service-learning* (pp. 87–98). Washington, DC: Council of Independent Colleges.

Eckel, P., Green, M., Hill, B., & Mallon, W. (1999). *On Change III: Taking charge of change: A primer for colleges and universities.* Washington, DC: American Council on Education.

Finkelstein, M., Seal, R., & Schuster, J. (1998). *The new academic generation: A profession in transformation.* Baltimore: Johns Hopkins University Press.

Finnegan, D. E. (1993). Segmentation in the academic labor market: Hiring cohorts in comprehensive universities. *Journal of Higher Education, 64:* 621–656.

Gaff, J. G., & Lambert, L. M. (1996, July/August). Socializing future faculty to the values of undergraduate education. *Change, 28:* 38–45.

Geiger, R. L. (1999). The ten generations of American higher education. In P. T. Altbach, R. O. Berdahl, & P. T. Gumport (Eds.), *American higher education in the 21st century: Social, political and economic challenges* (pp. 38–69). Baltimore: Johns Hopkins University Press.

Glassick, C. E., Huber, M. T., & Maeroff, G. I. (1997). *Scholarship assessed: Evaluation of the professoriate.* San Francisco: Jossey-Bass.

Huber, M. T. (2002). Faculty evaluation and the development of academic careers. *New Directions for Institutional Research, 114:* 73–81.

Hutchings, P., & Shulman, L. (1999). The scholarship of teaching: New elaborations, new developments. *Change, 31*(5): 11–15.

Kanter, R. B. (1985, April). Managing the human side of change. *Management Review, 4*(4): 52–56.

Kezar, A. J. (2001). *Understanding and facilitating organizational change in the 21st century: Recent research and conceptualizations.* ASHE-ERIC Higher Education Report Vol. 28, No. 4. San Francisco: Jossey-Bass.

Kuh, G. D., & Whitt, E. J. (1988). *The invisible tapestry: Culture in American colleges and universities.* ASHE-ERIC Higher Education Report Vol. 17, No. 1. San Francisco: Jossey-Bass.

Lynton, E. (1998). Reversing the telescope. *AAHE Bulletin, 50*(7): 8–10.

NERCHE. (2003). *New faculty: A catalyst for change.* Retrieved May 15, 2003, from *NERCHE Brief: New Faculty,* www.nerche.org.

O'Meara, K.A. (1997). *Rewarding faculty professional service.* Boston: New England Resource Center for Higher Education.

O'Meara, K.A. (2000). Climbing the academic ladder: Promotion in rank. In C. A. Trower (Ed.), *Policies on faculty appointment: Standard practices and unusual arrangements* (pp. 141–179). Bolton, MA: Anker.

O'Meara, K.A. (2002a, Summer). Uncovering the values in faculty evaluation of service as scholarship. *Review of Higher Education, 26:* 57–80.

O'Meara, K.A. (2002b). *Scholarship unbound: Assessing service as scholarship for promotion and tenure.* New York: Routledge.

O'Meara, K. (forthcoming). *Encouraging multiple forms of scholarship in faculty reward systems. Have academic cultures really changed?* Amherst, MA.

O'Meara, K., & Braskamp, L. (2005). Aligning faculty reward systems and development to promote faculty and student growth. *NASPA Journal, 42*(2): 223–240.

Prince, G. S., Jr. (2000). A liberal arts college perspective. In T. Ehrlich (Ed.), *Civic responsibility and higher education* (pp. 249–262). Phoenix: Oryx.

Ramaley, J. A. (2000). Embracing civic responsibility. *AAHE Bulletin, 52*(7): 9–13.

Rice, R. E. (1996). *Making a place for the new American scholar* (New Pathways Inquiry No. 1). Washington, DC: American Association for Higher Education.

Rice, R. E., & Sorcinelli, M. (2002). Can the tenure process be improved? In R. Chait (Ed.), *The questions of tenure* (pp. 101–124). Cambridge, MA: Harvard University Press.

Rice, R. E., Sorcinelli, M. D., & Austin, A. E. (2000). *Heeding new voices: Academic careers for a new generation.* New Pathways Inquiry No. 7. Washington, DC: American Association for Higher Education.

Richlin, L. (1993). Graduate education and the U.S. faculty. In L. Richlin (Ed.), *Preparing faculty for the new conceptions of scholarship.* New Directions for Institutional Research, no. 54. San Francisco: Jossey-Bass.

Ruscio, K. P. (1987). The distinct scholarship of the selective liberal arts college. *Journal of Higher Education, 58:* 205–221.

Schein, E. H. (1992). *Organizational culture and leadership* (2nd ed.). San Francisco: Jossey-Bass.

Seldin, P. (1993). *Successful use of teaching portfolios.* Bolton, MA: Anker.

Senge, P. M. (1990). *The fifth discipline: The art and practice of the learning organization.* New York: Currency Doubleday.

Sorcinelli, M. D. (2000). *Principles of good practice: Supporting early-career faculty.* Washington, DC: American Association for Higher Education.

Sorcinelli, M. D. (2002). Ten principles of good practice in creating and sustaining teaching and learning centers. In K. H. Gillespie (Ed.), *A guide to faculty development: Practical advice, examples and resources.* Bolton, MA: Anker.

Trower, C. A. (2000). *Policies on faculty appointment: Standard practices and unusual arrangements.* Bolton, MA: Anker.

Van Maanen, J., & Schein, E. H. (1979). Toward a theory of organizational socialization. In B. M. Staw (Ed.), *Research in organizational behavior* (pp. 209–264). Greenwich, CT: JAL.

Walker, C. J. (2002). Faculty well-being review: An alternative to post-tenure review? In C. Licata & J. Morreale (Eds.), *Post-tenure faculty review and renewal: Experienced voices* (pp. 229–241). Washington, DC: American Association for Higher Education.

Weick, K. (1995). *Sensemaking in organizations.* Thousand Oaks, CA: Sage.

Wergin, J. F. (1994). *The collaborative department: How five campuses are inching toward cultures of collective responsibility.* Washington, DC: American Association for Higher Education.

Wergin, J. F., & Swingen, J. (2000). *Departmental assessment: How some campuses are effectively evaluating the collective work of faculty.* Washington, DC: American Association for Higher Education.

Zahorski, K. J. (1994). *The sabbatical mentor: A practical guide to successful sabbaticals.* Bolton, MA: Anker.

Zahorski, K. J., & Cognard, R. (1999). *Reconsidering faculty roles and rewards: Promising practices for institutional transformation and enhanced learning.* Washington, DC: Council of Independent Colleges.

CHAPTER FOURTEEN

PRINCIPLES OF GOOD PRACTICE

Encouraging Multiple Forms of Scholarship in Policy and Practice

KerryAnn O'Meara

This chapter offers 10 principles of good practice for encouraging multiple forms of scholarship in higher education. For each practice I provide an inventory of actions that academic leaders, department chairs, and others can take to examine institutional practices. By examining campus policy and practices and selecting the complement of strategies that best fits institutional circumstances, academic leaders and others may be able to create environments that nurture and support the faculty's full array of scholarly contributions.

These best practices reflect a variety of different ways to support faculty involvement in the scholarships of teaching, discovery, engagement, and integration. Just as Boyer (1990) suggested that different types of institutions might emphasize different domains of scholarship in their roles and rewards, I argue that what works for one institutional type might not work for another. In addition, faculty in different disciplines will have more or less opportunity to en-

The author wishes to thank Larry Braskamp, Mary Huber, R. Eugene Rice, and Mary Deane Sorcinelli for their thoughtful feedback on this chapter as it was being developed.

gage in certain forms of scholarship (Adam & Roberts, 1993; Diamond & Adam, 1995); also, they will likely emphasize different forms of scholarship at different points in their careers (Rice, 1996). Accordingly, faculty and staff on individual campuses are the best judges of which strategies and practices best fit their cultures.

Encouraging multiple forms of scholarship requires partnerships between academic leaders and faculty to align missions, workloads, and reward systems, define or redefine scholarship in light of institutional mission, provide resources for faculty professional development, expand the criteria by which scholarship is evaluated, and nurture a culture that values a diversity of faculty contributions. Given the complex nature of academic reward systems and the diversity of institutional types, this task does not belong to the individual faculty member or department chair but rather to a collaboration among members of the academic community. In addition, campuses cannot effectively encourage multiple forms of scholarship without the active support of accrediting agencies, disciplinary associations, foundations, graduate programs that train future faculty, and national associations.

The 10 principles of best practices emerged from the American Association for Higher Education (AAHE) national survey of chief academic officers (CAOs), the nine campus studies from the "Reflecting on Best Practices Project," focus groups with CAOs in New England colleges and universities, reflections on more than a decade of institutional visits and consultations by R. Eugene Rice and me, case-study research (O'Meara, 2002), and an extensive review of the literature on organizational change in reward systems and faculty development. I have modeled presentation of the best practices after Mary Deane Sorcinelli's (2000) "Principles of Good Practice: Supporting Early-Career Faculty."

The principles move from an emphasis on socialization (Principles 1 and 2), to expectations for faculty (3 and 4), to assessment and evaluation (5 and 6), to resources (7), to collaboration and community (8), and finally to institutional identity and direction (9 and 10). Each of the sources that informed these principles pointed to these categories as critical to any examination of support for multiple forms of scholarship. For example, according to research on the socialization and preparation of graduate students, it is during graduate school that future faculty develop the values, work preferences, and personal commitment that will guide them throughout their careers (Tierney & Rhoads, 1994; Weidman, Twale, & Stein, 2001). Likewise, the first campus visits and subsequent meetings between a new faculty member and the department are crucial aspects of organizational socialization (Tierney & Rhoads, 1994). Thus, the process of socializing a future faculty member to a broader definition of scholarship must begin in graduate school and continue once the person becomes part of their new department.

Expectations are another critical component of supporting a broader definition of scholarship and faculty professional development. It is good practice to prepare faculty members for success by not expecting and rewarding an "overloaded plate" (Rice, Sorcinelli, & Austin, 2000). Colleges that engender a strong sense of faculty well-being provide fair, equitable, and ample rewards and recognition; whereas in colleges that burn out their faculty, perceived inequities in workloads and rewards contribute to a sense of lack of control over work (Hagedorn, 2000; Walker, 2002). Structures and policies need to be put into place to ensure that faculty do not feel that they have to excel in every form of scholarship simultaneously, and can work from their strengths.

Assessment and evaluation are critical aspects of supporting a broader definition of scholarship. Research shows that faculty are driven by a desire to achieve and attain excellence in the areas most important to them (Bess, 1977; Blackburn & Lawrence, 1995; Bowen & Schuster, 1986). Faculty who do not receive feedback on their professional work are likely to withdraw and feel isolated from their colleagues and frustrated with their work (Bess, 1977; Hagedorn, 2000; Walker, 2002). Given that many faculty who have become involved in the scholarships of teaching, learning, and engagement are working on disciplinary frontiers, it is perhaps even more crucial to provide them with useful, concrete feedback to the evaluation processes. Likewise, resources are needed to support faculty professional development in each of the four forms of scholarship. These resources should be targeted at scholarship most closely aligned with institutional mission, and should encourage growth, development, and professional writing.

Collaboration and a sense of community are crucial. Ernest Lynton (1998) discussed this strategy eloquently in his article "Reversing the Telescope." Lynton argued that in order to be responsive to institutional priorities and external demands, we need to take a collective approach to faculty evaluation. He suggested that units as opposed to individuals be evaluated for their overall scholarly contributions and other aspects of faculty work. Departments should create room for a diversity of faculty contributions and support these varied contributions as equitably as possible.

Finally, a broader conception of scholarship in faculty roles and rewards depends on a strong sense of institutional identity and direction. Faculty will not feel supported in pursuing alternative forms of scholarship if their institution's leaders and reward system are ratcheting up research expectations to enhance institutional prestige without regard to mission. Academic leaders must guard against mission drift, to ensure that faculty rewards, priorities, and workload are aligned with institutional mission and a shared sense of aspirations.

Ten Principles of Good Practice for Encouraging Multiple Forms of Scholarship

1. *Prepare faculty in graduate school for the variety of roles and types of scholarship in which they will engage.*

- If your institution is involved in doctoral education, consider ways to introduce graduate students to the scholarships of teaching and engagement through special seminars and grant projects.
- If your institution is focused more on the liberal arts and has few doctoral programs, consider partnering with a doctoral or research university for summer internships that enable graduate students to visit and intern at your institution. In addition to exposing graduate students to a different type of institution and perhaps different forms of scholarship, the program may become an effective recruiting tool.
- Many centers for teaching and learning are now providing special workshops and professional development opportunities for graduate student teaching assistants. By offering certificate programs, for-credit graduate courses, and other

opportunities, they help graduate students become better
teachers in the future.

- Consider asking departmental faculty to host a brown-bag
lunch discussion focusing on academic career paths. Possibly
invite program alumni who are now faculty members to discuss job searches and how faculty roles differ by institutional
type. Students can gain valuable information about careers,
and the program may cultivate better relations within the
department.
- Reward mid-career and senior faculty members for time spent
mentoring graduate students and creating opportunities for
students to engage in the scholarships of discovery, engagement, teaching, and integration.
- Encourage faculty advisors and others who work with graduate
students to discuss students' strengths and weaknesses in various forms of scholarship and teaching, as well as strategies for
professional growth.

2. *Socialize new faculty to the broader institutional definition of
scholarship.*

- In the recruitment process, before faculty are hired, employ
a variety of screening procedures, hold extended on-campus
visits, and host discussions about institutional expectations and
mission to ensure that candidates understand how the institution defines scholarship and which areas of scholarship may
be emphasized in the reward system.
- During new faculty orientations, highlight involvement in
multiple forms of scholarship and interdisciplinary work.
- Recognize and reward senior faculty members for time spent
mentoring junior colleagues in scholarship that supports the
unique mission of the institution.
- Review with candidates for tenure and promotion the broadened definition of scholarship, the kind of information they
need to document scholarship in each area, and the criteria
used to assess excellence.
- Make room for experimentation through new approaches
and a tolerance of failure when trying something new and
different.

- Encourage departmental brown-bag lunches for collegial discussions of work in progress or sharing scholarly projects in teaching and engagement.
- Hold department meetings in which faculty can share their scholarly agendas and plans and see areas for potential collaboration with each other.
- Encourage early career and senior faculty to mentor each other and work collaboratively on scholarly projects.

3. *Present clear expectations for scholarship in promotion and tenure guidelines.*

- Establish clear expectations for scholarship in official guidelines for faculty roles and rewards. Include what is and is not considered scholarship. Review faculty guidelines for promotion and tenure. Do the guidelines clearly distinguish effective teaching from the scholarship of teaching, or community service from the scholarship of engagement? Do they outline expectations for documentation, peer review, and dissemination of multiple forms of scholarship?
- In annual reviews, provide clear and constructive feedback on what is going well, and offer suggestions for improvement through discussions and written comments.
- Encourage candidates to meet with personnel committees before they submit their portfolios.
- Encourage departments to develop standards documents for scholarship, in each of the four domains, specific to their discipline.
- Solicit help from national and disciplinary associations in assessing rigor and establishing benchmarks for excellence. For example, the National Review Board for the Scholarship of Engagement (www.scholarshipofengagement.org) assists campuses in reviewing faculty engagement for promotion and tenure. The Carnegie Foundation for the Advancement of Teaching has several programs that support teaching scholarship, including the Carnegie Academy for the Scholarship of Teaching and Learning (CASTL) (www.carnegiefoundation.org).
- Provide copies of Glassick, Huber, and Maeroff (1997), *Scholarship Assessed,* and Braskamp and Ory (1994), *Assessing Faculty Work: Enhancing Individual and Institutional Performance,*

to faculty committees charged with amending promotion and tenure guidelines, and to candidates preparing their dossiers.

4. *Do not expect or reward the "overloaded plate."*

- Expectations for the amount of scholarship a faculty member contributes in any domain should account for time spent in teaching, advising, and service contributions. For example, a faculty member teaching four courses a semester and advising more than 50 undergraduates should not be evaluated for tenure based primarily on research contributions.
- Establish a committee on faculty workload to assess whether expectations for faculty contributions to scholarship are realistic, considering the balance of faculty responsibilities.
- Conduct focus groups across the institution to ascertain the degree to which faculty members feel that they have to excel in all areas of scholarship simultaneously. Brainstorm strategies for alleviating or changing these expectations and avoiding burnout.
- Develop flexible workload programs that enable faculty to concentrate on one or two areas of scholarship for an agreed-upon amount of time and to be evaluated based on that work.
- Provide incentives, rather than penalties, for collaborative work such as team teaching, coauthored publications, or grant applications. Working collaboratively can help faculty maximize their time and build community within departments.

5. *Assess the impact of scholarship on multiple beneficiaries and partners.*

- Create guidebooks that enable promotion and tenure committees and department chairs to assess the impact of scholarship. Scholarship should be assessed according to its effect on students, institutions, communities, professions, and the faculty member, as well as on and within a discipline.
- Over the past decade, several key resources have been developed for assessing the impact of scholarship on multiple constituencies; these should be offered both to candidates for promotion and tenure and to personnel committees. *Making*

the Case for Professional Service (Lynton, 1995) and *Making Out-reach Visible: A Guide to Documenting Professional Service and Outreach* (Driscoll & Lynton, 1999) are two excellent guides for documenting and assessing the scholarship in engagement and outreach. Likewise, two works by Hutchings, *Making Teaching Community Property: A Menu for Peer Collaboration and Peer Review* (1996) and *The Course Portfolio: How Faculty Can Examine Their Teaching to Advance Practice and Improve Student Learning* (1998), are excellent resources for documenting or assessing the impact of teaching on partners and beneficiaries.

- Department chairs can facilitate the external review process to ensure that faculty members involved in the scholarships of teaching, engagement, and integration are reviewed by others in their discipline involved in similar work.
- Academic leaders, department chairs, and senior faculty members should support the first strong "test case" of candidates for promotion and tenure who emphasize the scholarship of teaching or engagement. Be sure their portfolios stress the impact of their work in all of the areas mentioned.
- Encourage faculty members to design tools for classroom assessment and to document how they are using information about student learning to improve pedagogy, curriculum, discipline, and learning outcomes.

6. *Provide useful feedback to faculty during evaluation.*

- Make sure department chairs meet individually with faculty members to discuss their annual review and mini-tenure or post-tenure review feedback and discuss strengths and areas for improvement.
- Document all feedback, and offer information about resources that might assist faculty in meeting goals.
- Ask a department or school member involved in similar work to be a resource in helping the faculty member use feedback to their best advantage.
- For faculty members involved in the scholarships of engagement and teaching provide feedback about how they have disseminated their work and how it has been made public or available for peer review.

- Department chairs and personnel committees might use feedback to inform faculty members about colleagues doing similar work and suggest that they collaborate in related grant or disciplinary opportunities.

7. *Support pioneers with resources—structural and financial, training and development, political and symbolic.*

- Offer reduced course loads, incentive grants, and sabbatical options that target newer forms of scholarship.
- Make graduate assistants, space, and other institutional resources as available for multiple forms of scholarship as for discovery research activities.
- Encourage faculty members to work with teaching and learning centers on portfolio development, to document the scholarship of teaching.
- Promote the development of partnerships between junior and senior faculty members, and Academic and Student Affairs, on scholarly projects.
- Highlight exciting scholarly projects during annual faculty events, awards ceremonies, strategic planning exercises, and presidential presentations.

8. *Encourage scholarly contributions that build on strengths.*

- Manage departments so as to cultivate and acknowledge both individual and departmental strengths. Hold trainings for department chairs on how to organize workload to enhance individual faculty strengths.
- Deans might consider letting departments choose to be evaluated as a unit rather than individually. Departments that have attempted similar collective evaluation have found that it improves collegiality and productivity for individual faculty and the unit as a whole (Wergin, 1994; Wergin & Swingen, 2000).
- Faculty interest in various forms of scholarship is likely to change through career stages. Provosts, deans, and department chairs can support all faculty by creating programs that target needs and strengths at different stages. For example,

late career faculty have institutional knowledge and knowledge of students and curriculum that are assets for curriculum
redesign and classroom assessment projects. Programs that
create special opportunities to use these skills often enhance
the passion for teaching and improve student learning.

- Many early career faculty arrive with well-developed technology skills but do not know how to use them to improve and
study student learning. Possibly establish a technology fellows
program to engage new faculty in scholarly teaching projects
using advanced technology.
- Create opportunities enabling late career faculty members
who have won teaching awards or are strong researchers to
collaborate with early career faculty through team teaching,
grant writing, or development of a university-community
partnership.

9. *Define and emphasize scholarship in the context of institutional
mission.*

- Host open forums or campus dialogues on the institutional
definition of scholarship and how reflective it is of institutional mission, faculty workload, and rewards.
- Encourage ongoing departmental discussions about the
mission of the institution, department goals, the institutional
definition of scholarship, and related values.
- Provide opportunities through open forums and discussions
to examine hypothetical promotion and tenure cases, as a way
of improving understanding of issues and questions related
to the institutional definition.
- Revisit institutional missions from time to time. Engage the
campus in conversations that reconsider the institutional mission and how it relates to the priorities and aspirations of the
faculty.
- Encourage faculty to link their scholarship to the unique
mission of the institution, for example, through scholarship
aimed at increasing student learning.
- Support all forms of scholarship, but put institutional resources, such as allocation of merit pay and incentive grants,

behind forms of scholarship most closely related to the institutional mission or emphasis.

10. *Resist increasing research expectations to enhance institutional prestige.*

- Be vigilant about rewarding faculty for their talents and contributions to the institutional mission through highly visible processes such as merit pay evaluations, post-tenure review, and allotments of scarce department resources. When these processes are focused exclusively or mostly on numbers of articles or books published, amount of grant funding, or similar measures, faculty members involved in multiple forms of scholarship may be at a significant disadvantage.
- Academic leaders might use annual faculty conferences, letters to the faculty, or other formal occasions to affirm the institutional mission and how it relates to institutional direction and faculty rewards.
- At the institutional level, difficult decisions about resource allocation should rest on information that takes account of the full range of contributions that a faculty member makes to the mission. Avoid information that focuses exclusively on how many articles the faculty member has published but omits factors related to quality of teaching, community partnerships, and contributions to the profession.
- At the department level, chairs might work with faculty to create a list of standards and criteria by which faculty believe their work should be judged. These criteria should include accomplishments in all four domains of scholarship, mentoring and advising, and institutional governance.
- Create strategic opportunities, at the institution and within the department or college, to celebrate and reward characteristics that make the institution distinctive in how it carries out its mission, as opposed to simply more prestigious in the academic hierarchy.
- Faculty well established in their disciplines should urge accrediting associations and disciplinary associations to include the contributions of multiple forms of scholarship in the criteria by which excellence in academic programs is judged.

CONCLUSION

Given the critical need for discovery, integration, teaching, and application of knowledge in our society, as well as a wide variety of institutional purposes and the need to honor faculty and their contributions more equitably, it is crucial that campuses find concrete ways to institutionalize a broader definition of scholarship. Encouraging multiple forms of scholarship in policy and practice benefits individual faculty, institutions, and society.

References

Adam, B. E., & Roberts, A. O. (1993). Differences among the disciplines. In R. Diamond & B. Adam (Eds.), *Recognizing faculty work: Reward systems for the year 2000* (pp. 23–62). San Francisco: Jossey-Bass.

Bess, J. (1977, May/June). The motivation to teach. *Journal of Higher Education, 68:* 243–258.

Blackburn, R. T., & Lawrence, J. H. (1995). *Faculty at work: Motivation, expectation, satisfaction.* Baltimore: Johns Hopkins University Press.

Bowen, H. R., & Schuster, J. H. (1986). *American professors: A national resource imperiled.* Oxford: Oxford University Press.

Boyer, E. (1990). *Scholarship reconsidered: Priorities of the professoriate.* Princeton, NJ: Carnegie Foundation for the Advancement of Teaching.

Braskamp, L. A., & Ory, J. C. (1994). *Assessing faculty work: Enhancing individual and institutional performance.* San Francisco: Jossey-Bass.

Diamond, R. M., & Adam, B. E. (Eds.). (1995). *The disciplines speak.* Washington, DC: American Association for Higher Education.

Driscoll, A., & Lynton, E. A. (1999). *Making outreach visible: A guide to documenting professional service and outreach.* Washington, DC: American Association for Higher Education.

Glassick, C. E., Huber, M. T., & Maeroff, G. I. (1997). *Scholarship assessed: Evaluation of the professoriate.* San Francisco: Jossey-Bass.

Hagedorn, L. S. (2000). Conceptualizing faculty job satisfaction: Components, theories, and outcomes. In L. Hagedorn (Ed.), *What contributes to job satisfaction among faculty and staff* (pp. 5–20). San Francisco: Jossey-Bass.

Hutchings, P. (1996). *Making teaching community property: A menu for peer collaboration and peer review.* Washington, DC: American Association for Higher Education.

Hutchings, P. (1998). (Ed.). *The course portfolio: How faculty can examine their teaching to advance practice and improve student learning.* Washington, DC: American Association for Higher Education.

Lynton, E. A. (1995). *Making the case for professional service.* Washington, DC: American Association for Higher Education.

Lynton, E. A. (1998). Reversing the telescope: Fitting individual tasks to common organizational ends. *AAHE Bulletin,* 50(7): 8–10.

O'Meara, K.A. (2002). *Scholarship unbound: Assessing service as scholarship for promotion and tenure.* New York: Routledge.

Rice, R. E. (1996). *Making a place for the new American scholar.* Washington, DC: American Association for Higher Education.

Rice, R. E., Sorcinelli, M. D., & Austin, A. E. (2000). *Heeding new voices: Academic careers for a new generation.* New Pathways Working Paper Series, Inquiry No. 7. Washington, DC: American Association for Higher Education.

Sorcinelli, M. D. (2000). *Principles of good practice: Supporting early-career faculty: Guidance for deans, department chairs and other academic leaders.* Washington, DC: American Association for Higher Education.

Tierney, W. G., & Rhoads, R. A. (1994). *Faculty socialization as cultural process: A mirror of institutional commitment.* ASHE-ERIC Higher Education Report No. 93–6. Washington, DC: George Washington University, School of Education and Human Development.

Walker, C. J. (2002). Faculty well-being review: An alternative to post-tenure review? In C. Licata & J. Morreale (Eds.), *Post-tenure faculty review and renewal: Experienced voices* (pp. 229–241). Washington, DC: American Association for Higher Education.

Weidman, J., Twale, D., & Stein, D. (2001). *Graduate and professional student socialization: A perilous passage.* ASHE-ERIC Monograph 28(3). San Francisco: Jossey-Bass.

Wergin, J. (1994). *The collaborative department: How five campuses are inching toward cultures of collective responsibility.* Washington, DC: American Association for Higher Education.

Wergin, J., & Swingen, J. (2000). *Departmental assessment: How some campuses are effectively evaluating the collective work of faculty.* Washington, DC: American Association for Higher Education.

CHAPTER FIFTEEN

THE FUTURE OF THE SCHOLARLY WORK OF FACULTY

R. Eugene Rice

Few times in the history of American higher education have seen more intense pressure to rethink the scholarly work of faculty. This is a time of extraordinary opportunity and danger for the quality of academic work, as higher education struggles with monumental changes focused directly on the work of the professoriate and the structure of the academic workplace. The changes are as significant as those that ushered in the new American university at the opening of the 20th century or that, 50 years later, redefined the scholarly work of faculty in response to the GI Bill and the launching of Sputnik. Today, 50 years beyond that, we face another turbulent transitional period in how we think about and organize academic work.

Publication of *Scholarship Reconsidered* (Boyer, 1990) and the ensuing national discussion did not precipitate this transitional time: demographic and structural pressures did that. Boyer's book and the follow-up work chronicled in this volume did provide higher education with a head start, a conceptual framework, and initiatives to build on. Whether the advances will be sustained depends on a new cohort of leaders and coordinated endeavors that reach beyond the local campus.

PRESSURES FOR CHANGE

The substantive changes having a direct impact on the structure of academic work are, first, the generational change among faculty. Many faculty appointed during the expansionist 1960s and early '70s are beginning to retire, and they are being replaced by new faculty who are more diverse, more female, and more often appointed with contracts that are not on a tenure track (Rice, 2004). We have a rare opportunity to shape a new generation of faculty or, as is being widely proposed, choose a new configuration of academic staff that might include faculty but have the potential for greatly enhancing the substance and effectiveness of the scholarship that a changing society requires.

Technology is already having a major impact on the way faculty learn, pursue their research, and organize the teaching and learning process. The profound changes provoked by the new digital environment are only beginning to register. In addition, there is a real shift in student demography. Students are older and more diverse, and most are working while going to school. They represent a wide range of new communities, many of them recent immigrants from Africa, Latin America, and Asia. Faculty interactions with these students of widely varying backgrounds and interests introduce new issues and conflicts, raise different questions, and require new approaches.

Related to the demographic shift is the nature of what we are learning about learning. The National Research Council's important book *How People Learn: Brain, Mind, Experience, and School* begins, "Today, the world is in the midst of an extraordinary outpouring of scientific work on the mind and brain, on the processes of thinking and learning, on the neural processes that occur during thought and learning, and on the development of competence" (Bransford, Brown & Cocking, 1999, p. 1). Research advances now allow us to offer guiding principles for deeper, more durable, and more transferable learning—principles that can be applied in every classroom and every other educational setting where learning is expected to take place. Faculty need to know about what is being called "the science of learning" and be able to apply it in their work.

We are now experiencing a pedagogical revolution led by three significant developments: (1) collaborative learning, as expressed, for instance, in the strength of the learning community movement; (2) experiential learning, manifest in the rapid growth of service-learning and other forms of active engagement and reflection; and (3) technologically assisted learning, which is only beginning to reveal its power.

Two other critical challenges shaping the environment into which we are moving are the alternative (for-profit) providers and increased corporate involvement in the academic life of the college and university. The for-profit providers such as the University of Phoenix are leading the way, as they put it, in "unbundling the faculty role." This promises to have a major impact on the scholarly work of faculty. Corporate involvement in the financing and support of major aspects of curriculum development and research priorities raises serious questions about the intellectual autonomy of the academic enterprise. In Chapter 1, I quoted Derek Bok's excoriating charge that faculty who hold to the dominant notion of scholarship are insufficiently engaged in the important social issues. Recent alliances with the biotechnology industry and collaboration with pharmaceutical companies raise the specter of the "kept university," as the *Atlantic Monthly* recently put it (Press & Washburn, 2000); a kind of engagement is emerging that could seriously threaten the scholarly independence and professional autonomy required for valid and reliable academic scholarship. These changes are again posing the perennial questions of the limits of engagement and the importance of having an unfettered perspective. Engagement with public issues and intellectual independence stand in a delicate balance, whose relationship has yet to be worked out.

As we look to the future, the broader conception of scholarly work can be a potent resource in addressing the significant changes already identified. It has proven to be unusually valuable in aligning faculty priorities and institutional missions. It has made a major contribution by cultivating public recognition of the scholarly aspects of teaching and the development of the scholarship of teaching and learning. And it has significantly advanced the case for acknowledging the scholarly contributions of faculty who choose to address important civic issues.

Each contribution, however, has the potential for making matters worse, particularly for the faculty now being recruited and socialized into the academic profession. If we continue to take an incremental, additive approach to change, we may create a career that is increasingly less viable and inviting. Under the current arrangement, innovations are introduced, developed, and added on; reforms are advocated and refined, and become the responsibility of the most talented, who are usually already overcommitted (Rice, Sorcinelli, & Austin, 2000).

Additionally, we will have to examine how, indeed if, broadening the definition of scholarship can be accomplished at those institutions most ardently engaged in the pursuit of national prestige. The pernicious power of the national ranking system often manifests itself when there is a change in presidential leadership, which occurs much too frequently. An institution makes substantial gains in realigning its mission and its faculty's priorities; teaching and learning are advanced or faculty engagement in meeting the educational needs of the community begin to be recognized and rewarded; then there is a change in the presidency, and the old research agenda regains ascendancy as part of an effort to improve the institution's national ranking or profile. This is hindering the effort to encourage a fuller and more nuanced understanding of scholarship.

The prestige race is not the only big barrier to reform. A less visible but more insidious issue is the emerging gap between policy and practice. As the survey of provosts indicates, many campuses have policies supporting a broader definition of scholarship, but there is some indication that in practice—in actual promotion and tenure decisions and in how faculty are supported and rewarded in the larger institutional context—the public statements are not being acted upon. For example, in one large urban university, "second-generation issues" that emerged once the reform had been in place for a decade are being fundamentally reassessed; old, established criteria are regaining precedence.

A Radically Different Approach

We need a genuinely "transformative" approach to change. I use this term hesitantly, because it has been so overworked and inappropriately employed, but it is especially apt in reference to the academic career during this transitional period. Transformational change is more than additive. Its proponents do not assume that improvement can be made by only introducing another responsibility to work that is already required. Transformational change calls for rethinking the whole professional role and choosing among many important tasks. It could mean jettisoning some tasks long regarded as significant, assigning some work formerly seen as the responsibility of faculty to others, or devising new ways of organizing academic work. Clearly, although the profession values independence and autonomy, it will have to move toward much greater collaboration and cooperation. Evaluation processes and reward systems will need to shift attention from individual performance to the achievements of departments and the shared contributions of more comprehensive units. We cannot get to what is needed by more incremental change; we must begin to think in terms that are genuinely transformational.

Several critical issues have emerged from the extensive debate since the publication of *Scholarship Reconsidered.* A significant element in the original notion of a broader definition of scholarship was that the four primary dimensions of scholarly work—discovery, integration, teaching, and engagement—are fundamentally interrelated. As the different forms of scholarship have received increasing attention, however, there is a danger that the parts will be disaggregated, with each being viewed as a separate and independent form of scholarship. Some of the most recent discussion about the scholarship of teaching and learning borders on this kind of disaggregation. The scholarship of teaching and learning is being promoted as an independent form of scholarship, separated from the substance of the field. This could threaten gains made to break down the bifurcation of teaching into process, on the one hand, and the deep exploration of an area of study, on the other—the same dilemma that has haunted schools of education for so long.

As each form of scholarship develops strength and new constituencies, it risks this kind of separation. The scholarship of engagement, under the impetus of service-learning as an organized movement and the growth of community-based research, will need to guard against the pressures to take on a life independent of the other forms of scholarship. The scholarship of integration and synthesis, however, has gained so little attention that the temptation to develop autonomy has not been a problem; also, its primary thrust is centripetal, with connection and interrelationships being the central theme.

Pressures to return to the scholarship of discovery, as the only form of scholarly work to be recognized and counted, are almost insurmountable. Particularly striking about the national survey of provosts discussed in Part Three of this book is that, while the scholarships related to teaching and engagement have gained demonstrably in value, there is, at the same time, a growing emphasis on the scholarship of discovery, whose prestige remains undiminished. Those fearing that the broader definition of scholarship would lead to a "zero-sum game" in which research would lose support obviously have little to be concerned about.

If the interconnectedness of the four forms of scholarship disappears, one of the primary intents of *Scholarship Reconsidered* will have been lost. It is not an accident that the four forms of scholarly work are incorporated into the mission statements of colleges and universities across all sectors of American higher education. The sectors are committed to a particular combination of scholarly capabilities, and all assume some blend of the four. For instance, research universities, by design, have large numbers of undergraduate students; for while research is central to the mission of the institutions, teaching and learning are vital to their academic integrity. Community colleges focus mainly on student learning and engagement with the educational needs of the local community, but their faculty must be continually engaged in learning and in producing some kind of scholarly work that can be publicly critiqued by knowledgeable peers. A dynamic learning community can flourish only where the four forms of scholarly work are actively interrelated. This brings us to one of the most formidable challenges in reconfiguring the academic workplace.

Scholarship Reconsidered articulated a view of the faculty role that was later identified as the "complete scholar." Ideally, a faculty member might concentrate on one aspect of scholarly work at a particular time but, over the length of a professional career, would practice all four forms of scholarship, leading to an integrated wholeness unique to the person. Such a pattern would accommodate what we have discovered through recent studies of adult and career development—the need to grow and change throughout a lifetime. These "ideal" faculty could provide institutional coherence in a time of dramatic change, have a sense of the whole, and contribute to the hard work of institution building in the years ahead.

The vision of the complete scholar remains compelling, particularly to those considering an academic career. Yet, it may be a notion that flourishes most in the imagination of those of us attracted to it, for much of higher education is moving in another direction, toward what the University of Phoenix first tagged "unbundling the faculty role." Technology is a primary driver behind this development. Teams of experts—not all of whom are faculty—design online courses in a digital environment that makes the unbundling possible and perhaps even inevitable.

What we are learning about learning requires a new mix of participants in the learning process. Learning communities rely heavily on student affairs and housing personnel. Service-learning, by making the walls of the university and college more permeable, opens the way for students and faculty to move into the larger community and learn from the wisdom of practice, and for people on the outside to play a key instructional role.

Established faculty, particularly in research universities, are already deeply implicated in this unbundling process. Many institutions have outsourced the lower-division advising function. Much of the instruction done by graduate teaching assistants can be viewed in this light. Rather than being genuinely mentored in the practice of teaching and learning, teaching assistants are often engaged primarily to free senior faculty from their responsibilities for undergraduate teaching and to make time for specialized research. Medical schools are already committed to specialization, not only by field but also by function: teaching, researching, or practicing.

The most persuasive argument for differentiated staffing, or unbundling the faculty role, emerges from interviews with early career faculty in the American Association for Higher Education's (AAHE) New Pathways project "Heeding New Voices" (Rice, Sorcinelli, & Austin, 2000). Asked about the future, new faculty responded, quite consistently, by citing issues related to their "overloaded plate." In graduate school, most prospective faculty are socialized thoroughly into the research priorities of academic life, the scholarship of discovery. When they take their first appointment, they usually find themselves in a different kind of institution, confronted with an entirely new set of priorities: teaching and learning, engagement, and the responsibilities of integration and synthesis—the other forms of scholarly work. In a small way, the success of *Scholarship Reconsidered* has contributed to the sense of having more responsibilities added to a full plate. In a tight labor market in which the standards for tenure are being continually ratcheted up, and each individual is evaluated on the basis of performance in all four forms of scholarship simultaneously, the faculty career is becoming less attractive and increasingly regarded as hardly tenable, certainly not the kind of career that could attract the best of a new generation.

We urgently need cost-effective strategies for sharing the load and encouraging greater collaboration. Unbundling the faculty role is one persuasive response. Another is differentiated staffing, which Kansas State University prefers to call "flexible allocation of time and talent." Other institutions are experimenting with alternatives. Increasingly we will need to rely on personnel other than faculty in reorganizing the university and college for learning. Already, new bridges are being built to student affairs offices, information technology centers, and libraries. AAHE is beginning to talk about new academic networks that will collaborate in the development of effective learning environments.

There is a way to sustain the vision of the complete scholar while addressing the problem of the overflowing plate. This can be accomplished through individual professional agreements, formerly called "growth contracts," which would be negotiated periodically in a department or academic unit. They would enable department and college goals to be met while allowing individual faculty to shift academic responsibilities and develop other parts of their scholarly selves, thus sustaining the commitment to the notion of the complete scholar. This would alter academic culture radically, and require faculty to learn to collaborate, something often absent among current faculty, for whom autonomy is a primary value.

This approach could help faculty work more closely with other academic staff and external contributors to the learning process, open the way for significant budget savings, and potentially enhance the quality of learning. Although this combination of individualized planning and unit evaluation would be complicated and time consuming for deans and department chairs, it holds promise for the future of a higher education where multiple forms of scholarship can flourish.

In thinking about the change levers for encouraging multiple forms of scholarship, one approach immediately comes to mind. The scholarly priorities of the professoriate are firmly rooted in graduate school socialization. Interviews with graduate students and early career faculty disclose a serious mismatch between the doctoral preparation that most receive and the needs of the universities and colleges in which they are likely to be employed. Graduate students serious about careers in higher education need to be more adequately prepared for scholarly work extending beyond the scholarship of discovery, as important and essential as that is. Graduate school, the starting point of the professional career, is where the largest difference can be made.

Given current generational changes in the faculty and other dramatic shifts noted early in this chapter, there could not be a better time to reframe our approach to preparing future faculty. The long-term potential is enormous. In Chapter 3 of this book, Jerry Gaff describes work in graduate education being done to encourage multiple forms of scholarship. The new Center for the Integration of Research, Teaching, and Learning (sponsored by the National Science Foundation) established at the University of Wisconsin-Madison in collaboration with Michigan State and Penn State has a major initiative focusing on the science-based disciplines. The Carnegie Foundation's Initiative on the Doctorate, directed by George Walker, has also taken up the challenge. Resources and energy are being appropriately directed.

CONCLUSION

That we are still pursuing ideas first launched in a small Carnegie report in 1990 is amazing. The challenge is to keep the initiative alive, productive, and intellectually vital, which will involve an ongoing process that requires continuous attention. Institutions need to systematically rehearse and renew their commitment to overcome entrenched resistance within their ranks. The work and perseverance of individual campuses, though vital to the cause, will need to extend nationally and even internationally, for, as we have been reminded throughout this project, the scholarship of teaching and learning and the scholarship of engagement must become portable and cosmopolitan if they are to take hold. Indeed, some of the most serious efforts to enlarge our understanding of the scholarly work of faculty are now being pursued abroad, in places such as Australia, Canada, Portugal, and the United Kingdom. As systems of higher education around the world expand their missions, and more countries take up the struggle to recognize and reward multiple forms of scholarship, this important initiative will have become genuinely global in perspective and scope.

References

Boyer, E. L. (1990). *Scholarship reconsidered: Priorities of the professoriate.* Princeton, NJ: Carnegie Foundation for the Advancement of Teaching.

Bransford, J., Brown, A., & Cocking, R. (1999). *How people learn: Brain, mind, experience, and school.* Committee on Development in the Science of Learning, Commission on Behavioral and Social Sciences and Education, National Research Council. Washington, DC: National Academy Press.

Press, E., & Washburn, J. (2000, March 20). The kept university. *The Atlantic Monthly, 285*(3). http:www.theatlantic.com/issues/2000/03/press.htm

Rice, R. E. (2004, March-April). The future of the American faculty: An interview with Martin J. Finkelstein and Jack H. Schuster. *Change, 36*(2): 26–35.

Rice, R. E., Sorcinelli, M., & Austin, A. (2000). *Heeding new voices: Academic careers for a new generation.* New Pathways Working Paper Series. Washington, DC: American Association for Higher Education.

APPENDIX

SURVEY TABLES

TABLE A.1 CATALYSTS: REFORM-INSTITUTION CAOs

"Please check if, and to what extent, the following catalysts and/or conditions influenced your institution's decision to change faculty evaluation policy to encourage and reward multiple forms of scholarship."

Question	Major Influence (%)	Minor Influence (%)	No Influence (%)	Not Applicable (%)	Did Not Respond (%)	Total (%)
Leadership by this institution's president	35	35	19	5	6	100
Leadership by this institution's provost	57	24	4	10	5	100
Leadership from other administrators	28	38	21	7	6	100
Leadership by unionized or organized faculty	9	10	31	44	6	100
Grassroots efforts by faculty	25	45	18	6	6	100
General dissatisfaction among faculty	10	40	31	13	6	100
Need to align reward system with mission to meet institutional goals	49	29	11	6	5	100
Institutional commitment to teaching	73	17	2	2	6	100

Institutional commitment to engagement and professional service	44	38	9	4	5	100
Models from other colleges or universities	12	52	22	8	6	100
Ideas generated by discussion of Boyer's *Scholarship Reconsidered*	32	31	19	12	6	100
Faculty or administrator involvement in national movement to redefine faculty roles and rewards (for example, Forum on Faculty Roles and Rewards)	17	31	32	14	6	100
Pressures from state legislature, parents, and trustees for greater accountability	8	18	49	19	6	100
Partnerships with industry	6	24	43	21	6	100
Encouragement from accreditation agencies	13	31	38	11	7	100
Other	5	1	1	16	77	100

TABLE A.2 BARRIERS: ALL CAOS

"Please mark if, and to what degree, any of the following issues have acted as barriers to your efforts to encourage multiple forms of scholarship."

Question	Major Barrier (%)	Minor Barrier (%)	No Barrier (%)	Not Applicable (%)	Did Not Respond (%)	Total (%)
Desire by academic leadership to move institution up in Carnegie classification	4	15	56	19	6	100
Ratcheting up of research expectations to improve institutional or department rankings	15	29	35	14	7	100
Stance of disciplinary associations in some fields	9	32	41	11	7	100
Resistance from faculty members	4	5	24	60	7	100
Difficulty in documenting multiple forms of scholarship for promotion and tenure	22	40	27	5	6	100
Greater confusion and ambiguity for faculty about what really counts for promotion and tenure	24	47	18	5	6	100
Confusion about definitions of teaching, research, and service as scholarship	24	40	25	4	7	100
Political nature of faculty evaluation	18	37	31	7	7	100
Excessive paperwork for faculty evaluation	9	36	43	6	6	100
Insufficient training for department chairs and deans	22	46	20	5	7	100

Vested interests of some faculty in maintaining the status quo	32	40	17	4	7	100
Research orientation of newly recruited faculty	13	38	37	6	6	100
Fear that changes in the reward system will make faculty careers and programs less marketable or "transferable" to other institutions	12	37	36	8	7	100
Faculty graduate school training and socialization favoring traditional definitions of scholarship	27	40	20	7	6	100
Faculty concerns about unrealistic expectations that they excel in all areas at the same time	27	47	14	5	7	100
Difficulty in expanding a consistent definition of scholarship across the university	27	43	19	5	6	100
Uneven application of new criteria and standards within and across units	22	40	24	8	6	100
Rejection of the reform or change because initiated by the administration	11	29	40	13	7	100
Turnover of key advocates or change in institutional leadership	7	28	47	11	7	100
Change in institutional priorities	8	28	44	11	9	100
Other	2	1	1	16	80	100

TABLE A.3 INCREASES AND IMPROVEMENTS FROM REFORM: COMPARISON OF ALL, REFORM-, AND TRADITIONAL-INSTITUTION CAOs

"Please rate the extent to which your efforts to encourage multiple forms of scholarship have influenced this increase or improvement."

Question	All CAOs		Reform-Institution CAOs		Traditional-Institution CAOs	
	Major Influence (%)	Minor Influence (%)	Major Influence (%)	Minor Influence (%)	Major Influence (%)	Minor Influence (%)
Faculty satisfaction with roles and rewards	13	19	18	25	4	7
Retention and satisfaction of women faculty	11	23	15	31	1	7
Retention and satisfaction of faculty of color	6	13	9	17	1	4
Faculty recruitment efforts	21	21	29	28	5	5
Attention to the quality of undergraduate learning	33	23	45	29	7	9
Relationships with the community	16	23	21	31	4	6
Ability of the institution to meet its goals and objectives	26	21	36	26	6	8
Faculty involvement in the scholarship of engagement and professional service	17	24	21	31	9	9

Faculty involvement in the scholarship of teaching and learning	29	22	42	30	3	7
Faculty involvement in the scholarship of integration	15	21	18	27	8	8
Congruence between faculty priorities and institutional mission	22	19	31	24	4	8
External funding	18	19	25	25	4	6
Faculty presentations at national conferences	19	23	26	31	5	7
Grant applications	18	21	25	27	4	8
Faculty publications	16	25	22	33	4	7
Applications for promotion from associate to full professor	6	13	7	17	2	5
Probability of a favorable tenure decision	9	12	12	17	2	4
Probability of a favorable decision to full professor	6	14	7	18	2	6
Evidence of senior faculty vitality	7	15	9	19	2	6
Faculty involvement in service-learning	17	20	23	26	5	6
Student contact	12	16	17	21	3	5
Other	1	2	1	1	1	3

TABLE A.4 WHAT COUNTS FOR FACULTY EVALUATION: COMPARISON OF ALL, REFORM-, AND TRADITIONAL-INSTITUTION CAOs

"For purposes of evaluation, do the following faculty activities count more or less today than they did 10 years ago?"

Question	Count More (%)	Count About the Same (%)	Count Less (%)	Not Applicable (%)	Did Not Respond (%)	Total (%)
Publication productivity						
All CAOs	51	40	3	2	4	100
Reform	54	34	5	1	6	100
Traditional	45	50	.4	4	1	100
Teaching						
All CAOs	35	59	2	.3	4	100
Reform	39	54	1	.2	6	100
Traditional	26	70	3	.4	1	100
Engagement/professional service						
All CAOs	31	59	4	2	4	100
Reform	39	51	3	1	6	100
Traditional	12	77	6	4	1	100
Service to the institution/citizenship						
All CAOs	19	67	8	2	4	100
Reform	23	62	8	1	6	100
Traditional	9	79	9	2	1	100
Service to the profession/discipline						
All CAOs	19	69	6	2	4	100
Reform	23	63	6	2	6	100
Traditional	10	81	4	4	1	100

Note: Due to rounding, percentages may not equal 100.

TABLE A.5 CHANGE IN REWARD SYSTEMS: COMPARISON OF ALL, REFORM-, AND TRADITIONAL-INSTITUTION CAOs

"Please indicate if any of the following events have increased, stayed about the same, or decreased over the last 10 years."

Question	Respondents	Increased (%)	About the Same (%)	Decreased (%)	Not Applicable (%)	Did Not Respond (%)	Total (%)
Chances to achieve *tenure* for a faculty member who *excels in teaching* and completes adequate research	All CAOs	24	60	3	10	3	100
	Reform	30	54	2	9	5	100
	Traditional	10	73	6	11	0	100
Chances to *be promoted to full professor* for a faculty member who *excels in teaching* and completes adequate research	All CAOs	26	62	6	3	3	100
	Reform	31	55	7	2	5	100
	Traditional	14	75	6	5	0	100
Chances to achieve *tenure* for a faculty member who *excels in engagement and professional service* and completes adequate research	All CAOs	17	58	8	14	3	100
	Reform	22	54	7	12	5	100
	Traditional	4	68	12	16	0	100
Chances to *be promoted to full professor* for a faculty member who *excels in engagement and professional service* and completes adequate research	All CAOs	19	61	10	7	3	100
	Reform	24	57	9	5	5	100
	Traditional	8	68	13	11	0	100
Number of faculty who are *tenured or promoted* based primarily on the scholarship of *teaching and learning*	All CAOs	23	55	10	9	3	100
	Reform	28	52	7	8	5	100
	Traditional	11	61	16	12	0	100
Number of faculty who are *tenured or promoted* based primarily on *engagement and professional service* with the community	All CAOs	10	54	15	18	3	100
	Reform	14	55	11	15	1	100
	Traditional	3	50	23	24	0	100

TABLE A.6 CRITERIA USED TO EVALUATE SCHOLARSHIP

"What degree of influence do the following issues have on the final decision by faculty committees to recommend or deny tenure and promotion today?"

Question		Major Influence (%)	Minor Influence (%)	No Influence (%)	Not Applicable (%)	Did Not Respond (%)	Total (%)
Whether scholarly products are published	All CAOs	59	30	0	6	5	100
	Reform	57	31	0	6	6	100
	Traditional	63	28	0	6	3	100
Where scholarly products are published	All CAOs	38	45	8	4	5	100
	Reform	35	47	8	4	6	100
	Traditional	46	39	8	4	3	100
Impact of scholarship on the local community and state	All CAOs	11	59	20	5	5	100
	Reform	15	58	17	4	6	100
	Traditional	4	61	27	5	3	100
Impact of scholarship on the profession and discipline	All CAOs	39	46	6	4	5	100
	Reform	37	48	5	4	6	100
	Traditional	45	40	9	3	3	100
Impact of scholarship on the institution	All CAOs	26	54	11	4	5	100
	Reform	31	51	7	4	7	100
	Traditional	15	60	18	4	3	100

Impact of scholarship on students	All CAOs	42	42	7	3	6	100
	Reform	47	38	5	3	7	100
	Traditional	30	52	11	4	3	100
That the scholarship resulted in significant external funding	All CAOs	27	43	19	6	5	100
	Reform	27	44	18	5	6	100
	Traditional	27	42	21	8	2	100
Originality of the scholarship	All CAOs	38	44	9	4	5	100
	Reform	34	48	8	4	6	100
	Traditional	46	36	10	5	3	100
Mission of the institution	All CAOs	51	33	6	4	6	100
	Reform	56	29	4	4	7	100
	Traditional	39	43	10	4	4	100
Priorities of the academic unit	All CAOs	39	40	10	5	6	100
	Reform	43	37	8	5	7	100
	Traditional	30	46	15	6	3	100

Note: "Scholarship" refers here to any piece of work put forward by faculty as scholarship for promotion and tenure.

TABLE A.7 SUPPORT FOR A BROADER DEFINITION OF SCHOLARSHIP

"How would you rate the level of support for an expanded definition of scholarship among the following groups, during the past five years?"

Question	Respondents	Very Supportive or Supportive (%)	Neutral (%)	Opposed (%)	Not Applicable (%)	Did Not Respond (%)	Total (%)
Faculty in the social sciences	All CAOs	70	14	5	3	8	100
	Reform	77	12	1	1	9	100
	Traditional	57	19	10	7	7	100
Faculty in the humanities	All CAOs	64	18	7	3	8	100
	Reform	70	15	5	1	9	100
	Traditional	50	25	11	7	7	100
Faculty in professional schools (education, business, engineering)	All CAOs	62	14	3	13	8	100
	Reform	68	13	2	8	9	100
	Traditional	50	15	6	22	7	100
Faculty in the natural sciences	All CAOs	46	25	18	3	8	100
	Reform	52	25	13	1	9	100
	Traditional	32	24	29	8	7	100
Junior faculty	All CAOs	71	13	5	3	8	100
	Reform	76	12	2	1	9	100
	Traditional	60	17	9	7	7	100

Mid-career faculty						
All CAOs	63	21	5	3	8	100
Reform	71	17	2	1	9	100
Traditional	46	29	11	7	7	100
Senior faculty						
All CAOs	42	29	17	3	9	100
Reform	46	30	14	1	9	100
Traditional	34	27	25	7	7	100
Deans						
All CAOs	73	8	4	6	9	100
Reform	80	5	1	4	10	100
Traditional	59	14	10	10	7	100
President or chancellor						
All CAOs	69	13	4	5	9	100
Reform	76	10	3	2	9	100
Traditional	54	22	7	10	7	100
Department chairs						
All CAOs	60	21	4	6	9	100
Reform	68	17	1	4	10	100
Traditional	43	29	10	10	8	100
Board of trustees						
All CAOs	40	31	2	18	9	100
Reform	46	27	2	16	9	100
Traditional	27	40	3	23	7	100

TABLE A.8 ACCEPTANCE OF MULTIPLE FORMS OF SCHOLARSHIP WITHIN INSTITUTIONAL CULTURES

"Please indicate your level of agreement or disagreement with each statement."

Question	Strongly Agree (%)	Agree (%)	Disagree (%)	Strongly Disagree (%)	Not Applicable (%)	Did Not Respond (%)	Total (%)
At my institution, it is commonly believed that many aspects of college teaching may be defined as scholarship							
All CAOs	19	43	26	3	1	8	100
Reform	23	48	19	1	1	8	100
Traditional	11	33	41	5	3	7	100
At my institution, it is commonly believed that many aspects of engagement and professional service may be defined as scholarship							
All CAOs	12	45	29	3	3	8	100
Reform	15	52	21	1	2	9	100
Traditional	5	31	45	7	5	7	100
At my institution, it is commonly believed that integrating and synthesizing existing bodies of knowledge into interdisciplinary contexts may be defined as scholarship							
All CAOs	20	58	11	1	7	3	100
Reform	23	59	9	0	8	1	100
Traditional	15	57	17	1	3	7	100
At my institution, participatory-action research and other, newer forms of research are considered scholarship							
All CAOs	16	51	15	2	8	8	100
Reform	20	53	11	1	7	8	100
Traditional	8	46	24	4	11	7	100
Over the last 10 years, faculty have developed a more complex, nuanced view of scholarship							
All CAOs	18	53	17	1	4	8	100
Reform	24	55	11	1	1	8	100
Traditional	6	49	29	4	5	7	100

INDEX

A

AAHE. *See* American Association for Higher Education (AAHE)

AAUP. *See* American Association of University Professors (AAUP)

Absentee professors, 1

Academic counselors, 136

Academic reward system: at Albany State University, 119, 124–125; at Arizona State University, 220; best practice in, 294, 300; challenges to reform of, 57–58, 263–264; definition of, 21; effects of change to, 264–269; faculty's perception of, 56; at Franklin College, 78, 84–89, 93; at historically black colleges and universities, 130; increased attention to, 57; institutional support for reform in, 70; at Kansas State University, 166; at Madonna University, 102; in medical schools, 233–234; for minority faculty, 116; at Portland State University, 191, 206; recommendations for, 58–59, 64; at South Dakota State University, 146–147, 157–159; at University of Colorado School of Medicine, 235–242; at University of Phoenix, 136

Academic Senate, 221

Academy of Management, 27

Accountability, 193–194

ACEPT. *See* Arizona Collaborative for Excellence in the Preparation of Teachers (ACEPT)

Achievement gaps, 122–123

"Achieving Excellence in Faculty Roles" (South Dakota State University), 150

Action research, 121

Adam, B., 22–23, 291

Advising, 136, 151

Age, of students, 132–133

Albany State University: academic reward system at, 119, 124–125; action research at, 121; challenges at, 126–127; collaboration at, 124; enrollment at, 113, 114; expectations at, 118; faculty morale at, 127; faculty responsibilities at, 118; faculty roles at, 114–115; first-year students at, 121–122; history of, 113; including faculty in discussions at, 116–117; mission of, 113–114, 274; overview of, 112–113; problems at, 117; professional development at, 120, 122, 127; reflection at, 120–121; response agenda at, 119–125; results of, 126–127; retention at, 113–114; scholarship of application at, 123–124; scholarship of discovery at, 122–123; scholarship of integration at, 123–124; supplemental learning at, 123; teaching focus of, 120–121; technology use at, 120, 122, 127; tenure at, 127; work-based learning at, 121

Albany State University study: implications of, 128–130; methods of, 125; overview of, 6–7

Aldersley, S. F., 257

Kansas State University study: findings of, 172–184; methods of, 171–172; overview of, 171
Kanter, R. B., 274
Katz, J., 24
Kayongo-Male, D., 146
Keillor, G., 5
Kern, D. E., 233
Kerr, C., 49
Kerrigan, S., 40
Ketcheson, K., 196
Kezar, A., 2, 11, 263, 268, 280, 281
Klein, J., 49
"Knowledge and Teaching: Foundations of the New Reform" (Shulman), 25
Knowledge, stages of, 50
Knowledge transfer, 195
Knudsen, C., 49
Kolodner, K., 233
Kotter, J. P., 181
Kroenke, K., 232, 234, 249
Kuh, G. D., 172, 268, 269
Kuhn, T., 210
Kuttner, R., 232

L

Lambert, L. M., 267
Lang, M., 217
Language, 80–81, 83–84, 177–179
Lawrence, J. H., 292
Lazerson, M., 35
Leaders: and challenges to reward system reform, 57–58; recommended actions for, 58–59
Leadership: at Arizona State University, 222–227; at Franklin College, 75–76; and policy changes, 262–263; at Portland State University, 187, 189–190, 194–195; support for expanded scholarship definition by, 268–269
Leadership development, 278, 282
Learner-centered teaching, 213, 215–216, 304–305

Learning: increased attention to, 35–36; mainstream nature of, 34; problems of scholarship in, 37–38; shifted emphasis to, 132–133
Learning communities, 214, 309
Learning paradigm, 133–134
The Learning Paradigm conference, 132
Legal testimony, 139–140
Lenker, L., 3
Levinson, W., 230, 231, 232, 233, 234, 249
Lewis, R., 50
Liberal arts colleges, 257, 293
Library materials, 127
Light, D., 22
Limoges, C., 49
Lowenstein, S. R., 230
Lowery, B. J., 232
Luckey, W., 2, 3, 256, 257, 265, 279
Ludmerer, K. M., 232, 249–250
Lynton, E., 28, 40, 41, 184, 185, 259, 278, 282, 292, 296–297, 297
Lyons, N., 34

M

Madonna University: academic reward system at, 102; curriculum at, 109; enrollment at, 97; faculty partnerships at, 273–274; history of, 96–98; lack of traditional scholarship at, 98–99; mission of, 96–97, 98; name change at, 98; obstacles to accomplishing scholarship at, 104; prioritization of scholarship at, 103; redefining scholarship at, 105–107; scholarship definition at, 99–100; scholarship expectations at, 102–103; scholarship of application at, 107; scholarship of discovery at, 106; scholarship of integration at, 109; scholarship of teaching at, 107; service-learning at, 108; support for scholarship at, 105,